GUEST EDITOR

ASHON CRAWLEY University of Virginia

EDITORS

EVE TUCK (Unangax̂) Ontario Institute for Studies in Education (OISE), University of Toronto
K. WAYNE YANG University of California, San Diego

MANAGING EDITOR

LEKEISHA HUGHES University of California, San Diego

PUBLICATIONS COMMITTEE

FATIMA EL-TAYEB University of California, San Diego
SHANA GRIFFIN Critical Ethnic Studies Association
SYLVESTER JOHNSON Northwestern University
SONIYA MUNSHI Borough of Manhattan Community College, CUNY
AMRAH SALOMÓN J. University of California, San Diego
LEE ANN S. WANG University of California, Berkeley
K. WAYNE YANG University of California, San Diego

EDITORIAL BOARD

GLEN COULTHARD (Yellowknives Dene First Nation) University of British Columbia
DENISE FERREIRA DA SILVA University of British Columbia
MICHAEL J. DUMAS University of California, Berkeley
ROXANNE DUNBAR-ORTIZ California State University, East Bay
NIRMALA EREVELLES University of Alabama
KALE BANTIGUE FAJARDO University of Minnesota

CANDACE FUJIKANE	University of Hawaiʻi at Mānoa
ALYOSHA GOLDSTEIN	University of New Mexico
MACARENA GÓMEZ-BARRIS	University of Southern California
NOELANI GOODYEAR-KAʻŌPUA (Kanaka Maoli)	University of Hawaiʻi at Mānoa
LISA KAHALEOLE HALL (Kanaka Maoli)	Wells College
MICHAEL HAMES-GARCÍA	University of Oregon
MARC LAMONT HILL	Morehouse College
AILEEN MORETON-ROBINSON (Goenpul, Quandamooka First Nation)	Queensland University of Technology
SCOTT LAURIA MORGENSEN	Queen's University
NADINE NABER	University of Illinois, Chicago
MIMI THI NGUYEN	University of Illinois, Urbana-Champaign
JESSICA BISSETT PEREA (Dena'ina)	University of California, Davis
LEONIE PIHAMA (Te Ātiawa, Ngāti Māhanga, Ngā Māhanga a Tairi)	University of Waikato
JASBIR K. PUAR	Rutgers University
SHERENE RAZACK	University of California, Los Angeles
KARYN RECOLLET (Cree)	University of Toronto
JUANA MARÍA RODRÍGUEZ	University of California, Berkeley
STEVEN SALAITA	American University of Beirut
DEAN ITSUJI SARANILLIO	New York University
MISTINGUETTE SMITH	Black/Land Project
THOMAS MICHAEL SWENSEN (Tangirnaq Native Village)	Colorado State University
LISA YONEYAMA	University of Toronto

Journal of the
Critical Ethnic Studies Association

VOLUME 4 · ISSUE 1
SPRING 2018

EDITORS' INTRODUCTION

Introduction by the Journal Coeditors — 1
EVE TUCK AND K. WAYNE YANG

Introduction to the Academy and What Can Be Done? — 4
ASHON CRAWLEY

ESSAYS

Subjunctively Inhabiting the University — 23
JIGNA DESAI AND KEVIN P. MURPHY

Queer of Color Space-Making in and beyond the Academic Industrial Complex — 44
PAOLA BACCHETTA, FATIMA EL-TAYEB, JIN HARITAWORN, JILLIAN HERNANDEZ, SA SMYTHE, VANESSA THOMPSON, AND TIFFANY WILLOUGHBY-HERARD

More than "Two Worlds":
Black Feminist Theories of Difference in Relation — 64
LISA KAHALEOLE HALL

American University Consensus and the Imaginative Power of Fiction — 84
COURTNEY MOFFETT-BATEAU

The Order of Disciplinarity, the Terms of Silence — 107
JOSHUA MYERS

Higher Education and the Im/possibility of Transformative Justice — 130
SHARON STEIN

Robin D. G. Kelley and Fred Moten in Conversation 154
MODERATED BY AFUA COOPER AND RINALDO WALCOTT

REVIEWS

Letters in Black, Care of Christina Sharpe:
Book Review of *In The Wake: On Blackness and Being* 175
CORNEL GREY

Introduction by the Journal Coeditors

EVE TUCK AND K. WAYNE YANG

To say that we begin with gratitude is to do it every time. To do this every time does not make it less meaningful; it is to make it a practice to pause to describe, as much as we can remember, the labors crisscrossing space and time to make this journal come to be.

When we were named the editors of this journal, sometime in the spring of 2015, or maybe it was the fall of 2014, we inherited a digital folder, an electric archive of all of the planning that went into the founding of the journal. The names of the authors of those documents are those whose scholarly works we read, scholars in and out of the university whom we greatly admire, writing the mundane work of proposing the creation of the journal to University of Minnesota Press, including establishing timelines, publishing agreements, and plans for the peer review process. In issue 1.1, John Márquez and Junaid Rana describe the founding of the journal, the collective organizing efforts and intracollective politics, the tensions between radical intellectual work and its appropriation, the piles and piles of planning notes and memos and contracts, so we won't recount that history here. Instead, we point simply to the dimensional aspects of radical intellectual work for those working in, toward, or away from the university: sometimes our writing is soaring, sometimes our writing is boring.

In some academic departments, scholars write into their fields with opposing views on topics like the commitments of Black studies, the compositions of Indigenous feminist theory, and what makes critical ethnic studies indeed critical. Yet, though their writings may bring readers to the brink of understanding these imperative aspects of their fields, these same scholars may also participate together in the humdrum of university life: admissions committees, search committees, promotion and tenure reviews, academic planning, selecting art for the library.

Some of the most partisan disagreements about the very purpose, foundational theories, and politics of scholarship play out in these mundane labors.

Also occurring are some of the most unlikely acts of solidarity, in the everyday labors of people supporting others whom they vehemently disagree with and quite possibly dislike. Acts of subverting the typical processes of the academy (and their typical results) can also be quite mundane. Our theories—especially those against white supremacy, against settler colonialism, against antiblackness, against homophobic and trans-exclusionary practices, toward abolition, toward decolonization, toward queer futurities—show up as we make decisions about which students to admit, which colleagues to hire, promote, and award, which art to display in the library.

This is perhaps why service loads for some of us are so heavy, especially for women of color, and especially for Black women. This service, frequently described as "invisible labor," is part and parcel of our very presence in the academy, at least for some of us. Universities make public commitments to effective sexual violence policies, to diversity, to "indigenizing," to welcoming more Black faculty and students, to improved gender diversity policies and supports; yet, it is clear that they can't possibly do this without the already overburdened presence of people of color, sexual violence survivors, Black people, queer people, nonbinary people, gender-nonconforming people, and Indigenous people (of course, these are not mutually exclusive peoples!). Universities that herald these needed changes as part of new and emerging definitions of excellence thus are legitimated by the presence of those who have historically been systematically and purposefully excluded; indeed, those upon whose backs entire disciplines have been forged. So the term "invisible labor" isn't quite doing it, if it ever did. Instead we are talking about the laboring presences that make universities legitimate—without them, they can, and do, burn.

We say thank you to those who carried out the mundane task of reviewing for this themed issue on "the academy and what can be done," often in ways that were extraordinary. Reviewers for *Critical Ethnic Studies* understand the stakes of this journal, and their responsibilities to authors, yes, but also to the communities from which and toward which authors write. Managing editor LeKeisha Hughes continues to facilitate the review process and much of the correspondence for the journal, all the while deftly demonstrating what we gesture toward in this brief essay as practicing theory/putting theory into practice. Boké Saisi, Nisha Toomey, and Jane Griffith provided caretaking expertise in copyediting and manuscript preparation after authors submitted final drafts. Authors—both those whose works appear in this issue and those whose works did not ultimately get published—took seriously the double question imbued in this issue's theme: What can be done to change the academy? What can be done or finished about the academy? "Done" can mean acted upon, engaged, intervened upon, changed. "Done" can also be finished, completed, made to be over.

When we decided that this would be the theme, our very next thought was to reach out to the brilliant scholar and artist Ashon Crawley, to ask him to please partner with us as a coeditor for this issue. He said yes to doing all of the unremarkable work of making a journal issue happen, from cowriting the call for papers, advising the reviewer matching process, reading submission and reviewer reports, making decisions to request revisions or not, and ultimately accepting final manuscripts. His introduction, which immediately follows these words, is all but unremarkable—it is another example of Crawley's exquisite approach to theorizing, in body, in time, in place, in deep inflection of the world of sound and feeling that his work has attended to so astoundingly. To have had the opportunity to make relationship with Crawley, through collaborating to make this issue, but also to have discussed our writing, our intentions, and to feel them in the cadence of pages that follow, has been a kind of making possible. Writing, both in this journal and *outside*, both the soaring and the workaday, can be what opens us up to one another for abounding connection, even for friendship; and this is surely what working with Crawley has reminded us.

EVE TUCK (Unangax̂) is a member of the Aleut Community of St. Paul Island in Alaska. She engages in theories of decolonization in a series of collaborations, including with K. Wayne Yang, the Black/Land Project, the Super Futures Haunt Qollective, and the Land Relationships Super Collective.

K. WAYNE YANG writes about decolonization and everyday epic organizing, particularly from underneath ghetto colonialism, often with his frequent collaborator, Eve Tuck, and sometimes for an avatar called La Paperson. He is excited to collaborate with the Land Relationships Super Collective, the Black Teacher Project, and Roses in Concrete.

Introduction to the Academy and What Can Be Done?

ASHON CRAWLEY

The academy and what can be done? This is more than a merely rhetorical question or an abstract concern. It has material weight and texture and depth. I write to you from Charlottesville, Virginia, just a couple of weeks after white supremacists—a new-old thing reemerging in our times, times that have never quite gone away though they may have quieted in flow and become more pronounced in ebb—marched on the campus of the University of Virginia. I joined the faculty here in July of 2017 and was not prepared to see the campus encroached upon from the outside. What has now made Charlottesville resonate on an international stage—I was in London and Exeter and was questioned if I lived in *that* Charlottesville; *yes, I do*, I'd say—is the relation of inside and outside the university. There have been white supremacist rallies of the spectacular sort in May, July, August, and October of 2017. But only the one in August, dubbed A11–12, had the outsiders march on the interior of the campus.

OUTSIDE

Such a word, "outside," we know by now, is a misnomer and an imprecision of stunning proportion and measure. *Outside* the university would presume the categorical distinction of—and possibility for pure practice, pure space, pure thought for—something called an *inside*. Yet we who are committed to Black studies, Indigenous studies, Asian American studies, Latinx studies, women and gender studies, *Critical Ethnic Studies* have witnessed and extended a thought tradition that have each in their own ways demonstrated with an acuity and precision that the very concepts of inside and outside, private and public, are creations, creations in the service of the project of white supremacism and its epistemological limits. The capacity for the distinction—inside/outside, private/public—would come to be racialized by those that could, according to Western thought traditions, be self-possessed and, thus, possess things. The distinction would obtain for those that have the capacity to own things. Epistemological delimitation, the capacity for purity and thus an inside and outside, is a modern construction of thought, a modern construction of a way to think resistance to relation, a modern construction for a way to think *a*sociality.

Yet it would not be going too far or be inaccurate to say that primarily cisgender white male-identified persons walked past my apartment building not minutes from the university campus with the intentional and expressed purpose of ongoing colonizing, antiblack racist, antiqueer practices of fearmongering and terrorizing. What I mean to say, in other words, is that there is no presumed inside and outside the academy, even if there is an inside and outside of my apartment. The university and white supremacists that seek to keep ongoing white racialist violence and terror know this, know this delimitation of thought no longer works in the service of a thought project and tradition of pernicious, rapacious, and stunningly old but never inconsequential violence. White supremacists have always been inside the university. That they walked the corners of my university makes very real the urgency of this issue if it had not been previous.

DISORIENTATION

Scenes and sights and sounds that recede into the normative and quotidian, that recede into memory, recede because of current moments of unfamiliarity. But they are unfamiliar only insofar as they mark what we have allowed to recede, what we have allowed to go unnoticed. It is easy to think of white supremacist rallies on campuses—in Charlottesville, or protests in Berkeley, or the racial terrorizing in Boston, campuses all—as spectacular because they are unfamiliar.

Yet, the unfamiliar is the spectacular such that the division between—the categorical distinction of—the spectacle and the mundane are disoriented, undone. Disoriented and undone like the (non)distinction between the inside and the outside. The counterintuitive is intuitive for someone else. Disorientation, in other words, names orientation for others, orientation otherwise. The distinction between the two is not categorical, not constant, certainly not about being, not about existence. But disorientation does, at the moment of feeling, mark connection to pasts, connections to that which could be otherwise.

This themed issue of *Critical Ethnic Studies* slips between the presumption of safety that the supposed distinction between outside and inside is thought to provide, that the distinction between the spectacular and mundane is supposed to hold. We seek, in this themed special issue, to interrogate knowledge production in academia, to consider the ways disorientation is what is necessary, disorientation as a kind of making of the mundane spectacle, allowing the quotidian and ordinary to flash before us, in haptic force, as a perpetual moment of crisis.

Disorienting first, then slipping between the space, diving in the break, the essays consider what is possible, which alternative structures and logics can be practiced and performed, what otherwise modality of thought, enfleshed, collective, improvisational action can emerge from the space of the neoliberal university. To extend conversations about the efficacy of Black studies, Indigenous studies, Asian American studies, Latinx studies, women and gender studies, critical ethnic studies, to extend and enlarge the conversations to a material practice of thinking and breathing and performing the plural possibility of alternative logics is urgent in these times. Such plural possibility would be boldly irreducible. Such plural possibility would be the *grounds* of operation. The neoliberal university is a choice that vivifies the political economy, a choice that the political economy thus in reciprocity vivifies for the university. But as a choice, it is but one of an infinite range of choices that could be made.

The university is a site of struggle and contestation. And what the university attempts is against the flourishing of survivance and abundance. The line and root of the word "abundant" marks relation to an overflowing quantity, a large number, marks an exorbitance of sufficiency, an exorbitance of plenty. The university thrives in the antithesis to abundance, thrives in producing knowledge as a limited resource and good, a limited supply and store. The university is as much a place of inhabitation and dwelling for neoliberal logics of privatization and financialization as it is an idea, a concept, a way to think antisociality as the grounds for relation.

The university is a gathering of resources but in our neoliberal world, such gathering is at the expense of the intensification of displacement and degradation through settler colonial logics of land acquisition, privatization of knowledge production and the adjunctification of faculties, the making students into customers, and the financialization and profitability of research projects. In its normative function and form, then, the university exists to make some knowledges major and others minor, and then to short-circuit and extinguish minor knowledges, minor epistemologies, because they constitute an ongoing, *thoroughgoing*, and unceasing variation around a theme: the performative force of the critique of Western civilization. The university, in its normative function and form, is against the flourishing of abundance. Of course, in music at least, major and minor scales mark a relation to normative Western knowledge regimes, such that the very concept of the major and minor would be interrogated by otherwise music epistemologies. The minor knowledges the university attempts to extinguish, in other words, are only minor insofar as they mark relation to otherwise modalities of thought and practice.

So we turn to what minor knowledges do to the university, what such epistemological displacements produce as a disruption within and without the university, minor knowledges as a meditative practice of collective improvisation as a knowledge project of the commons. So we write and think and imagine otherwise possibility, the *as if* of Derrida. The *as if* that Derrida describes imagines that what the university is and what it could be is a space of distinction.

Riffing on Derrida, the university professes the truth, and that is its profession. It declares and promises an unlimited commitment to the truth. No doubt the status of and the changes to the value of truth can be discussed ad infinitum ... But these are discussed, precisely, in the university and in departments that belong to the humanities. These immense questions of truth and of light, of the Enlightenment ... have always been linked to the question of man, to a concept of that which is proper to man, on which concept were founded both humanism and the historical idea of the humanities.[1]

We are always struggling, in other words, over the conceptual object that allows to cohere the thought related to such an object. To think about the academy and what can be done is to interrogate what—no, really, *who*—is supposed to occupy the space of the university, who is its pedagogies and plans created to satiate, who is its imagined audience, who is its imagined thinker that would come to learn, and in the service of what kind of world is such learning, such audience, such pedagogy, created? We are precisely always at the concerns that critical ethnic studies elaborates as an interdisciplinary field, as a way of thought, a way of life. We must now interrogate and make disoriented the very *man* that is considered to occupy the space of thought and action from within the university. But we must now also interrogate and make disoriented the man who produces the conceptual possibility of a hermetically sealed place of thought as well.

Turns out, it's the same concept, the same subject, dancing around and producing itself, thinking itself into being. Derrida wants to treat the university as if it is what it says it is, as if it is a space of flourishing thought, as if it is a place of critical inquiry. And this against its modernization, its corporatization, its militarization. How to work within, think within, practice poetics of peace and equity from within the space while also remaining critically aware of how the space would attempt to exploit the very projects against the university in the service of the flourishing of the neoliberal logics of the university? This is the challenge. It is also the opportunity. It is a gap to which we must be mindful, a space and break of possibility.

It is in that space that the flourishing of radical thought and mood and movement can occur. I follow Cedric J. Robinson's line and root, his theorizing of the Black Radical Tradition as the thinking that charges my imagination for imagining what can be done with the university. Robinson, in *The Terms of Order: Political Science and the Myth of Leadership*, offers that though myths exist that order the normative world, because they are mythical, they can be changed. What he offers, in other words, is a way to consider otherwise possibilities for thought, that the myths that order the normative world are but a choice made. And there is hope insofar as we can choose differently, choose alternatives.[2]

In this way, the essays collected are not just about what the university has excluded, what it has produced in terms of pain and suffering—though the university as concept and as a space of operation certainly has produced pain and suffering—but they are also about what can be done, how we can think, what we can be by utilizing the university as a site of inquiry and object of knowledge. We attempt ways to reimagine, to recast, to think myth differently of the university. This is a practice and process of imagination.

And we can do this imagining as practice and process because the university that emerges from within Western knowledge regimes, epistemologies, and mythologies lacks the capacity to make impossible, to make a connection. We can reimagine and create otherwise mythology because connection as possible remains with us, is that which we seek and desire and outpour and extend. It is this failure, the failure to produce severance, a failure that produces the occasion for flowering in which we find joy, pleasure, knowledge as a collective project and practice. And, following the theorizing and thought Robinson made available for my own thinking, the essays collected here are not to exhaust the possibilities of discussing the problems or potentials of the modern university, but simply to suggest that therein is a potential for otherwise, for alternatives, to what is known and conceded as normative. We are not exhausting the conversation but suggesting that otherwise possibility has already been realized, is already *there*.[3]

THE UNIVERSITY...

The logics of the modern university have always been mired in the project of racial thought, categorical distinction, and the exploitation of labor. This exploitation is dual pronged through the colonization of land that necessitated the removal of Indigenous people through genocide, thus veiling the labor produced to make the land available for use—a colonization process that is still with us, that remains, that echoes and reverberates and has material consequence in our times—*as well as* the importation of Africans as free labor to continue to work the purportedly "available" land for the project of racial purity.

Such a project is of concern to the university because it is at once a thought project, a way to think the world and refuse relationality, a way to think the world and the possibility of discovering a modern liberal subject, unencumbered by crises it throws into place. Sylvia Wynter would call this the "coloniality of being/power/truth/freedom," would say that this is the problem of modern Man, that such an entity is created by thinking one's genre of the human as the *only* and the *perfectability* of the human, a genre that would be a gift of white, landed gentry.[4]

The university in its modern constitution was constructed for this entity, for modern Man as first a theocentric, then political, then biogenic thing. We might even begin to think of disciplinarity and the way it is utilized in the university to sequester knowledge, to make it categorically distinct and, thus, pure knowledge. We might then say, after Wynter, that the problem of the modern university is disciplinarity and its overrepresentation. The overrepresentation of disciplinarity occurs by a genre-specific thinking that relation of knowledge and enclosure, the relation of knowledge and borders, are natural, axiomatic, universal. This discrete form of knowledge production is genre-specific, produced by modern Man, and produced as the *only* way to produce knowledge and, thus, overrepresents itself. We must disorient relations to knowledge production, we must make the quotidian and mundane aspects of thought projects available for analysis, we must think the relation between the quotidian and spectacular eruptions of the logics of white supremacist thought.

With the current order of neoliberal administration for universities, diversity, inclusion, and multiculturalism are each used with varied intensities to leave the racialist logics in play and place, to leave the logics of racial hierarchies and the ordering of knowledge production along the streams of divisibility and purity. Such a university during flashpoints of spectacular crises—

think lawn fire torches being marched on public or private campuses while marchers proclaim "blood and soil"—call upon the diversity, inclusion, and multicultural forces of the university for public relations that faces outward, that does the work of marketing and calls upon sequestered knowledges that are purported to be specifically "about race" or "about gender" or "about sexuality" to manage such crises.

Such knowledge is not considered to be more than a response to spectacular crisis. This because the modern university does not consider its very existence as an instantiation of a long crisis, as old as Lisbon 1442 *before* 1492 and Cristoforo Colombo's oceanic traverses on the blue. And current institutional arrangements make apparent the fact that the various thought projects that fit under the name and heading of critical ethnic studies— in their variousness and plurality—are both needed as exploitable resources to prove a kind of diversity and multiculturalism but also are knowledges sequestered to the margins. We seek not simply a centering of marginal voices and knowledge productions but an obliteration of the very choreographies of marginality and violence that emerge from geographies of normativity.

This means struggling against settler colonialism and new world enslavement as not just a problem that arrives on campus but one in which campuses participated. For example, Craig Steven Wilder in *Ebony and Ivy: Race, Slavery, and the Troubled History of America's Universities* states, "Colleges arrived in the Americas in response to European nations' attempts to seize territories and hold off rivals. European powers deployed colleges to help defend and regulate their colonial possessions and they turned to African slavery and the African slave trade to fund these efforts" and that we should think expansively beyond the campus itself because, "The American college trained the personal and cultivated the ideas that accelerated and legitimated the dispossession of Native Americans and the enslavement of Africans."[5] That is, thought practices on college campuses included colonizing anti-Indigenous and antiblack racist *logics* and *logistics* as the formation for knowledge production for the making of the normative, liberal scholar-subject. Learning *about* and being trained *in* colonizing and antiblack racialist logics would be a means to producing a learned subject, one that was prepared for the world that would include the proliferation of such logics, the making normativized and quotidian the practices of violence, violation, dispossession, displacement, and exclusion. Knowledge, in other words, was produced in the university in order to justify and make entrenched the logics of coloniality and its racialist hierarchies of exclusion.

... AND WHAT CAN BE DONE

To ask what can be done with and about the academy, the university, is to become an antagonism for its current survival. It is to ask how knowledge production can be reorganized to account for the history of racial capitalist violence and exclusion, it is to ask to give an accounting that cannot be easily folded into the logics of inclusion, diversity, and multiculturalism. To ask what can be done with and about the academy is to reach back and consider epistemological foundations for the *space* and *place* of the university as a modality through which knowledge was presumed to be produced. To ask what can be done with and about the academy, the university, however, is *not* to ask if knowledge will end. Rather, we move toward the end of a knowledge production that produces *as it is produced by* modern Man, the genre-specific man and its overrepresentation. Sylvia Wynter says the problem of the current epistemological ordering is "the overrepresentation of Man as if it were the human," and the knowledge produced by such overrepresentation is what we seek to unsettle.[6] What will knowledge be once it is released from its being enclosed by the logics of the very possibility of universality, abstraction, stilling. We are after a poetics, a practice, that unsettles, disorients, imagines otherwise possibility.

To ask what can be done with the academy is to ask what can be interrogated, and in Sylvia Wynter's terms—unsettled—about and within the academy as a space and place of thought. Honing in on the presence of Black studies, and black people, on college campuses, Wynter offers, "Blacks would be allowed on the campus as a group, admitted to have even a culture, as long as this 'culture' and its related enclave studies could be made to function as the extra-cultural space, in relation, no longer to a Wasp, but now more inclusively to a White American, normatively Euro-American intra-cultural space; as the mode of Chaos imperative to the latter's new self-ordering."[7] Here then too is the idea that the presence of minoritarian difference is harnessed by the academy, not to unsettle, but to produce anew the occasion for white self-ordering, the very possibility for white thought, something perhaps like—after Toni Morrison's Africanist presence in American literature—a minoritized presence of the academy.[8] We might go as far as to say that self-ordering itself is the project of white supremacist capitalist patriarchy, the project of Western thought-theological, Western thought-philosophical, Western thought-historical, Western thought-ethical. Self-ordering is "the 'ground' of our present order of knowledge in which [the biocentric, Western superstition] belief system is narratively articulated on the basis of the premise that the human is a natural organism or a purely genetic being."[9]

Self-ordering is consistent with, and extends, what Sara Ahmed would come to offer regarding the models of diversity and inclusion, keywords of the modern neoliberal university. "I suggest that diversity can be offered as a narrative of repair, as what allows us to 'recover' from racism by recovering the very signs of injury ... my aim is not to suggest that we should stop doing diversity, but that we need to keep asking what we are doing with diversity."[10] What this means is, like Wynter's self-ordering, diversity too is a conceptual frame and tool for the ongoing settlement, the ongoing colonizing logic, of the academy to be what it has always been. Diversity as narrative repair seeks to enclose difference in the service of the management of crisis difference it is considered to carry. What to do when our presence is crisis, when we carry crisis in the flesh, and also how to produce a crisis against the crisis of neoliberalism and its current iteration in the university? That is, how can we be in the university as a fundamental antagonism that is not immediately captured in the logics of its enclosure, the logics of diversification and disciplinarity?

Again, the challenge but also the possibility.

The academy has never been a benign space but was and continues to be a staging ground, a site of struggle and contestation, over the meaning of knowledge production. Piya Chatterjee and Sunaina Maira underscore the imperialist logics—always deeply connected to settler logics—of the academy:

> We argue that the state of permanent war that is core to U.S. imperialism and racial statecraft has three fronts: military, cultural, and academic. Our conceptualization of the imperial university links these fronts of war, for the academic battleground is part of the culture wars that emerge in a militarized nation, one that is always presumably under threat, externally or internally. Debates about national identity and national culture shape the battles over academic freedom and the role of the university in defining the racial boundaries of the nation and its "proper" subjects and "proper" politics. Furthermore, pedagogies of nationhood, race, gender, sexuality, class, and culture within the imperial nation are fundamentally intertwined with the interests of neoliberal capital and the possibilities of economic dominance.[11]

The imperialist impulse, the colonizing logic, of the academy is in need of interrogation that moves beyond the rhetorical flourish because such a flourish is easily and quite often incorporable into the project of the neoliberal university, such interrogation is often the mark, the trace, the evidence of diversity, inclusion, "freedom of speech," "free thought," and the like. But Wynter warns, again, "our present order of knowledge can give us no knowledge" of the possibility for unsettling, of what can be done, with the academy. Such knowledge would be the practice of freedom, would be a kind of knowing, following Denise Ferreira da Silva, *at the limits of justice*.[12] It would be a knowledge that is not cognized according to the perspective, the vantage, the space-time of the normative epistemology for Western knowledge production.

The university is a site of contestation and struggle because what is being argued over, and argued against, is epistemology itself, the method of knowing and the path to such knowability. Epistemology is a theory of knowledge, a theory for thinking itself, and is a way to investigate how knowledge is produced in particular ways to think the world. To separate the world out through racial, classed, and gendered distinction is European in its line and root. The epistemology of dividing the world into types, types that receive benefits, is a product of European thought. This issue of *Critical Ethnic Studies* stages possible interventions into the university without a kind of naïveté that believes thought is neutral, that attempting to critique the university from inside the academy cannot be easily folded into the project of neoliberalism.

Yet, we do not give up. Eve Tuck and K. Wayne Yang argue that the university is "one of the last places for legitimated inquiry," but that, by calling on the university, "we are invoking a community of practice that is focused upon the propagation and promulgation of (settler colonial) knowledge."[13] To produce knowledge as a practice of resistance, to produce knowledge behaviors that can unsettle the university, to produce, following Tuck and Yang, "knowledge that the academy does not deserve," is to engage in a dance and play and sonification—which is another way to say, a poetics practice—of otherwise possibility.

OTHERWISE POSSIBILITIES IN THIS ISSUE

How to practice a way of life against the "fraught relationality to the persistence of settler colonialism, which always threatens to reappropriate, assimilate, subsume/consume, and repress Indigenous voicings and visuality, their forms and aesthetics, within its hegemonic logic of domination."[14] We recognize the constraints only insofar as we seek to overcome them; we recognize constraint in order to creatively inhabit, unsettle, and dispense with them.

This is what Jigna Desai and Kevin P. Murphy call for in "Subjunctively Inhabiting the University"; they call us to an attention to failure. For those of us who are concerned with ethnic, gender, women, sexuality, feminist, and queer studies, according to Desai and Murphy, "unlike other arts and humanities, [these disciplines] are seen as constitutively failed in that they cannot account for themselves intellectually and ontologically as disciplines." Moreover, they argue, "The logics of quantifiable metrics and the positivist calculus of diversity are always indexed to the supposed indebtedness, lack, and failure of ethnic and GWSFQ studies." But what can be made from purported failure, what does failure produce, what is the generativity of failure? We might be in the terrain of folks like Jack Halberstam, who writes convincingly of failure as a queer art, failure as the practice of queer imaginings, queer longings, queer potentialities. Attending to failure does not mean that we are at the end *in general* but perhaps the end of a knowledge project that assumes the genre-specific overrepresentation of Man. That failure, then, would be a gift.

Perhaps collectivity is a way otherwise. We have included in this issue a statement by Paola Bacchetta, Fatima El-Tayeb, Jin Haritaworn, Jillian Hernandez, SA Smythe, Vanessa Thompson, and Tiffany Willoughby-Herard—a collective—titled "Queer of Color Space-Making in and beyond the Academic Industrial Complex." What are the possibilities for writing in a collective voice, and how can such writing produce a failure of the neoliberal project of the university, a failure to produce modern Man and *his* singular, individual, enclosed thought? The writing that the form takes is just as much of the argument as the content in this statement about making space against the settler logic of taking and claiming and owning space through displacement. While taking critical aim at a universalist "We," they still utilize the nomenclature for such writing, marking the tension between the world as it is and the world as it is imagined otherwise. To critique the "We" while utilizing it is to redeploy it, is to think *as if* it were not enmeshed and entrenched in a settler logic of knowledge production and its genre-specific humanism. Their collective writing a gift, they state:

> The strategies we invent divest from the competitive values of the colonial neoliberal university, and from its racially skewed logics of merit, respectability, and gender and racial exceptionalism, and instead invest in polyglot, heterotopic community. Our strategies affirm the lives of queer and trans people of color, and of all others treated as raw material for theory production, rather than fostered as present and future knowledge reproducers.

They have to invent a way to exist in the university because they attend to the knowledge that it was not created with them in mind. They inhabit *as if* the university were without condition in order to produce thought while at the same time writing against the university *as it is* full of contradiction, *as it is* with condition. Such condition is the grounds for the emergence of the intellectual, the thinker, the subject, the genre-specific Man. The voice of the collective is included to interrogate the university *as it is*.

How does one think relation in and against the university, in and against the academy? Lisa Kahaleole Hall takes this up in "More than 'Two Worlds': Black Feminist Theories of Difference in Relation." It is a meditation that considers the relation between Black feminist theory and Indigenous studies as a feminist practice and way of life. Kahaleole Hall writes about the university as a space of relationality. And in this, we might begin to detect that one problem with the overrepresentation of the genre-specific human Man and its knowledge production is precisely because this genre-specific human is *against* sociality, *against* relationality. And this, being against, is in the service of the realization of an enclosed self. If the university is a site in which relation happens, this would be true against the very constitution of the university. Violence attends the practice of renouncing what it fundamentally must do and be and is, produce and practice and have relation. Kahaleole Hall takes us on a journey of the personal, bespeaking how relation with Black feminist thinker Barbara Christian opened up worlds for her. And if for her, then worlds for us all.

Courtney Moffett-Bateau's essay, "American University Consensus and the Imaginative Power of Fiction," cautions against the idea that the existence of the university is fundamentally to produce, promote, and help proliferate social justice. We know this to be true through various studies. What is unique in Moffett-Bateau's essay is the way she takes of the literary in order to produce the occasion for thought. We're not abandoning literature or even literary criticism when we call for an unsettlement of, a disorientation with, the university. We are, rather, asking how we can redeploy and repurpose in the service of a practice that would produce something like a non-empty, nonsimplistic but full of complexity and texture, justice. Literature can produce a tear or rip or break in the way it can incite imagination. I know, for me at least, when I read literature, I have to imagine sensual experiences: how will this feel on my skin—skin that is brown; how would such a thing taste; how does that thing described smell; is that odor heavy or light, sweet or bitter?

Moffett-Bateau uses Ralph Ellison's *Invisible Man* and Mat Johnson's *Pym*, staging a conversation across texts in order to intervene into a pernicious violence in which "pain experienced within the Political is justifiable because of its promise of inclusion." Inclusion can come in the form of tenure, and the essay considers what happens when one is granted, or denied, tenure. The main character of *Pym*, Chris Jaynes, is denied tenure, and his "hope in the political project of the university dies," Moffett-Bateau says. The death of the political project of the university, a failure. A failure, then an opportunity. We keep running into this, into this pernicious idea, this idea that failure is not *the* end but *an* end. It is also an occasion. What worlds can be imagined from failure, failure of a particular political economic project? It is to this that Moffett-Bateau, and the other authors in this issue, attend.

I hear a sound. The sound I hear is made possible by what I've backgrounded, what I believe is *not* there. Silence is a quality but not a reality, at least not in space-time wherein humans must breathe. Silence only exists in vacuums, so when we speak of silence, we speak of a certain inattention to a certain ceaseless pulse and noise. To attend to silence and its being backgrounded, to attend to sound that foregrounds itself, Joshua Myers offers a meditation on the music, the sound, the collective practice of black thought in "The Order of Disciplinarity, the Terms of Silence." Meyers's essay excites because he stages an intervention against the conventional wisdom, the sort of anectodal narrativity, of Black studies. He offers that it is "reductionist and misleading to conceive of the whole of Black intellectual history as a corrective to the silences that make Western knowledges." So if Black studies, if Black intellectual history itself, is not simply a corrective, is not simply attempting to fill silence that makes Western knowledge, what is such a history and tradition? In another register, then, Myers is asking the question, is wrestling with the concern, that each of the authors are in their own ways thinking with and through and against: how to take the occasion of failure, constraint, or here, silence, and make something otherwise? These authors do not assume the finality and totality of such "bad" things but think their occasion as absolute—though not pure—possibility.

In mathematics, absolute values are considered to be the value's distance from zero. It is about relation, about space-time possibility then, about the way value and distance codetermine each other. These essays in this issue of *Critical Ethnic Studies* are each about absolution and the absolute; they each are in the direction of finding a ceremony, a ritual and performance, a collective improvisational intellectual practice and mode of life that is produced by life in the flesh, by the resistance of the object, life otherwise, life produced in and as minoritized knowledges. Sharon Stein cuts to the heart of the chase in her essay, "Higher Education and the Im/possibility of

Transformative Justice." Can we do anything from within this space? What is the purpose of even this issue if it is only a filler for curricula vitae and not for thinking about how we might inhabit worlds otherwise? Are these just rhetorical exercises?

Stein's essay is concerned with these questions. She notes the "colonial elisions in accounts of the neoliberal present that rest on nostalgia for a prior commitment to higher education as a state-sponsored means of educating enlightened citizens and ensuring social mobility" and cautions that the modern university is constructed with a genre-specific *student* in mind: "they are different versions of the same base modern subject, who is educated to rationally pursue affluence, maximize utility, and enact seamless progress and development through the supposedly universal governing architectures of the nation-state and global capital." The work we contend against, in other words, is varied, textured, difficult. If we are about the unsettling of the university, the becoming disoriented within the academy, it would have to be by way of a force that works on the university *as it works on us*, a force that works on the university *as if* it works on us.

Who is this "us"? Who would nominate oneself for such a status and position and station? And in the service of what, exactly, would such a nomination occur? This brings me, finally, to the conversation between Robin D. G. Kelley and Fred Moten, moderated by Afua Cooper and Rinaldo Walcott. They begin their conversation by responding to a question about a meditation on Black studies and Black politics, what they are and what they might be. When we begin to think about what something *might* be, we are in the terrain of the *as if*, we are in the hopes for the failure of the *what is*, we are desiring and imagining and sensing otherwise possibility. Moten thinks of Black studies as "not so much as an academic discipline or confluence of disciplines but as the atmosphere in which I grew up. And I love that atmosphere. I love the way that it felt, and I love the way that it smelled, and I love the flavors, and I love the sounds, and I love the movements." And Kelley comes on down the line, offering, "social movements have always been the catalyst for Black studies. When Fred was talking about Black studies as kind of a way of life, as an atmosphere in which he grew up and which I grew up and many of us grew up, that's so true. I never thought of it that way, but that is so true. In fact, if anything, Black studies is not a multidiscipline but a project, a project for liberation, whatever that means, and liberation is an ongoing project."

Can you hear it as you read? Have you sensed the sound from which my thinking emerges? Can you tell that I think with Fred Moten and Robin D. G. Kelley? Can you get a sense for the fact that what is offered in the pages to come has already worked on me, has already helped me practice life and the way I live it otherwise? Moten and Kelley key in on the sensuality of Black studies, which is to say the sensual experience the university seeks to harness only insofar as it transforms it into a knowledge object for its own existence, not a way to sense worlds, not a way to practice justice and equity and love. What these authors in their complexity, each of them, offer is the fact that we have to have a sense for this thing, a sense for otherwise possibility, have to make ourselves open and vulnerable to otherwise possibility while also protecting from harm the violence that attends being open and vulnerable.

Can we fail to live up to the university while showing up for each other? How can we go about an intentioned failure to produce the politics of the neoliberal academy while concurrently practicing a poetics of relationality, sociality, fundamental connection, and disorientation and unsettlement? It's felt in the music, in the poetics, in the forms minor life takes. To ask, in other words, what can be done with the academy is to question if we might currently be, what we might have been, what we might otherwise be. We displace linear time and space for a different relation to temporality. This difference would reconceptualize relation and sociality such that the genre of human's thoughts are allowed to flourish and, then, the knowledge production of otherwise genre-specific humanism would be taken as a way to practice, to perform, the joy and pleasure and liberation of thought otherwise.

ASHON CRAWLEY is an assistant professor of religious studies and African American and African studies at the University of Virginia. His research and teaching experiences are in the areas of Black studies, performance theory, sound studies, philosophy and theology, and Black feminist and queer theories. His first book, *Blackpentecostal Breath: The Aesthetics of Possibility* (2016), is an investigation of aesthetics and performance as modes of collective, social imaginings otherwise.

NOTES

1. Jacques Derrida, "The Future of the Profession or the Unconditional University (Thanks to the 'Humanities,' What Could Take Place Tomorrow)," in *Deconstructing Derrida: Tasks for the New Humanities*, ed. Peter Pericles Trifonas and Michael A. Peters (New York: Palgrave Macmillan, 2005), 12.

2. Cedric J. Robinson, *The Terms of Order: Political Science and the Myth of Leadership* (Albany: SUNY Press, 1980).

3. Cedric J. Robinson, *Black Marxism : The Making of the Black Radical Tradition*, Third World Studies (London: Zed Press, 1983), xxxii.

4. Sylvia Wynter, "Unsettling the Coloniality of Being/Power/Truth/Freedom: Towards the Human, after Man, Its Overrepresentation—An Argument," *CR: The New Centennial Review* 3, no. 3 (2003): 257–337.

5. Craig Steven Wilder, *Ebony and Ivy: Race, Slavery, and the Troubled History of America's Universities* (New York: Bloomsbury, 2013), 9, 10.

6. Wynter, "Unsettling," 267.

7. Sylvia Wynter, "The Ceremony Must Be Found: After Humanism," *Boundary 2* 12/13 (1984): 41, doi:10.2307/302808.

8. Toni Morrison, *Playing in the Dark: Whiteness and the Literary Imagination*, William E. Massey, Sr. Lectures in the History of American Civilization, 1990 (Cambridge, Mass.: Harvard University Press, 1992).

9. Sylvia Wynter, "A Black Studies Manifesto," *Forum N.H.I.: Knowledge for the 21st Century* 1, no. 1 (1994): 3–11.

10. Sara Ahmed, *On Being Included: Racism and Diversity in Institutional Life* (Durham, N.C.: Duke University Press, 2012), 17.

11. Piya Chatterjee and Sunaina Maira, *The Imperial University: Academic Repression and Scholarly Dissent* (Minneapolis: University of Minnesota Press, 2014), 7.

12. Denise Ferreira da Silva, "To Be Announced: Radical Praxis or Knowing (at) the Limits of Justice," *Social Text* 31, no. 1 (114) (March 20, 2013): 43–62.

13. Eve Tuck and K. Wayne Yang, "R-Words: Refusing Research," in *Humanizing Research: Decolonizing Qualitative Inquiry with Youth and Communities*, ed. Django Paris and Maisha T. Winn (Los Angeles: SAGE, 2013), 223, 232.

14. Jarrett Martineau and Eric Ritskes, "Fugitive Indigeneity: Reclaiming the Terrain of Decolonial Struggle through Indigenous Art," *Decolonization: Indigeneity, Education & Society* 3, no. 1 (May 20, 2014): 1, http://decolonization.org/index.php/des/article/download/21320.

ESSAYS

Subjunctively Inhabiting the University

JIGNA DESAI AND KEVIN P. MURPHY

This special issue gives us an opportunity to consider not only the university as an abstraction and as an institution, but, in particular, the interdisciplinary fields of ethnic studies and gender/women/sexuality/feminist/queer (GWSFQ) studies that have been highly self-reflexive in understanding their complex, sometimes complicit, and often contradictory institutionalizations within the university. We use the polynomial gender, women, sexuality, feminist, and queer studies as shorthand though the acronym GWSFQ does not capture the tensions and differences that are being held together here. We would suggest that one of the purposes of ethnic and GWSFQ studies is to bring into question the purpose of the university as both abstraction and institution. One might say, it is the work of ethnic and GWSFQ studies faculty to be, to adapt Sara Ahmed's phrase, institutional killjoys by disrupting through praxis the standard operating procedures and discourses of the university.

Ethnic and GWSFQ studies are critical spaces of knowledge production that theorize the fundamental links between freedom, university, knowledge, and difference. They also interrogate the relationship between the university, state, and communities in the formation of knowledge. In doing so, they question the continued workings of the institution itself. This essay considers questions of difference in the heterogeneous and hierarchical space of the neoliberal university and how we as ethnic and/or GWSFQ studies scholars work in and on it as an institution. We consider the ontological, affective, and epistemological facets of institutionalization as well as our attachments to it by thinking through the mood of our inhabitations within the university. We also imagine how ethnic and GWSFQ studies can be productive and powerful sites of theorization, practice, and engagement to challenge and reimagine the university.

The critiques, strategies, and knowledges that emerge from ethnic and GWSFQ studies vis-à-vis institutional transformation are often tossed into the dustbin of service through normative institutionalization. Too frequently this intellectual labor is disparaged and characterized as service (therefore labor from minoritized subjects). Moreover, this type of intellectual and affective labor has been consistently devalued precisely because it is feminized and racialized reproductive labor of the institution. When certain people think, it is theory. When others of us think, it is care. We write with the awareness of how knowledge, scholarship, and theory are gendered and racialized so that white and masculinist production is thought and theory, while other production is feminized and racialized as service and mentoring. It is intentional that we use the term "theorize" to delineate the work described here. In this moment, these interruptions of standard operating procedure must be seen as our intellectual work, not only as service, but identified as forms of knowledge through research, scholarship, teaching, mentoring, and field building. We must also elevate the racialized and gendered labor that is called service as well. Ethnic and GWSFQ studies must make critiques at a variety of scales from the level of the institution and knowledge to the level of our labor, knowledge, and service.

In this essay, we analyze ethnic and GWSFQ studies as they have been institutionalized—and have resisted institutionalization—within the neoliberal university. We show that these fields of study and areas of pedagogy have been marked as failures, in large part because they have been charged with doing "diversity work" within institutions that simultaneously invoke diversity and inclusion while resisting the kinds of transformative institutional changes that challenge the upward redistribution of resources and allow subaltern knowledge production. This essay then considers new strategies for inhabitation within the neoliberal university in an era of white supremacist backlash, namely by exploring experimental and collective ways to move between the informal and formal in order to work toward social justice and avoid co-optation. The essay grounds this analysis of institutionalization with a close examination of the formation of the Race, Indigeneity, Gender and Sexuality Studies (RIGS) collective and initiative at the University of Minnesota.

The University of Minnesota, Twin Cities functions as the site of our analysis for several reasons. It is an institution with which we have collectively four decades of institutional experience. The urban Twin Cities campus of the University of Minnesota is part of the larger state system and a land-grant institution (which means that it was established through settler colonialism); Minnesota is a state that has continued to provide moderate support for higher education including the University of Minnesota during the last decade of heightened defunding. It is not an exceptional institution in that it faces similar homogenizing corporate practices, funding and budgeting models, and management strategies deployed within many public universities. Justified by trends in public defunding, the collapse and merger of interdisciplinary units is a common strategy within the corporate university of managing difference and redistributing resources upward and elsewhere. Other common neoliberal management processes include death by a thousand cuts, scarcity models that pit units—especially interdisciplinary ethnic studies—against each other, and model minoritization of certain departments. One other strategy is the expansion of equity and diversity offices and staff within university administration, as opposed to academic units focused on ethnic studies and GWSFQ studies. This last strategy enables university administration to perform its commitment to diversity for university and non-university audiences alike by minimizing the role of faculty and students and without addressing or transforming the structural inequalities that constitute the university in the first place. Here is also where we break from critiques of the neoliberal university that disconnect the university from its longer histories of settler colonialism, enslavement, and unfreedom to suggest a recent fall from grace.[1] Ethnic studies students and scholars critique these neoliberal management strategies and renarrate them within the university's longer history located within larger structures of unfreedom and settler colonialism.

Throughout, we think through mood as it relates to successive iterations of the university. We rely on two meanings of mood: the first indicating affect or feeling and the second identifying a modality of verb use that identifies how we dwell within and on the institution. Specifically, in regard to the latter, the mood of the verb indicates the modality of the verb's expression. Mood—indicative, imperative, or subjunctive—distinguishes between an assertion, command, or wish, respectively. The indicative mood expresses an assertion, denial, or question; the imperative expresses a command, prohibition, or entreaty; and the subjunctive expresses an uncertain wish, suggestion, proposal, demand, or insistence. We conclude by theorizing how acting subjunctively might allow ethnic and GWSFQ studies scholars (including students) to conduct transformative work and enact responsibility to each other and the communities they value, even within a corporatized institution.

How we narrate ourselves in relation to the university is an issue of mood. Our mood for ethnic and GWSFQ studies is not the indicative (certainty) nor imperative (command), but one of the subjunctive (hope and doubt). We entered the university as graduate students and faculty with the understanding of it as an institution grounded in settler colonialism, white supremacy, imperialism, heteropatriarchy, and capitalism, and hence, with a sense of irony, distance, detachment, and hope. We continue to make use of the subjunctive in our narrations of the university because the tense indicates our openness to interpretation, possibility, and uncertainty of what may be. The subjunctive mood addresses provisional and partial inhabitations that are structured by uncertainty, but it also can indicate an investment to change something.

Scholars working within the often tenuous fields of ethnic and GWSFQ studies wrestle with the tension between the university as concept and university as institution. Sometimes there is slippage between the two. Scholars often distance themselves from their institution by drawing distinctions about their own complicity within the university in formulations stating, for example, that they are "in, but not of, the institution." We want to consider this formulation of being *in*—an ontological statement about location and dwelling within the institution, which is posed in contrast to being *of*—an ontological statement about the condition of existing as part of something.

But this hesitancy, this desire to separate oneself by being in, but not of, seeks to remove us from the contamination of the institution and thereby limits the possibility of recognizing our responsibilities within the institution. In *Community of Disagreement*, Danielle Bouchard, reflecting on this distinction to be "in" but not "of" the academy, states: "The problem of the general mode of describing feminism (and/or women's studies) as not 'of' the university is not that it underestimates the limitations of institutional membership but that it precludes recognition of responsibility to the enabling processes of institutional difference and division and thus, unwittingly, reenvisions the institution as a sovereign, discrete, self-present entity."[2]

So, we are in and of the institution whether we want to be or not. Our strategies that come from thought and action as praxis are not formed exterior to the university but are implicated within it. We may want to think about locations within the university as an inhabitation. The etymology of inhabit, *enhabiter*, guides us toward thinking about how we live and reside within the university. In this case, it emboldens us to consider with what affect and labor and toward what goals we have in the university. But, inhabit is also rooted in *habitare* (*habare*), which asks us to ponder what it is that we hold and have as we dwell in and on the university.

Ethnic and GWSFQ studies scholars address this question of the university, in part, by questioning institutionalization, disciplinarity, and formalization. While we are complicit in that our knowledge is produced through the university and its enmeshment in settler colonialism, imperialism, racism, capitalism, and heteropatriarchy, our fields offer us the opportunity to conceptualize different models for our inhabitations. For example, American Indian and Indigenous studies center decolonizing knowledge by questioning settler colonialism, land-grant missions, and the sovereignty of subjects and knowledge within the university. Similarly, Asian American studies might offer us opportunities to belong illegitimately, diasporically, and as perpetually out of place, not because we are not autochthonous, but because our knowledge, our affect, and our labors themselves seek to disrupt belonging, inhabitation, and knowing within the university. Put slightly differently, as fungible scholars we must deploy the critiques of ethnic and GWSFQ studies at all scales of inhabitation to address the institutionalization of these fields within the shifting ecologies of the land-grant university.

INDICATIVE MOOD OF THE LAND-GRANT UNIVERSITY

As we seek to understand our own inhabitations in the university, we must also examine the university's history and its constitutive place within white supremacy and the nation. In North America and elsewhere, institutions of higher education were produced and sustained through settler logic and processes. This is undeniably the case for land-grant institutions. When Abraham Lincoln signed the Morrill Land-Grant Act of 1862, it provided states with lands to settle and establish universities "without excluding other scientific and classical studies and including military tactic, to teach such branches of learning as are related to agriculture and the mechanic arts, in such manner as the legislatures of the States may respectively prescribe, in order to promote the liberal and practical education of the industrial classes in the several pursuits and professions in life."[3]

The act created a set of institutions that were funded with the purpose of the production of agricultural, military, and technically oriented citizens. The Morrill Land-Grant Act, Homestead Act, and Pacific Railroad Act all passed in the same year and hastened the expansion of white westward migration and settler colonialism. This expansion relied on the suppression of uprisings by American Indians and the claiming of land, rights, and privileges for white settlers. In essence, the Morrill Act and other acts passed during the Civil War were meant to interpellate industrial and agricultural workers into settler whiteness by offering new opportunities for prosperity in the West. As historian Kevin M. Gannon has argued, the Morrill Act was part of a larger federal movement to ensure that "the trans-Mississippi West would become the white man's land; government fiat and settlers' actions effaced the footprints of the region's indigenous, Mexican, and buffalo populations."[4]

The first Morrill Act, of course, made no provision for those living under the Confederacy. The Second Morrill Act, passed in 1890—aimed at the southern states—demanded that states demonstrate that race was not a limiting admissions criterion, or else create a separate land-grant institution for people of color. This act led to the establishment of the historically black colleges and universities, implicitly making the other universities historically white (though they are hardly ever labeled as such).[5]

Thus, the conditions for the formation of the land-grant university were structured through both settler colonialism and segregated forms of unfreedom. A century later, while imperial and racial imperatives continued to structure the Cold War university, the development and institutionalization of ethnic and GWSFQ studies was made possible, in part, from the actions of student, staff, and faculty who protested many of these imperatives with the aid of philanthropic funding institutions. These factors supported the emergence of centers and the formation of ethnic studies and women's studies programs and departmental units focused on difference in the 1970–90s.

The demand that the articulation and theorization of difference be institutionalized within specific curriculum and programs that began in New Left, Civil Rights, and student movements in the United States led to the institutionalization of ethnic studies and GWSFQ studies in many universities in the late 1960s and early 1970s. For example, the 1968 student strike at San Francisco State, the longest such strike in U.S. history, was but one of several hundred that occurred within a short timespan. The coalition of the Black Student Union and the Third World Liberation Front with the support of almost all students and local communities headed a five-month strike for increased access to public higher education, new curriculum, and senior faculty of color.[6] The students had a radical planetary vision grounded in anti-imperialism and anticapitalism while positioned against Cold War–era area studies. Their demands were broad and heterogeneous; they sought not only an increase in access but also new institutional space for intellectual and political knowledges. This strike led to the establishment of the College of Ethnic Studies at San Francisco State College in 1969. According to Robin Kelley, by 1971, 500 colleges and universities had ethnic studies units, and there were 1,300 colleges and universities offering at least one ethnic studies course; these numbers dropped so that in 1974 only 200 units existed. Twenty years later, there was an increased presence of ethnic studies in 700 institutions as liberal multiculturalism became unevenly institutionalized primarily through curricular additions.[7]

The same year, at the University of Minnesota, students occupied the main administration building, Morrill Hall, to make a number of demands calling for a transformation of the indicative Cold War university. The symbolism of the takeover of Morrill Hall as an occupation and disruption at the University of Minnesota extends beyond its local institutional meaning, given that the building's very name references the act that established state-funded public research universities. In fact, students who participated in the occupation insisted that a commitment to ethnic studies represented an obligation for the post-segregation land-grant university.

According to University of Minnesota professor John Wright, who participated in the occupation as a student, the takeover paved the way for the establishment of the African American and African Studies Department, as well as the Chicano/a Studies, American Indian Studies, and Women's Studies programs at Minnesota. We want to recognize that student and youth movements from the Third World Liberation Front to the contemporary Whose Diversity? student movement (discussed below) have been at the forefront pressing for institutional transformation. Additionally, we want to note that while it is rarely part of the narrative of any of these departments at the University of Minnesota, the emergence and formalization of these units are symbolically and institutionally linked. While narratives of solidarity are associated with the Third World Liberation Front movement within origin narratives of ethnic studies, at the University of Minnesota, the specific intellectual genealogies of Chicano and Latino studies, American Indian studies, Asian American studies, and African American and African studies have been kept separate over time through processes of institutionalization. It is not our goal to offer an origin narrative with an idealized student movement of solidarity at its foundation that ends in a ragtag collection of fractured units. There are multiple genealogies that can be traced and drawn here that recognize the complex birthings of these fields and the conditions for their emergence and growth within the university. We want to suggest that these longer-entangled histories encourage us to ponder our current inhabitations and formations by attending to the continuing solidarities and tensions that characterize ethnic and GWSFQ studies.

IMPERATIVE MOOD OF THE NEOLIBERAL UNIVERSITY

As the Critical Ethnic Studies Collective has argued, liberal multiculturalism increasingly became the technology for the management of difference within the university.[8] "As a liberal corrective to long-standing histories of exclusion, the contemporary regime of hegemonic multiculturalism nominally includes previously marginalized and exploited peoples in selective institutional sites of civil societies. This pluralist dispensation of rights has fabricated a universal, liberated (multicultural) subject from material histories of domination, displacement, and unfreedom. Critical ethnic studies attempts to interrogate the grand telos emplotted by the narrative of liberal multicultural inclusion, recognition, and equality."[9]

Indeed there is a price to seeking transformative knowledge production within institutions propounding liberal multiculturalism while confronting institutional precarity. The institutionalization of ethnic and GWSFQ studies addressed inclusion and difference—but institutionalization was often accomplished without redistribution of resources. Instead, institutionalization relied greatly on informalization and informal labor. Through this informal labor, new social ecologies, knowledges, and institutional formations came into being. All of this resulted from the care and labor of women, people of color, LGBTQ faculty, and allies who sought to produce knowledge differently and different knowledge at the same time that they worked to transform the university itself. In other words, they sought to work within and to work on the university. To work within and work on the university is to be in and of the university.

While we openly acknowledge and engage our complicities, inhabiting the neoliberal historically white "public" university in the last decade has been dominated by the urgency of addressing institutional precarity manifested through defunding, unit mergers and collapses, adjunctification and informalization, and/or erasures. With the increased corporatization of the neoliberal university, the mood of the university has shifted to the imperative with the command to account for oneself.[10] As ethnic and GWSFQ studies, like many arts and humanities disciplines, perennially come up short in this accounting, they are considered to be failed and or failing. However, unlike other arts and humanities, they are seen as constitutively failed in that they cannot account for themselves intellectually and ontologically as disciplines. Charges take different forms such as we have failed our activist roots, not adequately reached and transformed publics, or become too professional. But it is important to keep in mind that such discourses of failure reflect and contribute to larger narratives of institutional failure attributed to the neoliberal university in crisis.

How does the institution deploy technologies of power to work with and manage difference and its "insurgent possibilities?" How did fields like ethnic and GWSFQ studies gain institutionalization only to now find themselves narrated as having failed? The management of diversity maintains, rather than challenges, the distribution of resources requiring even further justifications in an age of debt, accounting, and metrics in regard to excellence, profit, etc. Ethnic and GWSFQ studies are compelled to respond to the demand for accountability in the face of indebtedness. The logics of quantifiable metrics and the positivist calculus of diversity are always indexed to the supposed indebtedness, lack, and failure of ethnic and GWSFQ studies.

While endowments grow, programs are, nevertheless, slashed. Simultaneously, narratives about the death of the liberal arts are used to justify defunding of the arts and humanities in the name of crisis of the university writ large. In January 2016, Kentucky governor Matt Bevin suggested that humanities students should pay more for their degrees than, say, engineering students. "All the people in the world that want to study French literature can do so," he asserted, adding that "they are just not going to be subsidized by the taxpayer." Private universities too are divesting from liberal arts and boosting support for programs intended to train workers in the neoliberal economy.[11] In the university of austerity, the departments of languages, arts, and interdisciplinary ethnic studies and GWSFQ studies have often been the biggest losers. In institutions throughout North America, programs have been collapsed or cancelled.

As argued above, there are many factors that contribute to ethnic and GWSFQ studies being read as failures within the university, even in relation to other disciplines within the liberal arts. Being read as failures often leads to even greater disinvestment and more vulnerability, as the units function without minimum resources, face excessive institutional demands, negotiate deficient structures of support, must chase and demand soft funding sources, and garner joint appointments for scholars of color.

The neoliberal university justifies its commands and prohibitions through its own statements about crisis. The narrative of institutional crisis is perhaps one of the most common narratives of austerity. Crisis mongering has been, of course, very useful within the neoliberal university to justify retrenchment, norm enforcement, and the consolidation of wealth, resources, and authority in fewer and fewer hands. For those who are on the receiving end, crisis or disaster channels our energies toward mere survival, promotes an affective comportment of misery, and requires that we do not ask for more than is "realistic." Moreover, crisis confers a commonsense justification for the redistribution of resources upward.[12] In austere universities, small departments are inefficient, and large departments, like banks, are too big to fail. In this era of the neoliberal public university, there has been an upward redistribution of resources and value to STEM-related initiatives, to administration, and to athletics. While equity and diversity have changed the communications and representation strategies of universities in the twenty-first century, managing diversity has meant that value has been placed elsewhere in staff and administrative positions.

The projects of ethnic and GWSFQ studies are also vulnerable to defunding, collapse, and erasure due to external pressures. In Arizona, Republican legislators banned the teaching of ethnic studies courses in the Tucson Unified School District, saying that the courses taught hatred of other races, taught misinformation about historical subjugation, and taught sedition. In January 2017, Arizona legislators emboldened by the Trump presidency went so far as to expand the state's "ethnic studies ban" to cover university and community college courses.[13] Although the Arizona bill has been tabled for now, we are already seeing new and emboldened efforts to achieve austerity through defunding programs and classes seen as hostile to the new world order set forth by the Trump and other right-wing nationalist regimes. We are sure to see the intensification of these practices from the racial state. In January 2017, for example, Trump tweeted that UC Berkeley should lose its federal funding for the campus protests against hate-mongering white supremacist and xenophobe Milo Yiannapoulous, who was planning to speak about a campaign against sanctuary campuses financed by the Horowitz Center.[14] Also, the threat to academic freedom wherein the Wisconsin state legislature has identified a six-week program on understanding masculinity called the Men's Project and a course called The Problem of Whiteness as reasons to reform the University of Wisconsin system and further cut its budget.[15]

Even prior to this moment of Trump administration intensification, apparently benign narratives of austerity (e.g., discourses suggesting that we cannot do everything in the university, that there are too many departments, and that departments are redundant) had already become "apolitical" common sense. As Stuart Hall and Alan O'Shea comment, common sense is "'what everybody knows,' takes-for-granted and agrees with—the folk wisdom of the age.... what they are really doing is not just invoking popular opinion but shaping and influencing it ... By asserting that popular opinion already agrees, they hope to produce agreement as an effect."[16] Administrative strategies such as uniform cuts across departments, supposedly resource-blind policies, and metrics are all commonsense technologies of neoliberal administration that sear disproportionately.

Within the neoliberal university, the question is framed as "Who has failed the university? Who lacks moral responsibility? Who is not accountable?"

We question this account and emphasis on failure. As we have mentioned, there are many ways that the narrative of failure and crisis works to reestablish hierarchies, manage difference, and invalidate and undermine the labor and affect of ethnic and GWSFQ studies faculty and students inhabiting the university. In spite of threats to their budgets and autonomy, ethnic and GWSFQ studies continue to be called upon to perform diversity work within neoliberal governmentality and are, therefore, seen as necessary to the project of difference within the university. But ethnic and GWSFQ studies are also assessed and measured by additional metrics associated with the management of diversity and inclusion within liberal multiculturalism. Difference within the university is seen as a problem, one that ethnic studies was institutionalized and positioned to manage. Put differently, the gift of institutionalization of ethnic studies within the university was accompanied by an indebtedness indexed to the inclusion of the other through the metrics of diversity. Diversity, in this form, is preoccupied with the biopolitical management through technologies of counting and tracking minority student enrollments. Ethnic studies in its inability to dismantle the impacts of white supremacy, settler colonialism, and imperialism of the university is seen as having failed its mission in managing diversity for and in the university.

IRONIC INHABITATIONS WITHIN CONDITIONS OF UNCERTAINTY

Ethnic and GWSFQ studies and scholars do not inhabit the university gently, comfortably, or safely. They do so within a mood of uncertainty, doubt, and wishfulness. This is not to forget that faculty inhabit with privilege, while our students do not. Ethnic and GWSFQ studies inhabitants are often outside of the norms and standard operating procedures of the university and are made to feel displaced in their dwellings. Doing diversity work, transforming the university through inhabitation, is difficult uncertain labor that requires laughter. Sara Ahmed has given this labor for transformation through inhabitation a name. "Firstly, diversity work can refer to work that has the explicit aim of transforming an institution; and secondly, diversity work can be what is required, or what we do, when we do not quite inhabit the norms of an institution. These two senses often meet in a body: those who do not quite inhabit the norms of the institution are often those given the task of transforming those norms."[17] Put another way, diversity work is also the care and labor that is provided in response to the administrative violence that is produced when one works on the university. Diversity work is often considered the invisible reproductive labor performed by minoritized faculty, staff, and students. It provides some critical support to withstand the systemic exclusions and administrative violences of the university, but it also allows us to remain within the university, subject to its administrative violences.

In this last section, we consider different modalities of inhabitation as diversity work, in particular, examining different moments of institutional praxis at the University of Minnesota. We know that ethnic and GWSFQ studies have deployed different strategies in confronting and inhabiting the institution. From being a killjoy to demanding reparations, performing institutionalization, and developing informal networks of sociality and care, strategies have shifted over the years as neoliberal universities themselves have produced technologies of administration such as liberal multiculturalism and diversity in their management of difference.

At Minnesota, as in many other institutions, we have witnessed repeated attempts to collapse ethnic and GWSFQ studies units and reduce their administrative and budgetary footprint, if not minimize their presence and visibility. At root, these attempts were based on the idea that we produce redundant knowledges, while the disciplines themselves are considered unique and distinct. Three central assumptions underlie the call for collapse: (1) humanistic and "soft" social science research and pedagogy must be made leaner in a time of austerity (and the "fat" to be cut is in softer areas of interdisciplinary inquiry often understood as "identity studies"); (2) ethnic studies and GWSFQ studies are essentially all the same or have only insignificant differences; and (3) the work of ethnic and GWSFQ studies has been successfully incorporated into disciplines and now lives within departments—it is ever-present and the same in traditional disciplines. The inclusion is marked as successful. Gender is done, and everybody works on race and diversity everywhere. In short, our units are finished and unnecessary.

This process of diminution played out in myriad ways at Minnesota. In addition to wholesale plans to collapse and reduce units, administrators put us in competition with one another for resources and even scholarly and pedagogical terrain. We were informed our classes were duplicative and were asked to discontinue the practice of having graduate students (from American Studies and from Gender, Women, and Sexuality Studies) teach or assist in ethnic studies units, for example. This divide-and-conquer ethos threatened to thwart the shared intellectual and social justice work across these units. Yet, divide and conquer is a key modus operandi of the neoliberal university; even interdisciplinary inquiry is institutionalized most often in individual departments and centers, each with its own chair/head (or "boss"), its own budget, and its own line of communication with upper administration.

In the climate of manufactured scarcity, unit heads are rewarded for looking after the interests of their own individual units in relation to the rest of the university. If one unit manages to eke out a new faculty line, for example, that unit (and its head) has succeeded whereas those units whose resources are reduced "lose." Finding ways to maneuver ethically and effectively in the neoliberal university is the overriding challenge for those who foment interdisciplinary and socially just scholarship. Solidarity and collaboration are structurally disadvantaged, and the institutionalized nodes meant to promote faculty governance—including faculty senates and special committees—have been weakened to the point of hardly mattering within corporate university bureaucracies.

In 2013–14, in response to these challenges, chairs of the threatened units came together to strategize, lament, and foment, often in that order, to form the Race, Indigeneity, Gender, and Sexuality Studies (RIGS) collective.[18] The gathering was experimental; there was no set goal, and we all understood that working together both with and against the administration would likely take multiple forms, including many that would prove ephemeral, unsuccessful, or effective only in very particular circumstances. Here the idea of operating in the subjunctive mood, of asking about what might be possible if we operated in ways less legible to the structures and ideology of the corporate university, became relevant. Questions framed in terms of "what if" led us to consider myriad fascinating speculative possibilities.

We should note that the acronym "RIGS" was also a product of playful, subjunctive experimentation. We liked that it has multiple meanings; to "rig" means, among other things, to "make work," "to make use of," or "to outfit," all of which spoke to our attempts to make the neoliberal university work in ways in which it was not already, to ends that confounded goals of merit-based "excellence," and for those who are so often not understood as priorities. We also like that to "rig" also connotes a fraudulent system, one that is manipulated to maintain its white supremacy, settler colonial, and heteropatriarchal formations.

We met informally to resist our collapse while strategizing collaborations that pursue our capacious visions of transformation. To this effect, we convivially organized around nodes of shared political and intellectual projects while forging institutional solidarities and collectivity both informally and formally. In doing so, we neither sought to erase distinct intellectual genealogies nor reify staid oversimplified solidarities. We dynamically and intentionally anticipated and addressed contradictions, incommensurabilities, and tensions arising from intellectual and institutional locations with varying levels of success. We understood the uneven modalities of our institutionalization as well as the incongruency of our fields intellectually and administratively. Nevertheless, we forged a shared space for collective disruption through theory and praxis. Our idea was to remain mindful about the uneven terrain upon which we operate. Technically, five of the units were departments, with Asian American Studies as the only program (no faculty tenure lines housed in the unit, a minimal budget, etc.). This uneven institutionalization has been, and continues to be, a topic of discussion. Also, American Studies and Gender, Women and Sexuality Studies, as PhD-granting units, have often been afforded greater status and more resources within the political economy of a Research 1 institution (albeit less than disciplinary departments). These units were assigned the task of successfully managing difference, while ethnic studies units were increasingly denied support and resources and were often described as old-fashioned or obsolete, based largely on a liberal critique of "identity politics" and skepticism about the value of deep community engagement and outreach. RIGS chairs critically engaged this uneven assignment of value and also addressed how working together might yield both a redistribution and an expansion of resources and more opportunities for collaborative work.

One key disruptive tactic became evident right away; insisting on a practice of inclusive meetings would work to thwart "divide-and-conquer" management efforts. We met as a group of chairs with administrators at every level in the university, and we did so under the RIGS banner before RIGS had any formal institutional standing. Institutional legibility emerged largely through our collective presence and through the fact of our acronym, which implied a more formalized inhabitation of the university. This legibility was incomplete, though, because a newly organized group of chairs insisting on collective recognition proved both novel and confounding. Even more confounding was that we advocated for changes that typically had been promoted on the unit level—such as the hiring of more faculty in Chicano and Latino Studies—as a priority for all of our units. Such a move appealed to some administrators because it spoke to the (often empty) discourse of interdisciplinarity even as it disrupted the calculus of faculty lines meted out on the basis of a unit's "success" (as measured by undergraduate student enrollments and other ostensibly transparent neoliberal "metrics"). There was power in making requests—and demands—as a group of six, but there was also value in retaining our autonomous statuses as department chairs in other sites, such as college-wide chairs meetings, in which having six seats at the table (and six votes) proved essential in terms of policy making.

This ever shifting relationship between individual and unit autonomy (in many ways legible within the corporate university) and collectivity/solidarity (often disruptive to the corporate university) became the hallmark of RIGS—in some ways a radical administrative openness—a subjunctive inhabitation of the university. We believe it reflects the radical potential and spirit of ethnic studies today: "In the purposeful absence of a static or prescriptive scholarly agenda that poses as a definitive redefinition of ethnic studies, the still-forming project of critical ethnic studies is in some ways better understood as a principled gesture toward a radical intellectual openness."[19] Revising, refining, and rethinking the relationship between autonomy and collectivity emerged as the ongoing project of RIGS participants as we pursued a variety of goals. Ironically, asserting collectivity in a defensive mode became essential for maintaining autonomy. We consistently insisted that we would not support or cooperate with any administrative effort to collapse our units or to disinvest or close any one of our units. For the time being, at least, this effort has been successful in that it helped bring about the cessation of such proposals or even suggestions.

Of course, gathering under the sign of RIGS also drew on a deep and growing commitment to intersectional analysis and politics among the faculty and students in our units. Intersectionality as analytical frame meant that many of us were working across departmental lines in our individual and collaborative projects. And intersectionality marked activist critiques of, and engagements with, the university, especially among graduate and undergraduate students enrolled in or affiliated with our units. For example, Whose University? (formed in 2010), a collective "organizing students, educators, workers, and community members to challenge the University of Minnesota's priorities in equal access and resources for underrepresented groups,"[20] and its later iteration Whose Diversity? (formed in 2014), an "autonomous collective [of] . . . students from marginalized and underrepresented communities from within the University of Minnesota," were premised on intersectional inhabitations of and challenges to the neoliberal university's promotional celebration of "diversity" even as students of color remained marginalized. "Being people of color, first generation (im)migrants, differently-abled folks, people of various spiritual beliefs, Indigenous people, LGBT people, means that the University of Minnesota reads us as people that can be exploited."[21] Although not actively coordinated, the demands of RIGS and Whose Diversity? overlapped, and both stymied efforts to manage difference through atomized departments and identity categories. The actions promulgated by Whose Diversity?, such as a new occupation of Morrill Hall to demand, among other things, substantive commitments to recruiting and retaining students and faculty from marginalized communities, informed, shaped, and reflected the emerging RIGS agenda. Most broadly, RIGS and Whose Diversity? advocate for knowledge production that will be transformative for subaltern communities and the university.

RIGS, as subjunctive and collective formation, fomented some significant changes. A major one was the 2015 launch of a cluster hire for four scholars "with interest in the intersecting categories of race, ethnicity, class, gender, and sexuality whose research agendas focus on topics and questions concerning African Americans, American Indians, Asian Americans, Chicanas/os, and Latinas/os." As the search was launched, RIGS (now identified as an "initiative") also secured an operating budget to support programming and curricular initiatives as well as support (in the form of course releases, space, and graduate assistant administrative support) to appoint a director. In this phase, RIGS became more formalized within the institution. That shift proved useful, perhaps even necessary, in that phase given the complexities of conducting such a major hiring effort as well as the work necessary to build networks across the university and with community partners and to develop and advocate for curriculum that responded to the needs of underserved communities of students. The first RIGS director, Catherine Squires, working with RIGS chairs and others, managed to conduct a search that resisted pressure to hire individuals who would be given tenure homes in disciplinary departments, put in place a search committee that was recruited and nominated by RIGS, and allowed hires to identify the units with which they would affiliate. All of those features were unconventional and pushed against the political economic imperatives of a university system that often awarded "diversity hires" (and diversity hire resources) to "strong" larger units that were often incapable of producing and sustaining the conditions that would allow those hires to flourish.

As Ferguson and others have noted, formalization always comes with the potential for peril, among them institutional interpellation.[22] And, as many of those who work within the university recognize, faculty lines are often hailed as the most valuable resource within the institution (among faculty, at least) and competition over this resource can encourage retrenchment when it comes to collaboration across units or specialties. To put it more starkly, faculty searches can bring out the worst qualities among tenure-line faculty and academic units. Although the results of the cluster search—the hiring of four extraordinary new faculty members—were excellent, the complexities of the search process, including disagreement over which underresourced units were in greatest need of new faculty members, did cut against efforts to "act otherwise" and deflated some of the subjunctive enthusiasm that animated the formation of the collaborative.

That we were seeking to formalize our entity without specifying its final institutional formation was not only tricky but difficult. Formalization occurred with the approval of a cluster search, but also in the creation of an administrative director position, programming and research budget, and staffing for the initiative. Indeed, formalization in this imprecise form meant that the burden of negotiating the byzantine machinery of the university fell on the intrepid director, who had to manage the perils of underresourcing, understaffing, and neglect. The obstacles of this kind of diversity work is perhaps best described by Sara Ahmed in *Living a Feminist Life*, recounting how the feminist in the university hits a wall while the system denies the existence of the wall.[23] She is bruised and ascribed with fragility when she articulates the administrative violence of the university. RIGS continues to be brought into question, its tense questioned. Institutionalization acts in the imperative, demanding that RIGS congeal into a set form of a center, an institute, or a school. We have had to think subjunctively about our inhabitation.

CONCLUSION: HOW MOODY ARE WE?

If we inhabit the subjunctive in the university, on the side, a clause, and temporally in the becoming, and not yet in our ambiguity and not quite placement, we inhabit a mood indicating that which is hypothetical, imagined, dreaded, wished for, and uncertain. Ethnic and GWSFQ studies scholars often employ the subjunctive as a mood of expressing what might be possible and that which is still unknown. Moreover, working collectively across our differences, knowledges, and institutional formations means that we are learning how to conjugate in each other's languages. If RIGS is a mood, it is the subjunctive. It is how we feel, care, labor, and think within the academy. We inhabit without certainty this formation and the university. It is a space that we must imagine to come together, to laugh in rather than smile politely within, to remake ecologies for racialized queer bodies, and to reimagine care not as individual self-care but as acts of collective survival within institutionalized life. While discourses of individual self-care are rampant within neoliberalism as responses to the violences of capitalism, white supremacy, and patriarchy, radical care and healing requires recognition of interdependence and collective response—*a singular individual being* a slow professor is not transformative as he merely transfers the labor elsewhere down the pipeline. We mean the survival of those not meant to survive. Our moods and affects are not inconsequential. We want to suggest that mood, rather than moodiness, was and is also critical to RIGS. Within our informal and formal collectivity, we experienced and expressed the roots of the etymology of mood—heart, spirit, pride, power, and laughter. Perhaps, most importantly, we dwelled in laughter, laughter in the face of diversity (and adversity). Our laughter is and was a shared response to the lack of new language to describe new modalities of inhabitations. To laugh collectively in the university requires labor, in that it indicates a form of ecological ontology that is not automatic; it is created and has to be maintained.

This laughter is not one of happiness and joy. There is a tendency and perhaps a need to laugh in the moment of tragedy and in the face of downsides and obstacles. It is an understanding that we are again facing the inevitable and that we have faced the inevitable before. Indeed obstacles are familiar and are sometimes the path itself. At Minnesota, one particular obstacle/path was a strategic plan called "roadmap to the future" by the dean of the College of Liberal Arts. As we struggled to see ourselves and our futures in this latest of many strategic plans, we laughed together at the notion that ethnic and GWSFQ studies were positioned as the roadkill on that roadmap; carrion without future. This kind of gallows laughter, the laughter at familiar plans that always redistribute upward, is not absolute; we always carry hope, complicity, and possibility—not of some stable institutionalization, but of the familiarity of resourceful stubbornness, which we refuse to call resiliency. Our laughter did not reflect faith in the institution, but rather hope for the fragile intimacies that arise out of them.

This practice of laughter, linked to our desire to inhabit the university in the subjunctive mood, is largely ironic laughter. We found, in our collaboration, that we shared a certain positionality vis-à-vis the university—and any powerful institution for that matter—that did not rely on a belief that the institution would act on its stated principles through its established processes, precisely because we know such institutions are formed through constitutive violences. The university is an institution of the state. We continue to inhabit them, are complicit within them, and seek to simultaneously transform them with hope and detachment. Informed by our backgrounds in activism, which include AIDS activism, environmental justice movements, and anti-carceral movements, among others, we understood the power of wealth to direct institutional priorities and practices. We also understand the limitations of earnest calls to principle in the production of meaningful change. Irony fosters both a helpful distancing from the disappointments of fights thwarted or lost as well as a reminder that the university as institution does not, and will never, align neatly with the extent of our commitments, our desires, or our selves. But irony also encourages us to laugh at ourselves and our own, often misplaced or exaggerated, beliefs in our influence or our power to reform or undo.

RIGS may oscillate between pessimism and optimism (or futurism). And we must have room in this. Moreover, we rarely see such lack of a future as tragedy. Inhabiting the university with uncertainty is different than attaching to expectations associated with institutionalization. Ethnic and GWSFQ studies interrogates, almost daily, its attachment to the university and the supposed promise of (the) good life. We have long known that the good life (property, citizenship, and security) for some is constituted through unfreedoms for others. Rage and laughter reflect mistrust; we doubt that which is promised by the university through meritocracy, labor, and success as we know it has been constituted through violence, unfreedom, and exclusion. Our optimism is "a scene of negotiated sustenance that makes life bearable as it presents itself ambivalently, unevenly, incoherently."[24] But we continue to dwell despite, not because of, the university as we seek transformation through knowledge production. We are, perhaps, not attached to nor seeking the good life, or even a good life. If we inhabit the university in the subjunctive, we seek the infinitive. In other words, we desire *buen vivir*, to live well or even live well enough. This is uncertainty as a wish in the form of action. We seek to make knowledge and live responsibly (i.e., do the work of ethnic studies) while placing survival, not the university, at the center of networks of affect, care, and intellectual labor. Our optimism is that ethnic and GWSFQ studies will provide the blueprint for a different university yet to come. Fuck the university; long live the university that is yet to be.

JIGNA DESAI is professor in the Department of Gender, Women, and Sexuality Studies and the Asian American Studies Program at the University of Minnesota. Her research interests include Asian American, postcolonial, queer, disability, and diasporic cultural studies. She has served as a board member of the Association for Asian American Studies and serves as a coeditor of the Asian American Experience book series for the University of Illinois Press. She is a founding member of the Race, Indigeneity, Gender, and Sexuality Studies Collective (RIGS) at the University of Minnesota. Jigna Desai and Dr. Kari Smalkoski collaborate to amplify youth voices through

10,000 Stories: Minnesota Youth Make Media—an engaged research project focused on media-making with youth in urban public schools (z.umn.edu/10000stories).

KEVIN P. MURPHY is professor of history and affiliate professor of American studies and gender, women, and sexuality studies at University of Minnesota. He is the author of *Political Manhood* (2008) and, as a member of the Twin Cities GLBT Oral History Project, *Queer Twin Cities* (2010). He has edited several anthologies and special journal issues focused on queer studies and history and is writing a book focused on the intersection of queer and public history. He served as the chair of the department of American Studies and is founding member of the Race, Indigeneity, Gender, and Sexuality Studies Collective (RIGS) at the University of Minnesota.

NOTES

We want to thank Lisa Park, the anonymous reviewers, and Ashon Crawley, Eve Tuck, and K. Wayne Yang for their incisive comments; our essay is the better for it, though all shortcomings remain ours. We dedicate this essay to the people who work, laugh, and imagine the university yet to be—thanks to Lisa, Eden, Keith, Jeani, Karen, Catherine, Elliott, and Tracey.

1. For example: Christopher Newfield, *Unmaking the Public University: The Forty-Year Assault on the Middle Class* (Cambridge, Mass.: Harvard University Press, 2009); and Christopher Newfield, *The Great Mistake: How We Wrecked Public Universities and How We Can Fix Them* (Baltimore: Johns Hopkins University Press, 2015).

2. Danielle Bouchard, *Community of Disagreement: Feminism in the University* (New York: Peter Lang, 2012), 5.

3. Transcript of Morrill Land-Grant Act (1862) Chap. CXXX, Sec. 4.

4. Kevin M. Gannon, "The Civil War as a Settler-Colonial Revolution," *Age of Revolutions*, January 18, 2016, https://ageofrevolutions.com/2016/01/18/the-civil-war-as-a-settler-colonial-revolution/.

5. See, for example, William H. Jeynes, *American Educational History: School, Society, and the Common Good* (Thousand Oaks, Calif.: SAGE, 2007), 193–202.

6. "History," College of Ethnic Studies, San Francisco State University, https://ethnicstudies.sfsu.edu/home2.

7. Robin Kelley, "Over the Rainbow: Second Wave Ethnic Studies against the Neoliberal Turn," Department of Ethnic Studies, University of California, San Diego, https://www.youtube.com/watch?v=w9MJAxpWKYA.

8. See Critical Ethnic Studies Editorial Collective, "Introduction: A Sightline," *Critical Ethnic Studies: A Reader* (Durham, N.C.: Duke University Press, 2016), 1–18.

9. Critical Ethnic Studies Editorial Collective, "Introduction," 6.

10. Miranda Joseph, *Debt to Society: Accounting for Life under Capitalism* (Minneapolis: University of Minnesota Press, 2014).

11. U.S. News & World Report, "In Kentucky, a Push for Engineers over French Lit Scholars, January 29, 2016 (available at *San Diego Union-Tribune*, http://www.sandiegouniontribune.com/sdut-in-kentucky-a-push-for-engineers-over-french-lit-2016jan29-story.html).

12. See, for example, Anthony Loewenstein, *Disaster Capitalism: Making a Killing out of Catastrophe* (London: Verso, 2015), and Naomi Klein, *The Shock Doctrine: The Rise of Disaster Capitalism* (New York: Picador, 2007).

13. "Arizona Bill to Extend Ethnic-Studies Ban to Universities Dies," *Arizona Republic*, January 17, 2017, http://www.azcentral.com/story/news/politics/arizona-education/2017/01/18/arizona-bill-extend-ethnic-studies-ban-universities-dies/96694610/.

14. "Trump Tweets at Berkeley: No Free Speech, No Federal Funds," *San Jose (Calif.) Mercury News*, February 2, 2017, http://www.mercurynews.com/2017/02/02/trump-tweets-at-uc-berkeley-no-free-speech-no-federal-funds/.

15. Scott Jaschick, "Wisconsin–Madison Criticicized for Men's Discussion," *Inside Higher-Ed*, January 5, 2017, https://www.insidehighered.com/quicktakes/2017/01/05/wisconsin-madison-criticized-mens-discussions.

16. Stuart Hall and Alan O'Shea, "Common Sense Neoliberalism," *Soundings* 55 (Winter 2013), xx.

17. Sara Ahmed, *On Being Included: Racism and Diversity in Institutional Life* (Durham, N.C.: Duke University Press, 2012) 175.

18. Jigna Desai (gender, women, and sexuality studies), Keith Mayes (African American and African studies), Kevin Murphy (American studies), Jeani O'Brien (American Indian studies), Lisa Park (Asian American studies), and Eden Torres (Chicano and Latino studies).

19. Critical Ethnic Studies Editorial Collective, "Introduction," 3.

20. "Whose University? Campaign, Film Project, and Event," https://sites.google.com/site/whoseuniversityfilm/.

21. Whose Diversity?, "About," http://whosediversity.weebly.com/about.html.

22. Roderick A. Ferguson, *The Reorder of Things: The University and Its Pedagogies of Minority Difference* (Minneapolis: University of Minnesota Press, 2012); Ahmed, *On Being Included*; Myrl Beam, *Gay Inc.: The Nonprofitization of Queer Politics* (Minneapolis: University of Minnesota Press, forthcoming 2018).

23. Sara Ahmed, *Living a Feminist Life* (Durham, N.C.: Duke University Press, 2017).

24. Lauren Berlant, *Cruel Optimism* (Durham, N.C.: Duke University Press, 2011), 14.

Queer of Color Space-Making in and beyond the Academic Industrial Complex

PAOLA BACCHETTA, FATIMA EL-TAYEB, JIN HARITAWORN,
JILLIAN HERNANDEZ, SA SMYTHE, VANESSA E. THOMPSON,
AND TIFFANY WILLOUGHBY-HERARD

We are a group of eight organic and professional queer and trans people of color (QTPOC) intellectuals, who had the opportunity to spend a quarter together at the University of California, Irvine in early 2017, thanks to a successful grant from the University of California Humanities Research Institute (UCHRI). Our residential research group (RRG) came together to discuss queer of color space-making in Europe and transnationally.[1] Over the course of ten weeks, we engaged with a broad range of topics related to queer of color spaces, including spatial segregation; gentrification; queer of color performance; trans of color politics; travels and translations; theorizing activism; social movements; anti-Blackness; Islamophobia; racisms and racialization; decoloniality; violence; carceral and border regimes; historiography and archives; queer family making and the state; and creative practices including film, visual art, dance, and creative writing.

But beyond *studying* oppressed peoples' spatial, political, and historic interventions, we were deeply committed to finding better ways of *making* and sharing space with each other. Our experiences and how we make and share space together are indexes of power and viable categories of theoretical analysis. For example, over the course of the residency, we built space with each other in many ways, which we discuss in this article. We also built space with other queer, trans, nonqueer, and nontrans people of color by attending events organized by them on campus and by organizing our own public event including participants from Southern California and Europe and with people of all colors resisting the newly elected regime at anti-Trump and pro-immigration marches in LA and Orange County, where the residency was based. This was especially important to those of us who had traveled

Southern California and other parts of Europe and North America as part of the fellowship.

One of the ways we created our own space was through collective writing. This took considerable trust. Some of us had known each other for years; others first met in week one of our RRG. Our group included professors, tenured at different ranks or untenured, PhD students, and folks currently debating whether or not to return to the academic industrial complex (AIC) as graduate students. We had spent varying amounts of time in the AIC, on both sides of the Atlantic, including the United States, Canada, Germany, France, Britain, Italy, and South Africa. Several of us had escaped from the unself-consciously white academies of Northwest Europe and moved to North America. This displacement felt both inevitable for us as activist queer and/or trans of color scholars, and deeply problematic. In the United States and Canada, we found that we were invited into complicity with a settler colonialism that continually erases its own foundational and contemporary violence by celebrating its territory as a haven for oppressed peoples from everywhere, and thereby further strengthening its U.S.-centrism, which is based on settler colonial empire. Simultaneously, the place accorded to us in North America continually confronted us with the assumption of Europe as white, and QTPOCs in Europe as nonexistent.

While we all situationally identify as queer and/or trans of color, we have different relationships to power and oppression along many axes, including anti-Blackness, Islamophobia, border imperialism, transphobia, class oppression, chronic illness and disability, sexism, racial-mixphobia, and work with the next generation including queer parenting and other forms of intentional kin building. We were determined to give these differences, and the crucial knowledges that they give rise to, space, and to acknowledge how they impacted our weekly interactions and daily lives in Irvine: from not being able to use any of the (gender-segregated) bathrooms in the building where we were meeting, to being mistaken for the group's only other Black trans person by UCI faculty, to being mistaken for another lesbian of color fellow, to eruptions of irresolvable conflicts about how we handled and mishandled blackness and Indigeneity. We understood early on that while the institutional space that we had applied for and gained was, like all institutional spaces in the AIC, deeply flawed, we did have the power to inhabit and share this space intentionally and expansively, prefiguring the world we want to live in. The UCHRI RRG provided a space-time to do precisely that.

We began by crafting a community agreement together in week one. Its many detailed guidelines included recognizing the specificity of anti-Black racism and the labor of Black women, Black queers, and Black trans people; respecting self-determination; gendering each other consensually; and creating access for folks with chemical sensitivities, food differences, and other requirements. We shared food and met each other's kids, cats, and partners. We experimented with ways to share resources between waged and unwaged members of the RRG. We engaged in material solidarity. One person had a car and drove everyone to dinner. Another had to leave for a few days, and several others took care of her cat in her absence. One found a way to provide free bikes to visiting fellows stuck in Irvine without cars. Some of us bore unequal burdens resulting from the ubiquitous precarity of trying to finance graduate education, which included driving hundreds of hours on one of the world's most dangerous freeways. We created ritual: each session began with a reading of the community agreement and a pronoun round and check-in that validated the importance of emotions and of what was happening in the world in this time of rising fascism, as personal, political, and part of QTPOC knowledge production.

Our period of residency at the UCHRI corresponded to the beginning of the Trump presidency, thus a moment when coloniality, white supremacy, hate, and war were spectacularly legitimized across the United States. Given the real-world consequences of peoples waking up to the statuary of the Lost Cause Campaign littering and marking every official building, school, and park in U.S. society, this moment lent itself to a more critical understanding of the ways that anti-blackness and suppressing the reality of settler society operates to produce spaces of legitimacy, learning and socialization, and recreation and leisure. We found ourselves in Irvine, a small planned city incorporated in 1971 and built on the land of the Tongva people (aka Gabrieleño and Fernandeño people, according to names adopted and resignified by the Spanish colonial missions that built on their land). "Tongva" means "people of the earth." We are grateful to them for the use of the land. While our RRG was about QTPOC in Europe and space, and most of our discussions were about people of color born in white-dominated Europe, as longtime or more recent citizens, migrants, or refugees, this all took place on settler colonized land. The members of our RRG have different kinds of relations to Indigeneity and to U.S. Indigeneity. Some are mixed with Indigeneity in the Americas. Others come from sites where the term "Indigenous" is used as a racial slur to signify (post)colonial populations who arrived in the center of empire from the colonies. All are faced in Europe with our construction as other, as perpetual and permanent foreigners, in relation to white nationalists' claims to their own (European) Indigeneity. And yet, on Tongva land, our university affiliations signify forms of class privilege and association with a settler colonial institution, even if as people of color—some U.S. citizens and some not—we are also perpetual outsiders to the white settler nation and its institutions. Such are the complexities with which we live.

Within the culture of trust and vulnerability that we created together, we could begin to share, first with each other and now in print, that the AIC, often hailed as the nicest arm of neoliberal governance, is an irretrievably harmful presence in our lives and our communities. We wrestled with how the AIC's investments in meritocracy and professionalism produce friction, competition, and forms of tokenistic racial violence, some of which are still far too difficult to acknowledge and talk about openly. Some of us only had our silence or our absence or our compliance to register what the AIC has done to us and in our name. We were able to talk about the personal impacts of the spaces in which we produce knowledge, and our assigned locations in these spaces, and the ways in which these are each deeply implicated in the racial, colonial, gendered, capitalist, carceral regimes we are up against. We were able to explore, also, how queers of color can present a disruptive force to the AIC, whose strategies bring us closer to an abolitionist horizon on learning and education. The following pages were birthed as part of this transformative encounter.

We hope that in these pages the reader will hear our collective voice in both its plural and combined singular dimensions. Our positions and narratives are ones that the university—as a hegemonic site of cultural analysis and knowledge production—actively tries to avoid engaging, derides as bromides, and belittles as *mere* personal experiences. This politics of minimizing our analyses has taken many faces over the years, most often cohering around the idea that we as queer and trans people of color lack the capacity to historicize or theorize how power operates on these lives. As Saidiya Hartman has explained: *We* were "sold [as] strangers; those outside the web of kin and clan relationships, nonmembers of the polity, foreigners and barbarians at the outskirts of their country, and lawbreakers expelled from society."[2] As strangers within and without, our freedom dreams do not usually conjure sympathy or compassion because the world that we fight for looks so vastly different from the one in which we currently reside. In the current world there is room for us only if our ways of being are disciplined and caricatured using abstractions that are wholly unrecognizable to us. The value of experience as marshaled here clearly reflects a deep investment in critique and struggle against social structures, practices, policies, statutes, and institutions that produce systematic and institutionalized quotidian violence and ever-new forms of brutality—symbolic, embodied, and material.³ We critique the unity implied in the universalized "we" that paradigmatically and paradoxically presents itself as a sovereign individual "I" in Western philosophy and offer a situated narrative that links the "we" and the "I."⁴ Of course, we are not into some unmediated notion of experience or, farther back, the idea of an unmediated subject of experience. Instead we are deploying situated narratives. Norma Alarcon's "The Theoretical Subjects of *This Bridge Called My Back*" explains "the displacement of . . . subjectivity across multiple discourses . . . the peculiarity of [such] displacement implie[s] a multiplicity of positions from which she was driven to grasp or understand [the self] and [the] relations with the real" reflect how universalization is critical to power.⁵ Moreover, the collective voice here is the result of deliberate crafting and a highly mediated decision to link ourselves and to "adjust . . . behavior to maintain membership in a group" of queer and trans people of color in order to interrogate the social structures, practices, and embodied understandings that constitute how we are produced, read, and denoted in the world.⁶ This "we" is a chosen political association, not a careless set of revelations. The classic approach of coming together to write erases the individual voices to write systematically at the highest level of abstraction possible, because individual voices are deemed divisive and untrustworthy and symptomatic instead of paradigmatic. However, part of the evidence of the trust that we extended to each other is to be found in our method of creative collective writing. We decided that the individual voice should not be erased in the collective. The movement between the "we" and the "I" in this essay is a political choice that reflects a commitment to not erase the multiplicities of subalternities and instead to allow the components of the collectivity their full existence. Our goal was not to pursue universalization; instead we tried to pay attention to what each other was saying. This gesture against universalization allowed each person in the collectivity their full existence and compelled us to practice inhabiting each other's space as we created a new one, collectively.

The differences and similarities in our group were also reflected in our academic trajectories. Some of us had always dreamed of becoming an academic. Maybe a teacher or elder deemed us bright. Maybe the smartest queer we'd ever met, whom we had a mad crush on, was doing a PhD. Maybe we thought that we could change the world, one classroom at a time. Maybe we wanted to make our parents and community proud by obtaining status and a stable financial situation, even through the lens of meritocracy that constantly stigmatizes the poor and people of color, and yet, due to colonial and racialized extraction and appropriation, the university is also simultaneously often the legal owner of the most important repositories of histories of resistance and rebellion that have been hidden from us. Other members of our group had never dreamed of becoming academics. Most of us had no idea what that even meant. For some of us school was an escape from other brutal realities. Many of us hated educational institutions from the minute we set foot in high school and later college. We hated the white, elitist, cis-heteropatriarchal version of "knowledge" they were forcibly imposing upon us, and the ways our white middle-class heteronormative and cisgender peers were being fostered as future reproducers of civilization, while we were trained to become wardens for the assimilation and control of other black and brown folks. We were silenced, disciplined, and reminded daily that we arrived uninvited, yet we persisted (sometimes barely), reclaiming resources and knowledge for our communities.

Many of us were already well aware that the neoliberal humanist heteronormative, cisgender, and misogynist project of the university is and has always been deeply tied to the genocidal, colonial, and enslavement episteme. We were cognizant of the fact that Man's overrepresentation, as Sylvia Wynter puts it, continuously reproduces epistemic regimes of otherness as inferior, criminal, and to be eliminated.[7] We knew not to trust the "murderous invitations" of the neoliberal university, which needs "diverse" bodies in order to beautify its racial/colonial capitalist and carceral agenda.[8]

We did not belong in the institution. We belonged in the movement, in the streets. But we loved reading, and in those moments when we were able to forget where we were, we loved learning. We read stories about Black feminist liberation and emancipatory struggles, accounts of movements that were often subsumed by official histories and progress narratives.[9] We read the book about the Black woman who went to Harvard via the Rosenwald Fund.[10] We read books that opened up worlds where it was possible to be queer and trans and belong in antiracist and anticolonial struggles. We read theory, and we realized we had long started writing it, too, as a form of poetry, or in other creative genres, that made interventions into dominant categories, ways of thinking, and logics. This kind of theory engaged everything about our queer racialized bodies.

Books were our home. Many of us had grown up odd, nerdy, queer, and, socially awkward—far more involved with books than with people. Some were lucky enough to come of age in times and places where we could join radical movements that affirmed our lives. For others, books were the first place where we could find any kind of community. In a world that treats trans people of color in particular as excessive to even the most radical community, reading and writing can save lives.

Many of us were under no illusion that working in the AIC would occur under favorable conditions. However, the jobs that we saw tended to be better than working in the supermarkets, factories, restaurants, libraries, museums, and sexual health and nonprofit organizations in which we had previously worked.[11] We were tired of seeing so many upper-class white professors making money and careers from teaching Eurocentric analyses of the oppression and exploitation that we and our ancestors had gone through. If we were going to be exploited for our community connections, at least there was a small chance we might eventually land a full-time job.

Being paid to think was, of course, an extremely attractive idea. We chose employment in the AIC both for economic survival and for the transformative possibilities that some of its sites—the classroom in particular—promised. We stayed in grad school despite financial difficulties and in the face of a lot of hunger—spiritual, physical, material, emotional. One of us made it through graduate school as a single mother. Another stayed despite being the only Black student in the philosophy department for six years. Another was undocumented and in political exile during most of her university education. Most of us lived far away from family and friends. Much of the time, we felt marginalized, invisible, and alone. We stayed in spite of the anti-Black gendered violence that pervaded our grad schools, and despite horrifying experiences of racism, Islamophobia, queerphobia, and transphobia from teachers, administrators, staff, and fellow students. The strength we found often came from simultaneous continued involvement in multiple activist movements.

Our devaluation, tokenization, and erasure as queer and trans of color intellectuals did not end with the PhD. Many of us experienced recurring racial, gendered, and sexual macro assaults and macro aggressions in the areas of employment, labor, housing, health, hiring, and admissions, that if named and leveraged could maybe actually change how we understand what on earth we are doing here.[12] We stayed even though our colleagues did not greet us in the corridor, or told us we were in the wrong corridor. Some of us took close to a decade to land our first tenure-track job. Some made it through the tenure process, and some to full professor, in the face of racist, cis-supremacist, and misogynist presumptions, often in the guise of "mentorship," that we are "incompetent."[13] Many of us have stayed for the students: for our POC students who feel they have no place in the university or in the world; for our QTPOC students who need to be in the company of somebody who will let them come out and come into themselves on their own terms and in their own language and who won't mind them hiding beyond middle-class aspirations like "getting into graduate school." At the same time, we are well aware of the neoliberal traps of "staying for the students." Thus, students, too—especially, but not only, those white, cis, and/or male students for whom our classroom is often the only place where they have to confront the facts of racial/colonial capitalism and cis-heteropatriarchy—have a hard time respecting us and regularly reinscribe us as affectable subjects.[14] When we help these students understand how their history was mutually created with and deeply imbricated with structures of oppression that entrapped and strangled people from other communities, our teaching is deemed too "political," even as the neoliberal university decorates itself with us. We regularly receive worse evaluations, and more complaints, than our white colleagues. We perform an enormous amount of free labor to compensate for the university's own inability to deal with race, coloniality, class, gender, and sexuality. Yet our service record, just like our skin, is always "too thin."

We have remained academics in spite of quickly learning that we can't always expect solidarity from all of our POC/WOC/QTPOC colleagues, many of whom play into the colonial divide and rule and manipulation tactics of white colleagues and the administration in power. For one RRG member, occupying academic space as a cis-femme Latina from a working-class background has meant being routinely subject to belittling "micro" aggressions from senior scholars and sexual harassment from white men administrators. Some members have received rape threats from students. Others have supported student survivors in the face of criminally neglectful university structures. For trans and gender nonconforming people of color, almost no spaces currently exist where our academic contributions are invited or welcomed. Trans people of color generally remain disposable even in spaces that gather under such rubrics as "queer of color" and "anti-racist feminist." Every time we step into a room we are forced to engage in a new humiliating fight for basic access, pronoun awareness, and washroom use. Allies are few and far between: even in the most radical associations, gender solidarity often stops at cis women's loyalty with fragile cis men, whose comfort and "defense" is prioritized over the possibility to organize with trans people, whose unique positionalities have so much to teach about liberating gender from racist respectability scripts and the colonial gender binary. Trans people of color also get divided and ruled between entrenched interests that have little genuine care for them—like in France and the United States, where white cis male colleagues mobilize toxic inclusion to recruit trans people to burnish their own legitimacy while failing to mentor them and secure them funding, leaving them to be trained and mentored by the same old antiracist cis feminists they abuse and disdain.

We stay in the face of skyrocketing tuition fees that make the university inaccessible and the notion of liberationist education a sham. We stay even though the university is built on stolen land, run on Native, Black, Latinx, racially mixed, and Asian women's labor and part of the global privatized war machine complex, all of which we actively work against. We stay even though our workplaces are sites of racial profiling and actively gentrify working-class neighborhoods. We stay even though our very presence here signals "progress," when really we are fighting tooth and nail just to hang on to spaces and resources long and hard won by the isolated generations of QPOC and POC that precede us. This is why the ethics of how we make space together are so important as principles to us.

From our impossible locations in the AIC, we invent various strategies to keep us and other gendered and racialized subjects here. The strategies we invent divest from the competitive values of the colonial neoliberal university, and from its racially skewed logics of merit, respectability, and gender and racial exceptionalism, and instead invest in polyglot, heterotopic community. Our strategies affirm the lives of queer and trans people of color, and of all others treated as raw material for theory production, rather than fostered as present and future knowledge reproducers. We are cognizant of the harmful effects of the AIC on our community members—both those who never jump the gates, and those who do, and who, too, deserve solidarity in surviving the toxic impact of the institution. We repurpose the resources of the neoliberal university to redistribute the land, wealth, and cultures extracted from our peoples back to our peoples and to build community in our classrooms and our hallways, even as we acknowledge the profound inequalities inherent in the process of labor under conditions of coloniality, racism, capitalism, cis-heteropatriarchy, and misogyny. We create cultures of appreciation that strive toward an honest and constructive division of labor, risks, and benefits and that value the shifts we do for each other as comrades.

We have been forced to fight. But our strategies include engaging in these struggles for our very existence and for the departments and research centers we have built (see the film *On Strike* by Irum Sheikh).[15] These struggles also take place beyond individual universities—translocally and transnationally. As Black and other people of color academics, queer, trans and otherwise, we, especially those of us who are based in the United States, are sometimes called into an academic space to talk about racism and intersectional postcolonial power "over there," and as such we are often interpellated to become complicit in the erasure of the colonial, racist, and intersectional power at work "here."[16] We resist becoming fly-in academics who dismiss antiracist and anticolonial struggles locally and exclusively orient ourselves to the white institution that invites us and pays for our flight. We enter into crunchy transnational conversations in order to hold each other accountable to travel ethically and in ways that uplift and orient themselves toward local struggles both in and beyond the institution. We strive to become community-accountable scholars who seek to counter the uneven power relations between the Global North and South, the United States and the rest, and the English-speaking and non-English-speaking world.[17]

We fight for the future and also to maintain what our earlier generations have already established, which is constantly under threat. We remember and call the names of those who have created these spaces for us.[18] Sometimes they were queer and trans people of color, and sometimes they were not. Those spaces and our solidarity have kept us here.

While ultimately seeking to liberate education from the AIC, we invent practical strategies that help us and our students survive the space of toxic institutions here and now. We ask each other to act as coexaminers and committee members and letter writers in order to protect our students from racist, sexist, queer and transphobic, classist, ableist violence whether enacted by the state, vigilantes, or interpersonally. We swap concrete teaching methods for dealing with white/male/cis/hetero/sexist students and ideologies in our classrooms. We use our academic positions to funnel university funds into community spaces where QTPOC needs are centered and we all can learn from each other. These are just some examples of the many crucial survival strategies we invent so our peoples may survive and thrive inside the academy and beyond.

We collaboratively produce scholarship to ease the isolation we experience as academics and to enrich the work with each other's multiple positionalities and perspectives. The process further deepens these critically necessary relationships. We introduce people who might share similar questions. We host events where strangers share hotel rooms and become friends—even if just for forty-eight or seventy-two hours. We send text messages asking things like "Have you eaten today?"; "Can my child sleep at your house?"; and my "Bio-Family came through with the wrecking ball again and so can you sage my house?"

We critically revisit the academic tools we were given. We reclaim the spiritual and the sacred in our relationships, scholarship, politics, and pedagogy.[19]

We take creative turns in our work and embrace artistry as a way of saving our lives.[20] We generate images and languages that the university can never fully discipline or incorporate.[21]

We remain here because of you and us. In the process, the "here" changes alongside the you and us.

The university space we want to build with you is a decolonial and abolitionist space. It works toward a world without the university. Because in that world, there will be no capitalist mode of production—no classes, no separate education, no avowed or unavowed colonial, racist epistemologies, no meritocracy, no need to select the more "talented," no need to assign human beings to a ruling, working, or middle class. This is our horizon. Through building collectively, we create a decolonial abolitionist university space from the margins to the center. There, we share our freedom imaginings, practices, and ways of being and knowing, in their difference, with their complexities. We build safety outside the system: safety that is not organized around violence, but around relations that need neither the state nor an inferiorized other. Our political, intellectual solidarities work to keep the lives of all QTPOC, especially the most subaltern (simultaneously often the most resistant), at the center, regardless of whether they are in the room.

In this decolonial and abolitionist space, we work to have each other's back as WOC, QPOC, TPOC, POC. We see each other's potential and take collective risks to foster it. We see the beauty in our vulnerabilities and vow not to exploit them. We nourish each other and our students. We remain connected with our communities and have the work we do there valued. We do not owe each other. We build this space and do these things because they affirm our integrity, how we want to be in this world and the next, and what we want to create now and for future generations.

We envision this university as a place where people meet, exchange, engage, share knowledge, creativity, and stories, write and think—where we make beginnings without borders. In this space, everyone fully acknowledges the Native land on which we stand and the peoples whose land it is and who have been displaced, not in the sense of the colonial logics of recognition but of self-determination. In this place, Native peoples and cultures are fully present. And all marginalized peoples are fully present. In this space, we feed each other's cats and hold each other's hands and babies.

Our vision of a constructive academic space leaves the Ivory Tower, with its logics of austerity, debt, and rising tuition. It's a university where Native scholars and Native studies are prioritized and are a central part of every person's training. It is a university where three-quarters of the faculty of color are not contingent labor. It's a university where colonial, raced, and gendered employment discrimination is not masked by neoliberal diversity goodwill initiatives, and administrators of color do not pit students of color and faculty of color against each other. In this university, the resources currently centered on "diversity" are applied toward advancing justice, and the enormous sacrifices demanded of our labor and mentoring are recognized and fairly compensated.

It's a university where classes are taken in public libraries, jails/prisons and immigration detention centers (as we also work to abolish them), K–12 school buildings, storefront churches and business parks, neighborhood recreation centers, sex work places, bus stops, book shops, cafés, nightclubs, and the streets—public buildings and openings in, between, around, and beyond buildings—that are not just the sequestered areas designated as college campuses.[22] One of the many forms it could possibly take is an autonomous Third World college that critiques all relations of power (coloniality, capitalism, racism, disability, gender, sexuality, speciesism).[23] A place where people's fears of poverty are not able to drive them into studying scientific methods and problems that they don't really actually care about. In this university, everybody gets to learn to read and write and consider what deep-thick-nested-entangled-seemingly-impossible freedom dreams and decolonial and abolition promises might be available to them and us—if they were just permitted to sit in them for a little while or preferably for a long while.

In this new academic spatiality as *place*, we abolish grades and use written evaluations. Abolish tuition and create funding for smaller classes. Open up the very definition of education to include many different kinds of experiences, curiosities, skills, and ways of knowing and being, and open enrollment to everyone. To do this, we need also to create a totally different economy. To do this, the abolitionist university meets the grassroots struggles in order to overthrow this economic system of accumulation of knowledge-based status for some through the dispossession of others.

Perhaps we will never be able to create such a university space—too lazy, too silly, too self-indulgent, too weepy, too hungry to heal what got wounded in us. But as the collective space we created in Irvine (of all places) has taught us, we have the power, more often than not, to go much further in resisting the neoliberal university—its hierarchies, its competition, its murderous pace, its scarcity. In the two and a half months that we shared, we were able to take back a space in which we were able to treat each other better and dream up futures. Manifesting our community agreement, we spoke candidly about anti-Blackness and Islamophobia, paid attention to gender pronouns, and asked hard questions about white nationalism, white republicanism, white leftism, white conservatism, white secularism, white religious conservatism, white queer and trans politics, homonationalism, and Black and brown heteropatriarchy and misogyny, historically and at present. We talked scrupulously about Blackness, shared honestly what we had learned about creating autonomous spaces, rode bikes, took walks together to the outdoor market, rode busses and trains together to anti-Trump rallies in Los Angeles, huddled under umbrellas together and bought and shared inexpensive dry socks as it rained on rallies, went to dinner together regularly, cooked for each other, soaked happily in the hot tub and swam in the pool at housing provided by UCHRI, listened to what is happening in each other's lives, and held space for ourselves and each other to feel and mourn and name what it means to be liminal and constantly displaced. We strove to make the UCHRI room where our weekly formal meetings took place accessible by watching our scents and caring for each other's dietary restrictions and differences. We shared what road we had taken to get into that space and what our bodies were revealing to us simply by sitting still in it. All this before/alongside/under/over/when/after we started talking about the film, essay, article, book, chapter, or social problem we meant to examine that day.

Ultimately, the spaces that we created together, and that we dreamed together and as yet are unable to create, (have) touched us, moved us, opened us, healed us, strengthened us, enraged us, in many ways. The experience we shared during the two and a half months of our work together has an afterlife in multiple directions, registers, and the ongoing coproduction of yet more critical and politically constructive space. We ended our time together with a creative writing session on the need to claim (physical) QTBIPoC spaces that took on the shape of a manifesto. In its publication, we collaborated with contemp+orary, a brilliant online project devoted to (and founded by) radical queer and women of color artists.[24] One residential research group member shared from an earlier draft of this article at the Racial (In)Justice in the Canadian University conference at the University of British Columbia that happened shortly after the research group ended.[25] Emboldened by the queer-affirming space in which they had participated, and by their and other trans members' attempts to openly discuss transphobia in it, they were able to raise awareness in this important multiracial space as the only person at the event who was trans-identified, and the only speaker who explicitly addressed queer issues.

Another member shared the RRG reading materials with her QTPOC students; they read the articles along with the UCHRI sessions. Additionally, in a seminar she taught on Fanon and Feminism, the majority of the students read the articles from the UCHRI sessions. They engaged in discussion about how QTPOC epistemological frameworks enable us to reconsider Fanon's analyses of the world. Not only has this work and the kinds of questions that the RRG shared been drawn into classrooms, but activists also made use of the materials and discussions to shape their activism in real time.

Two other RRG members were involved in cocreating and speaking at a decolonial antiracism LTQ POC day-long Town Hall in Paris, entitled "R-assemblage lesbien, trans, queer décolonial et anticapitaliste" (Lesbian, Trans, Queer Re-Assemblage) on March 18, 2017, just days after the UCHRI RRG ended. It took place as the finale of the (otherwise generally very white dominated) annual Queer Week in Paris. Held at a new POC open space in Paris, La Colonie (the word "Colonie" is barred), the town hall consisted of a film about QTPOC in the French context (*Diasporas/Situations* by Tarek Lakrisi), a panel on Black trans subjects and issues (organized by a RRG member), a panel on Decolonizing Sexualities based on a recent book publication with that title and in which three RRG members are contributors, and a keynote (by an RRG member) on how not to do alliances so we can begin to think about how to actually create alliances.[26] It was the first time ever in France that there was a panel on Black trans, and that there was such a broad dialogue across LTQ POC positionalities and issues. Following the town hall a broad coalitional group was formed among LTQ POC, called LTQ POColibris in French and Rainbow Birds in English. Also a few months later, in mid-July, a mixed group, called Claq: Collectif queer, trans, pédé, bi, gouines (Claq: queer, trans, faggot, bi, dykes collective. "Claq" means "slap" in French), was formed and spectacularly staged a solidarity protest with refugees and migrants, directly condemning the French government's anti-refugee and anti-migrant position and policies.

Another member was deeply encouraged by the space we created to center the experiences and theories of QTPOC scholars and activists at the final and main panel of the conference "Securitization of Society: Queer-Feminist and Race Critical Perspectives" organized by the Women's and Gender Studies Section of the German Sociological Association (a deeply white institution), which she co-organized with other QPOCs and critical white members of the section.[27] This panel was not about presenting "lived experiences" as an add-on but about taking over the space and about teaching who can *really* speak about abolitionist justice, which is never based on systemic violence (like policing and carceral regimes) and about who needs to listen, including cisgender POCs.

It is our hope that this text, as a coauthored, cocreated QTPOC spatiality itself, will have its own afterlife, invoking ever more freedom promises and desires, ever more critical and creative analytics and practices, and provoking further effects with, in, and through everyone who is engaged, as readers, and as coauthors. We offer these pages up for the wider collectivity, even if as trace, inscription, moving assemblage, or fantasy.

Between Elon Musk and the seven "earth-like" planets NASA recently discovered, we ended the creative writing session that gave rise to this article by fantasizing that rich white people will get out and start fucking up the next planet, leaving us behind. That would be a good start.

PAOLA BACCHETTA is professor of gender and women's studies and vice chair of pedagogy at University of California, Berkeley. Her books include *Co-Motion: Situated Planetarities, Co-Formations and Co-Productions in Feminist and Queer Alliances* (forthcoming); *Femminismi Queer Postcoloniali: Critiche transnazionali all'omofobia, all'islamofobia e all'omonazionalismo* (with Laura Fantone, 2015); *Gender in the Hindu Nation: RSS Women as Ideologues* (2004); *Right-Wing Women: From Conservatives to Extremists around the World* (with Margaret Power, 2002). She has published over fifty journal articles and book chapters on critical analytics of power; postcolonial, decolonial, anticapitalist feminist and queer theories and practices; political conflict; and queer of color, decolonial feminist, antiracism, and right-wing social movements. Her areas of specialization are France, India, and the United States. See academia.edu/PaolaBacchetta.

FATIMA EL-TAYEB is professor of literature and ethnic studies at the University of California, San Diego. Her work deconstructs structural racism in "colorblind" Europe and centers strategies of resistance among racialized communities, especially those that politicize culture through an intersectional, queer practice. She is the author of three books and numerous articles on the interactions of race, gender, sexuality, religion, and nation. She is active in black feminist, migrant, and queer of color organizations in Europe and the United States.

JIN HARITAWORN is associate professor of gender, race, and environment at York University. Their publications include two books, numerous articles (in journals such as *GLQ* and *Society&Space*), and several coedited collections (including *Queer Necropolitics* and *Queering Urban Justice*). Their book *Queer Lovers and Hateful Others: Regenerating Violent Times and*

Places (2015), on queer Berlin, addresses both academic and non-academic readerships interested in queer of color spaces and communities. Jin has keynoted in several fields on both sides of the Atlantic, including gender, sexuality, and transgender studies, critical race and ethnic studies, and urban studies, and has made foundational contributions to various debates, including on gay imperialism, homonationalism, queer gentrification and criminalization, and trans and queer of color space. Together with a team of awesome Torontonians, they organized the third Critical Ethnic Studies conference in Toronto in 2015.

JILLIAN HERNANDEZ is a transdisciplinary scholar interested in the stakes of embodiment, aesthetics, and performance for Black and Latinx women and girls, gender-nonconformers, and queers. She is completing her first book, *Aesthetics of Excess: The Art and Politics of Black and Latina Embodiment*, and expanding her theorizing on raunch aesthetics into a second book project. Hernandez teaches courses on racialized sexualities and girlhood at the University of California, San Diego in the ethnic studies department and critical gender studies program. Her scholarship is based on over a decade of community arts work with Black and Latinx girls in Miami, Florida, through the Women on the Rise! program she established at the Museum of Contemporary Art in North Miami. She is continuing this work in San Diego in collaboration with Yessica Garcia and Hilda Gracie Uriarte through the Rebel Quinceañera Collective. Hernandez is also an artist and curator of contemporary art.

SA SMYTHE is a Black genderqueer writer living between London and LA, constantly scheming up new ways for us to get free. They earned a doctorate in history of consciousness from UC Santa Cruz and are currently UC President's Postdoctoral Fellow in gender and sexuality studies at UC Irvine. Their academic scholarship concerns dispossession and Black poetics in the Mediterranean. SA is publishing editor for *THEM—Trans Literary Journal* and an editor at *ScarfMagazine*. They have poetry published (and/or work forthcoming) in *phren-Z, the nines, Johannesburg Salon, Strike!,* and *Black Trans Love Is Trans Wealth: An Anthology*. Their writing has been featured in *Critical Contemporary Journal, okayafrica*, and elsewhere. SA also does translation work in several languages and organizes globally in Black queer and trans abolitionist writing collectives. Their next poetry collection is tentatively titled *but do you have reparations money?*, and their writing is archived at www.essaysmythe.com and on Twitter @essaysmythe.

VANESSA E. THOMPSON is a research associate and finishing doctoral candidate in the department of social sciences at Goethe University, Frankfurt, Germany. Her research and teaching are concerned with Black political theory, with a focus on Black formations and resistances in Europe, social movements, decolonial and postcolonial queer-feminist theories, theories of spatialities, and abolitionist theories and activism. Vanessa has written articles on black social movements and racism in France, the relation between postcolonial power and recognition politics, and racial profiling and policing in Europe. She is a cofounder of the initiative of Christy Schwundeck and the abolitionist grassroots initiative copwatch-ffm.

TIFFANY WILLOUGHBY-HERARD uses the resources available at the University of California, Irvine to participate in Black liberation. She has been concerned with how Black women and Black women's political consciousness has manifested itself in critical approaches to knowledge, culture, and associational life. Moving between political theory, history of knowledge, and Black movement politics, she has been active in countless social forums on race, class, gender, sexuality, political education, and political economy. She is concerned with theorizing how survival politics matter and what is to be learned by the way we actually treat the people we are in closest proximity to. She is a formally trained academic researcher, a formally trained choral singer, an untrained poet and dancer and creative writer—who has sought out these modes as a means for flourishing and communicating with others and with the natural world. She was raised in Detroit and is ever grateful to the Wildcat Generation who used print culture to overthrow American apartheid by naming its pyschic burdens and costs but also through organizing against it and taking over and founding newspapers to share their political ideas and principles.

NOTES

1. The RRG was called *Queer of Color Formations and Transnational Spaces in Europe*. A description can be found at https://uchri.org/awardees/queer-color-for mations-translocal-spaces-europe/. More on the themes and provocations that gave rise to the group can be found in a coauthored article by the group's convenors: Paola Bacchetta, Fatima El-Tayeb, and Jin Haritaworn, "Queer of Color Formations and Translocal Spaces in Europe," *Environment and Planning D: Society and Space* 33, no. 5 (2015): 769–78.

2. Saidiya Hartman, *Lose Your Mother: A Journey along the Atlantic Slave Route* (New York: Farrar, Straus and Giroux, 2006), 5.

3. Linda Martín Alcoff, *Visible Identities: Race, Gender, and the Self* (New York: Oxford University Press, 2006).

4. Viola F. Cordova, "Ethics: The We and the I," in *American Indian Thought: Philosophical Essays*, ed. Anne Waters (Hoboken, N.J.: Wiley-Blackwell Press, 2003), 173–81.

5. Norma Alarcón, "The Theoretical Subjects of *This Bridge Called My Back* and Anglo-American Feminism," in *Criticism in the Borderlands: Studies in Chicano Literature, Culture and Ideology*, ed. Hector Calderón and José David Saldiva (Durham, N.C.: Duke University Press, 1991), 140–52.

6. Cordova, "Ethics," 174.

7. Sylvia Wynter, "Unsettling the Coloniality of Being/Power/Truth/Freedom: Towards the Human, after Man, Its Overrepresentation—an Argument," *New Centennial Review* 3, no. 3 (2003): 257–337.

8. Jin Haritaworn, Adi Kuntsman, and Silvia Posocco, "Murderous Inclusions," *International Feminist Journal of Politics* 15, no. 4 (2013): 445–52. See also Sara Ahmed, *On Being Included: Racism and Diversity in Institutional Life* (Durham, N.C.: Duke University Press, 2012); Gayatri Chakravorty Spivak, *An Aesthetic Education in the Era of Globalization* (Cambridge, Mass.: Harvard University Press, 2012); Roderick Ferguson, *The Reorder of Things: The University and Its Pedagogies of Minority Difference* (Minneapolis: University of Minnesota Press, 2011); Grace Kyungwon Hong, "'The Future of Our Worlds': Black Feminism and the Politics of Knowledge in the University under Globalization," *Meridians: Feminism, Race, Transnationalism* 8, no. 2 (2008): 95–115.

9. Toni Cade Bambara's novels and short stories reflect on Black women who refuse to participate in doing the labor for charlatans passing as leaders in *The Salt Eaters* (New York: Vintage, 1992), 25–41; see Toni Cade Bambara, "The Organizer's Wife," in *The Sea Birds Are Still Alive* (New York: Vintage, 1982), 12. See also Alice Walker, *Meridian* (New York: Pocket Books, 1986); Gloria Naylor, *The Women of Brewster Place* (New York: Penguin, 1986); Paule Marshall, *The Chosen Place, The Timeless People* (New York: Vintage, 1982). If it is anything, *Meridian* and *The Women of Brewster Place* are fictional accounts of the lives of a generation of young Black women advocating voting rights and housing rights and anticolonial activists, too raucous and unruly in the early framing of the post–Civil Rights Movement generation to be included in schoolchildren's national history of the rebellion against the ubiquitous violence of Jim Crow. These were not saintly women; they lacked respectability, rank, children with all the proper paternal stamps of approval, and addresses on Strivers Row. Instead they had made political and social mistakes as well as fighting epic and incredibly long local battles within the constraints of black heteropatriarchy, white feminine solidarity politics, and racially planned environmental disasters. Their rebellion, though not fundamentally delinked from that of Dorothy Height and the formal political work of national Black women's organizations, was targeted in broad sweeps and became the center of hysterical masculinist national discourses from Daniel Moynihan's discourse about their economic autonomy being a sign of a "tangle of [family] pathology" to President Clinton's Crime Bill and Welfare Reform Bill, both signaling these women's refusal to cooperate with the normative expected

gendered political channels and protocols. In the North and South their organized dissent was deemed scandalous and antithetical to the kind of knowledge formation that is critical to state making. Marshall's protagonist orchestrates history plays and carnivals and is beloved by the children in her Caribbean community while she stymies and refuses to be accepted by the adults who afford no room to her queer sensibilities.

10. Rose Browne and James W. English, *Love My Children: An Autobiography (The Education of a Teacher)* (Des Moines: Meredith Press, 1969).

11. See also Michelle Dizon, "Institutions, When Will You Open Your Doors?," *Brooklyn Rail*, March 9, 2017, http://brooklynrail.org/2016/02/criticspage/institutions-when-will-you-open-your-doors.

12. We purposefully are troubling the language of micro aggressions. Though the interactions that the term includes are nuanced and interpersonal, they constitute forms of legalized discrimination, injustice, oppression, repression, dispossession, and other violence.

13. Gabriella Gutierrez y Muhs, Yolanda Flores Niemann, Carmen G. Gonzalez, and Angela P. Harris, eds., *Presumed Incompetent: The Intersections of Race and Class for Women in Academia* (Logan: Utah State University Press, 2012).

14. Denise Ferreira da Silva, *Toward a Global Idea of Race* (Minneapolis: University of Minnesota Press, 2007).

15. *On Strike! Ethnic Studies, 1969–1999*, dir. Irum Shiekh (San Francisco: Center for Asian American Media, 1999), DVD, 30 min.

16. Vanessa E. Thompson and Veronika Zablotsky, "Rethinking Diversity in Academic Institutions," *Wagadu: A Journal of Transnational Women's and Gender Studies* 16 (2016): 77–95.

17. Organizations and Members of the Black Communities in Germany and Austria, "Community Statement: 'Black' Studies at the University of Bremen," 2015, https://blackstudiesgermany.wordpress.com/statementbremen/.

18. Ruth Nicole Brown, *Black Girlhood Celebration: Toward a Hip Hop Feminist Pedagogy* (New York: Peter Lang, 2009); Zora Neale Hurston, *I Love Myself When I Am Laughing and Then Again When I Am Looking Mean and Impressive*, ed. Alice Walker (New York: Feminist Press at CUNY, 1989).

19. Jacqui M. Alexander, *Pedagogies of Crossing: Meditations on Feminism, Sexual Politics, and the Sacred* (Durham, N.C.: Duke University Press, 2006).

20. Ruth Nicole Brown, *Hear Our Truths: The Creative Potential of Black Girlhood* (Urbana: University of Illinois Press, 2013).

21. Gloria Anzaldúa, *Light in the Dark/Luz en lo Oscuro: Rewriting Identity, Spirituality, Reality* (Durham, N.C.: Duke University Press, 2015).

22. Toni Cade Bambara figures several sites of this kind of intergenerational learning in her works of fiction. From the Academy of the 7 Arts and the Southwest Community Infirmary to the salt marshes in *The Salt Eaters* (New York: Vintage, 1992; 106–7, 26–41, 42–54, 63) to "Broken Field Running" in *The Sea Birds Are Still Alive* (New York: Vintage, 1982), Bambara documents how the university is not the sole or the primary location where communities archive and share their alternative knowledges, principles, modes of contestation, and interpretation.

23. "Decolonizing the University" (workshop at University of California, Berkeley, February 26–27, 2010).

24. GENS QTPOC Collective: Fatima El-Tayeb, Paola Bacchetta, Jin Haritaworn, Jillian Hernandez, SA Smythe, Vanessa Thompson, Tiffany Willoughby-Herard, "On the Need to Claim (Physical) QTBIPoC Spaces," *Contemp+orary*, October 24, 2017, http://contemptorary.org/qtbipocs_spaces/; Jin Haritaworn, "Adventures of a Trans of Colour Professor," *Contemp+orary* (forthcoming).

25. Jin Haritarworn, panelist, "The State of the Academy: Issues, Policy & Effects on People," conference, "Racial (In)Justice in the Canadian University: The Politics of Race, Diversity, and Settler Colonialism," Vancouver, University of British Columbia, Traditional, ancestral, unceded Musqueam Territory, March 16, 2017, http://www.facultyassociation.ubc.ca/assets/media/Equity-Conference-Program_FINAL_web.pdf.

26. Sandeep Bakshi, Suhraiya Jivraj, and Silvia Posocco, *Decolonizing Sexuality* (London: Counterpress, 2016).

27. Jin Haritaworn and Alexander Weheliye, "Ethnic Studies in Deutschland? Über die Grenzen und Potenziale der universitären Institutionalisierung von minorisierten Wissensformen," in *Geschlossene Gesellschaft? Exklusion und rassistische Diskriminierung an deutschen Universitäten* [Closed society? Exclusion and racist discrimination at German universities], ed. Kien Nghi Ha, Noa Ha, and Mekonnen Mesghena (Berlin: Heinrich Boell Stiftung, forthcoming).

More than "Two Worlds"

Black Feminist Theories of Difference in Relation

LISA KAHALEOLE HALL

This essay began as a talk for the Native American and Indigenous Studies Association (NAISA) annual conference, which explored the concept of the "Two Worlds obsession" within the U.S. racial imaginary, defined by Amero-African community-based cultural activist Toni Cade Bambara as the overwhelming tendency for racialized communities to reference themselves and be referenced by others in relation solely or primarily to whiteness.[1] When first proposing my talk, I had thought of it as a critique of some of the assumptions of the Black feminist analysis that had been simultaneously so important to my development as an activist and intellectual, yet had such an absence of engagement with Indigenous-specific issues. But as I returned to the foundational work of these artists and intellectuals, I realized that what I needed to say was not, in fact, about a weakness in their critique but rather their and our collective failure to take their important and hard-won critical insights about difference and relationality and continue to expand their application. Here I use the word "failure" descriptively, rather than pejoratively, because many of the scholars and artists who gave us so much died much too early under the spiritual, physical, and intellectual burden of the conditions of their knowledge production and the multiple oppressions that gave birth to their politics and thinking. In reacknowledging the grief of these losses I realized that just as I try to keep their work alive in my classrooms, I needed to keep it highlighted in my writing.

I describe my current book project expanding on these issues, *Making Relations in the House of Difference*, as a "theory memoir" about my history in ethnic studies, women's studies, queer studies, and the spaces in between that is shaped by an Indigenous studies–inspired framework of genealogy (the histories, influences, and forbears shaping specific work), recognition/relationality (who and what is legible and/or acknowledged in that work), and survivance (Gerald Vizenor's term for the active assertion of agency and resistance). I bring to this essay the re-memory of my graduate school mentor, the literary scholar Barbara Christian, and key writers whose work she both materially supported and critically engaged with: Audre Lorde, Toni Cade Bambara, and June Jordan. What links them was their commitment to transformative political intellectual and creative work that far exceeded an academy that sometimes housed them. Each situated herself in multiple webs of relation at different moments: Black, Afro-American, African American, Caribbean, Caribbean American, women of color, African Diasporic. Each produced work that challenged the boundaries of what the U.S. academy considered legitimate in both form and content. Each changed many lives through the power of their insights. Each died much too young from cancers that destroyed their bodies. Their work is foundational to how I think about identity, difference, and the causes of what I have come to call the siloing of knowledge within activist academic communities.

In reanimating the implications of their insights, and in homage to the capaciousness of their worldviews, I hope to direct our attention to the relationships within and between those we consider a part of our various "we's", and away from the well-trodden paths analyzing "us" and "them." In an Indigenous studies context, Indigenous identity and who is part of an Indigenous "we" can be a highly fraught issue, dealing with who is recognized by the state, the Indigenous nation, and/or the particular Indigenous community. But the most salient definition of Indigenous belonging, and one that resonates across many other contexts, is that it rests not only on "who you claim, but who claims you." So these thoughts are about what it might look like to focus on a multiplicity of "we's," the multiple places where people claim a place and are claimed back, however contentiously and contingently. This is a place that is very difficult to talk about because land mines lie all around, and because as Audre Lorde's work has so powerfully shown we are collectively well conditioned to respond to difference as threat and to employ binary thinking as a norm.

I was uncertain how my talk about Bambara's and other U.S. Black feminists' work would be understood and received in the context of the international Indigenous audience of NAISA, but I was heartened by both the enthusiastic audience response and the number of people who subsequently told me they had never heard of Bambara before but were going to go find her books to read. This reinforced my belief that telling stories that recognize others and build new relationships must be central to our work as scholars, artists, and activists. Explicit or implicit sets of binary relations create knowledge silos. From the Indigenous studies knowledge silo, the operative binary of settler colonial states such as the United States, Canada, and New Zealand would be settler versus Indigenous, a distinction being contested in Canada by some Canadian immigrant groups of color and supported by others unpacking the complexities of a "settler of color" identity. In the United States the very concept of "settler colonialism" is largely absent from the epistemologies of anyone who is not Indigenous-identified or explicitly involved in Indigenous studies. Only those who have conscious relations with others who exist in other silos grapple with the existence of those silos, though not all do; those relations are a necessary but not sufficient precondition for this work. My own personal and institutional history has required me to live and work between and within multiple silos—the double-edged sword of my Hawaiian name, meaning both "homeless" and "without a single home": having many homes.

In her autobiographical essay "The Education of a Storyteller," Bambara tells of her twelve-year-old self bragging about what she had learned that day at school to the "grandmother who was in fact no kin to me, but we liked each other."[2] "Grandma Dorothy or Miss Dorothy or M'Dear" first asks Bambara to tell it to her in call-and-response mode, then failing that, in a story song, then failing that, in a way that highlights the theory's freedom message. When Bambara is unable to do this, M'Dear asks her who else holds this knowledge and who she could teach it to. Bambara responds:

> "Well, my girlfriends don't know it. Cynthia don't know it and Rosie don't know it and Carmen don't know it—just I know it."
>
> And she say, "Madame, if your friends don't know it, then you don't know it, and if you don't know that, then you don't know nothing. Now what else are you pretending not to know today, Colored Gal?"[3]

All of the elements of this anecdote—the multiplicity of names for Bambara's elder that connote their different overlapping relationships, the priority the older woman puts on communal knowledge, and the different modes of teachable knowledge she asks Bambara to share—highlight Bambara's understanding of the pedagogical and political centrality of storytelling and relationship to deepening our understanding of the world and our responsibilities to that understanding.

Stories are active—there is always a choice of who will be acknowledged in what contexts. The activity is crucial in creating and reinforcing both relationships and knowledge. Stories help us remember who we are and how we are related, but they also create those relationships.

THE ACADEMY AS A SITE OF KNOWLEDGE RELATIONS

Iconic poet, scholar, and activist June Jordan was one of few in the U.S. academy to explicitly address the theoretical implications of the history of academic exclusion and to foreground the concrete manifestations of racial, gender, and class hierarchies that permeate the university system, controlling what is taught, who is teaching, and with what resources and validation. In this context it is not insignificant to note that there were academics who fought against Jordan's hiring at University of California at Berkeley on the grounds that she was not a scholar. There were also those who never respected the phenomenal achievement that was her creation of the multi-sited Poetry for the People project, which produced a stunningly powerful and diverse cadre of poet teachers in the university and community. Jordan's acute analyses of language, difference, and power in highly accessible and often beautiful forms made her suspect to those critics. Jordan's essay "Finding the Haystack in the Needle" examines the vast disparity between the resources allocated to the different tiers of California's public higher education system and points out that the legacy of a segregated intellectual system is profound ignorance about everything other than the dominant:

> Until quite recently, the regular rule of thumb for measuring excellence in higher education was pretty crude stuff indeed: the smaller the eye of the needle, the better the school. The more people your standards of admission could reject, the more people and cultures and histories and spoken languages other than your own that you could exclude from your core curriculum—or patronize—the better the school.
>
> The best higher education available in the U.S.A. has meant that you could graduate *summa cum laude* certainly knowing about the fictive tragedy of King Lear, but absolutely ignorant about the actual prayers, the chants, the dances, the burial mounds, and the deeply reverent and unifying perspectives of Native Americans. You would definitely memorize the dates of major Anglo-Saxon battles, but you would remain unable to name or explain a single Chinese dynasty. You would never ever split an infinitive or end a sentence with a preposition, but you could not understand why other people—for example African-Americans and Puerto Ricans and Amerasians and Vietnamese and Japanese and Lebanese and Senegalese and Chinese

and Chicanos and Pakistanis seemed so stubbornly dependent upon and even rooted to their own "weird" mother tongue. [4]

This ignorance is the cornerstone of maintaining systems of oppression; historical amnesia and the erasure/devaluation of entire groups and cultures exist in reciprocal relation. The history of censorship, ignorance, and denial has differing toxic consequences for all, and for discourse on race, racism, and racial formation. Though this point may seem obvious, even progressive-identified academics generally have not dealt with their own institutionally constructed ignorance about "others" as a primary problem for their scholarship and analysis.

When I began my PhD work at the University of California at Berkeley, the Ethnic Studies Graduate Group had only existed for three years. Though the ethnic studies graduate program was explicitly created to be cross-racial and multidisciplinary, all of its faculty were monodisciplinarily trained and focused on a single racial grouping. Thus graduate students were often left to create our own paradigms and ways to connect the disparate narratives we were taught. But what we did have in abundance was something precious and rare, though I did not understand its rarity at the time—solidarity and a shared sense of purpose and kinship. The three existing cohorts contained a multitude of individuals—Native, Asian, Chicano, Caribbean, African American, and two white students—with very different histories and interests who came from a wide range of racial, ethnic, geographical, and political histories. For the most part our differences were lateral, not hierarchical; there was no sense of overt competition or cliquishness. By and large we supported each other within and outside of the classroom. We all knew that our previous educations had been impoverished by the racial segregation, censorship, and omissions of our previous curriculum; we all saw ourselves as part of the solution to that history in what we were learning and then teaching. We had potlucks, a graduate group, and shared resources both formally and informally. Our scholarly work had purpose and meaning for ourselves, and we hoped for others. That this sense of solidarity and purpose existed did not strike me as particularly notable at the time, partly because of the external assaults we were facing in the first round of the anti-"multiculturalism" wars of the late 1980s and early 1990s, but as I heard more stories throughout my academic career of the hazing, posturing, and jealous insecurities that permeated many of my colleagues' graduate school experiences, I grew more and more grateful for my own. We learned with and from each other—proximity enables informal learning that is often more powerful than that of the classroom, or at least enables that of the classroom to be more fully realized.

At the time I entered graduate school the community-produced feminist small press anthology *This Bridge Called My Back: Writings by Radical Women of Color* had entered the university classroom, powerfully naming the multiplicity of struggle with lived contradictions that those erased from or exceeding conceptual binaries are forced to constantly reckon with. Coeditor Cherrie Moraga described the epistemological and political process as creating "theory in the flesh"—where "the physical realities of our lives—our skin color, the land or concrete we grew up on, our sexual longings—all fuse to create a politic born out of necessity. Here, we attempt to bridge the contradictions in our experience."[5]

I was fortunate enough to be taken under the wing of a scholar who supported intellectual and cultural production inside and outside the academy and whose own work was often a powerful example of theory in the flesh: Barbara Christian was a deeply cherished mentor who later became my dissertation chair. Though she had no real knowledge of or deep interest in Pacific issues, she had a generous capacity for supporting a wide range of intellectual projects. Through her I became an African Americanist. As a literary critic who both loved artists and appreciated the materiality of cultural production, and as a scholar who was fully cognizant of the urgent need to pass on our knowledge, Barbara had a profound impact on my intellectual development as she did for so many other students across all racial-ethnic and disciplinary lines. The literature—fiction, creative nonfiction, poetry, and polemics of Black community, Black feminism, and African American studies—helped decolonize my mind.

Barbara showed her students that pleasure and beauty were legitimately desirable elements of art and scholarship; that art and politics were not separate arenas; and as she pointed out in her critically undervalued essay, "The Race for Theory," that "the finger pointing out the moon is not the moon."[6] That essay reminded us that peoples of color have always theorized, and that the many rich forms of that theorizing have been overshadowed at best or delegitimized at worst by the constant invocation of one very particular genealogy of theory originating in France and Germany and glossed as High Theory in the U.S. academy.

A precocious genius who began her undergraduate work at Columbia at the age of fifteen, Barbara was the first Black woman at Berkeley to receive tenure, the first to receive the campus's Distinguished Teaching Award, and the first to be promoted to full professor. She was known for her advocacy for both undergraduate and graduate students and was profoundly influential in the scholarly development of students based in English, rhetoric, history, ethnic studies, Afro-American studies, Africana studies, African diaspora studies, and law. Her home—filled with the paintings, sculpture, and music of the contemporary artists she supported—was the site of many visitors, whether neighbors, students, or the superstars of the African diaspora. Her hospitality was bountiful, her pleasure in a good party infectious. She exposed her students to a larger world of political and cultural production, to intellectual and artistic conversations inside and outside the university system.

She understood the fragility of archives. For those early years of graduate school in her course on African American women's literature, we often worked with photocopies of out-of-print books bound at Kinko's. She reminded us of Alice Walker's role in reviving the memory and importance of Zora Neale Hurston as an artist and anthropologist by researching and writing about her in "In Search of Our Mothers' Gardens." We took nothing for granted about our access to these foremothers' words, understanding what Barbara had had to go through to document that they existed in her groundbreaking studies *Black Women Novelists: The Development of a Tradition, 1892-1976* (1980); *Teaching Guide to Accompany Black Foremothers* (1980); and *Black Feminist Criticism: Perspectives on Black Women Writers* (1985).

She sat on committee after committee—MA, PhD, university fellowships, national fellowships. She knew there was no one else to do many of the things she did because of her oppressive singularity. She was determined to be a bridge to bring others into the academy and hoped they would lighten her burden and continue the hard work of providing access, resources, and mentorship to others who had been kept out of the system. Several months before her death, a colleague friend spotted her, ill and in pain, arms heaped with folders to read.

So much of what Barbara taught us had to do with the dynamics of erasure and forgetting, reclamation, and reassertion. Her controversial essay "The Race for Theory" attempted to elucidate her discomfort with these issues in the context of the commodification of particular forms of theory in the academy. Ironically, her plea that theory be more carefully contextualized and historicized was read as an antitheoretical polemic. Her scholarly work focused on both recovery of past forgotten or never acknowledged literary work of Black American women and on the encouragement of contemporary literary production and critical attention to that production. The project of recovery highlights the limitation of theory that ignored at worst or had no access to at best to a multitude of voices, histories, and perspectives commonly marginalized and erased. She was unusual in her conscious awareness of and attention to the contemporary means of production—supporting small presses and independent radio and buying art from artists.

Having already been a fan of Toni Cade Bambara's short stories and their celebration of the humor and critical intelligences embedded in everyday Black community life, as a graduate student I was thrilled to meet her in Barbara's living room. I adored the workings of Bambara's mind, her openness to genre, her insistent emphasis on community and self-education, her refusal to let education be elite, sterile, or impractical. Bambara once asked me if I thought I could turn my dissertation into a board game, and the very asking of the question expanded my mind in ways that had not previously been possible. The late Rudolph Byrd wrote lovingly of his experience recruiting her to be a visiting instructor at Carleton College, where she similarly upended his expectations and understandings.[7] She refused to teach entire semesters, and she refused to give course assignments that were not useful to a larger community beyond the classroom. She abhorred the idea of a paper that would only be read by a professor.

Even as she was a brilliant practitioner of fiction and nonfiction prose, Bambara never marked herself off as an artist or writer apart from her community-based identity. She was a community-oriented educator and activist in whatever modes she was operating within, and she was committed to sharing media production knowledge with youth and community groups. I still show my students a video clip of an opening she used to do before book readings—a call-and-response rendition of "Goldilocks and the Three Bears"—that strips the veneer off the story to reveal its exploitative and colonial underpinnings in a painfully hilarious fashion. She narrates the traditional tale while repeatedly stopping along the way to ask her campus audience what we call people that break into other people's houses and mess up their things and other related questions. At the end of a series of escalating pointed queries about the events of the story she asks the students in a mock academic style whether Goldilocks asked for help in dealing with the wreckage she had caused to the bears' home from her parents, "who were presumably adults capable of analyzing and combatting the normative assumptions that had given rise to the sociopathic behavior of their little offspring." She then asks in yet another register, "I mean—did she engage in principled self-criticism?!" A deadly pause as she looks slyly at the audience, then slowly drawls in a quintessentially Black southern style, "No. She said some bears were chasin' her."[8]

In revisiting Bambara's work I found the seeds of what I and many others need to help bring to fruition. I look to her life and work within the explicitly Black feminist and women of color feminist contexts in which she situated herself to see what spaces of relation they provide us. Her editing of the first U.S. Black feminist anthology, *The Black Woman*, in 1970 and her foreword to *This Bridge Called My Back* celebrated the sites of both "Black women" and "women of color" as imagined communities, not based on essentialist, univocal, and/or biological criteria, but on a matrix of shared political relations within and through difference. For *Bridge* she wrote: "*This Bridge* can get us there. Can coax us into the habit of listening to each other and learning each other's way of seeing and being.... Quite frankly, *This Bridge* needs no Foreword. It is the Afterward that'll count.... The work: To make revolution irresistible."[9]

Bambara understood at a deep level the structural blockages that have prevented variously marginalized groups from learning about and with each other and this was core to her longtime commitment to independent filmmaking and community-based spaces of learning. She trenchantly described the binary mindset that prevents us from examining the meanings and consequences of our situationally privileged and/or subordinated relations to a host of other others as the "Two-Worlds obsession":

> Still half-asleep, I rummage around in dualisms which keep the country locked into delusional thinking. The Two-Worlds obsession, for example: euro-Ams not the only book reviewers that run the caught-between-two-worlds number into the ground when discussing the works by Maxine Hong Kingston, Leslie Marmon Silko, Rudolfo Anaya, and other POCs, or rather, when reducing complex narrative dramas by POCs to a formula that keeps White World as a prominent/given/eternal factor in the discussion.

Bambara understood the way in which this obsession functions to make different peoples of color, and especially Indigenous peoples, invisible to each other:

> Two-Worlds functions in the cultural arena the way Two-Races or the Black-and-White routine functions in the sociopolitical arena. It's a bribe contract in which Amero-Africans assist in the invisibilization of Native Americans and Chicanos in return for the slot as *the* "indigenous," the former slaves who were there at the beginning of the great enterprise called America.[10]

She understood that shifting the emphasis away from either yearning for or avoiding a white gaze would radically refigure the direction of our work. I believe it was a phone conversation that we had late one night that prompted her to go on to inquire:

> What might happen if, say, Amero-Africans pitched our work toward Pacific Islander readers and spectators? We'd have to drop the Two-Race delusion, for one. What is and can be the effect of this swap meet, now that one out of every four persons in the U.S. is a POC? A reconceptualization of "America" and a shift in the power configuration of the USA.[11]

The asking of this question remains underexplored and unanswered decades later. What I describe as the "siloing of knowledge" has been evident throughout my travels and my formal and informal sites of education—deep rich and complex work being done by and about different intellectual and activist communities that doesn't travel across to others to engage and be engaged with. Who people know and/or whom they have been exposed to is the unacknowledged foundation of our assumptions about the world and the knowledge base we build from this. Relationality is the bedrock of knowledge production, and this is the deep significance of relationality in Indigenous contexts. Far from being "identity policing"—an attempt to cage, immobilize, and regulate—the grounding of self in both geographic place(s) and networks of relationship is a beginning, not an end, to individual and community articulations of identity and interrelationship. Who you know and whom you conceive of as kin/akin shapes three important intellectual dimensions: what knowledge surrounds you and forms the context for your own assumptions and beliefs; what knowledge you have the authority/responsibility to incorporate, acknowledge, and transmit; and what knowledge you perceive as having value.

Bambara's own work and political commitments were broad and deep in their associations and interconnections. As she traveled she incorporated her awareness of and engagement with multiple others into her work. Her short story "The Seabirds Are Still Alive" from the collection of that name explored the legacies of Vietnam;[12] her novel *The Salt Eaters* modeled the necessity of revolutionary interconnections between the Sisters of the Yam, Corn, and Rice in order to be well; her appearance as the neighborhood *griot* in Frances Negron Muntañer's film *Brincando El Charco* connected the histories of Puerto Rico and Black Harlem.

There were sometimes interesting gaps in her connections. During one of our discussions of racial identity, she told me that her mother was "part Indian," and I was confused by this framing of her mother as different than herself. "How do you think of your mother as being "part Indian," but not yourself?" I asked, baffled. She in turn was confused by my question. But when she stopped to think more deeply about it, she remembered that her mother was recognized and hailed by Indian women who had never met her as they walked about town, an experience that Bambara did not share. Community recognition and phenotype shaped their identities and identifications differently. Though she was as "part-Indian" as her mother, she did not live this genealogical relation in the same way. (To me this is similar to the ways the Asian ancestors within June Jordan's Caribbean lineage are neither denied nor highlighted.) Toni Cade Bambara was a quintessential storyteller, community educator, and teller of tall tales. Her loss, like that of so many others that we are missing, is not solely of her irreplaceable singularity but her web of connection with others and the multiplicity of issues and viewpoints that her work encompassed. The holding of that awareness is hard spiritual, intellectual, and emotional work, the pain and possibility debilitating the physical body. No coincidence shapes how many we have lost too soon.

Community as a Site of Knowledge Production

In trying to envision Northern California before my arrival for graduate school I had heard a lot from East Coasters, almost all of which was wrong. Oakland was a place East Coast white people shuddered over, a fantasy of Angela Davis, Black Panthers, and urban blight, all of which existed but not in the modes of their aversive imaginations. But Oakland is as big as ten Berkeleys together, rich Oakland, poor Oakland, gourmet ghettos and people ghettos, trees and lakes, bullets and concrete. The beauty of Oakland lay in the multiple levels of difference that coexisted. Oakland pulled me to its crossroads, where refugees of race and desire come together and combine and collide. Oakland in specific and the Bay Area in general shaped me at levels impossible to calculate. In Oakland, it was clear that there were far more possibilities than Black and white; in Oakland, it was clear that there were far more possibilities than gay and straight; in Oakland, it was clear that there were far more possibilities than male and female. This does not mean everyone liked this clarity—of course, racism, sexism, and homophobia were ever-present. But what was important to me was that the social reality—the everyday assumptions from which people operated—recognized that these possibilities existed. Because if you can't even get anyone to recognize your existence, everything else is an impossible battle.

The multiplicitous rather than homogenous space of "women of color" organizing provided me a space of alliance, recognition, and misrecognition.

My autobiographical essay from that time period "Eating Salt" used Bambara's incisive question in *The Salt Eaters*—"Are you sure, sweetheart, that you want to be well?"—to explore the complexities of how I was hailed and interpellated into many forms of kinship.[13] The assertion to me of West Indian ancestry in our Hawaiian family genealogy by a great-aunt during my early twenties was not the beginning of a complex dynamic of inclusion/erasure but merely compounded my inability to feel as if I could narrate myself and my relationships in anything but partial and contingent ways. I remain deeply grateful for Black kinship, women of color kinship, Pacific kinship, Indigenous kinship, queer kinship, and many other forms of relationship that the Bay Area of the 1990s made space and place for.

I do not romanticize this time and place, but I cherish its aliveness. I was so very tired of being entrapped in ludicrous binaries I experienced during my East Coast Ivy League education that the multiplicity of identities and political positions in the Bay Area came both as a welcome relief and a spur to learn more and more about the things I had not experienced and knew nothing about. Even before I read Audre Lorde's call for us to stop fearing difference but to instead recognize it as a great creative force, I had been living its creativity throughout my diasporic Hawaiian, multiracial, geographically dispersed military experience, and thus her articulation of the problem has stayed with me throughout my life. What if we appreciated rather than ran from, or tried to eradicate, or copied difference; what if we could be related through difference as well as similarity; what if we could enjoy difference without commodifying it or "eating the other"; what if we could be in solidarity with difference without trying to eradicate or appropriate it? In the Bay Area fear was there, to be sure, but also curiosity, pleasure, and a certain kind of exhilaration in making new connections and new communities, and in recovering and reclaiming old ones.

I do not romanticize this time and place, nor claim that all was recognized. The decades-long struggle of Rosemary Cambra, Corinna Gould, and other Ohlone and allies to first prevent and then commemorate the destruction of Ohlone graves and shell mounds to build a shopping center in Emeryville, the uncontested romanticized monuments to California mission histories, and focus on federally recognized tribes as the mark of "authentic" Indianness—all highlight the ongoing exclusion and erasure of California Indian peoples whose colonizers were first Spanish and Mexican. Esselen/Chumash poet Deborah A. Miranda's memoir *Bad Indian* creates chilling worksheets where elementary school children are instructed how to build craft models of the Dachau concentration camp and a Mississippi slave plantation with pasta noodles and sugar cubes in the same cheerful tones commonly used to describe the missions.[14] It is important to note that it was not only the white children that received and took in these lessons. The "Two-World obsession" that Bambara named is an outgrowth of white supremacy, where love or hate fixates on and revolves around whiteness but is also a mode of avoidance of analyzing our own relations of complicity and imbrication in forms of oppression we do not share. The difference between slogans supporting immigrant rights such as "We are all immigrants here" versus "#NoBansOnStolenLands" reflect the refusal of one marginalized group to participate in the political and cognitive erasure of another.

In thinking about how to navigate very real differences between and among us, I must always return to Lorde: the Black feminist foremother, simultaneously the most valorized by those who value activism and intellectual work, and taken the least seriously on a theoretical level by many who cite her legacy (an overlapping but not identical population). Lorde's meditations on and incisive analyses about difference and its creative potential have sparked innumerable responses by those who came after her, but I believe there is so much more to be done with her work. In her "biomythography" *Zami: A New Spelling of My Name*, she names her nascent awareness:

> Being women together was not enough. We were different. Being gay-girls together was not enough. We were different. Being Black together was not enough. We were different. Being Black women together was not enough. We were different. Being Black dykes together was not enough. We were different.... It was a while before we came to realize that our place was the very house of difference rather than the security of any one particular difference.[15]

Lorde's political insight about living in the house of difference could be fruitfully used in all social movements and intellectual projects. Lorde's subsequent revolutionary recasting of difference as necessary creative energy, similar to that of the sparks created from the friction between stones, gave us options other than only being able to see difference as the cause of inevitable division. Difference is inevitable, but Lorde notes that it is not difference itself but its denial that leads to distortions and disrupted relationships.

The mainstream conception of difference that Audre Lorde critiqued is very different than that which she offered. The mainstream conception is always overtly or covertly hierarchical—one thing is not just different than another, it is cast as superior or inferior. In this system difference is always the site of an oppressive dichotomy, and privileges are gained by being included on the "superior" side of this. In a racist society, those who are deemed white benefit. In a sexist society, those who are deemed male, heterosexual, gender-normative, and gender-conforming benefit. In an ableist society, those who fit physical, mental, and emotional "norms" benefit. In a xenophobic nationalist society, those deemed citizens and patriots, etc., etc. So how do we attempt to pull apart this tangle of overlapping privileges and oppressions?

THE DIVISION OF THE WORLD INTO "WE" AND "THEM"

I want to call for a moratorium on talking about "them," so we can talk about "we's." It is probably too much to ask those of us raised within relentlessly oppositional and binary frameworks to completely stop focusing on a "them," but as both a political strategy and a spiritual practice, I ask if we could try to spend at least 50 percent of our intellectual, emotional, and political energy on understanding and expanding the multitude of "we's" that each of us inhabits. The dehumanization and refusal of subjectivity to those deemed Other is a dynamic that cannot be resolved within a we/them framework because it both originates in and is promulgated by that framework.

Some people fear that moving attentional focus away from a "them" lets that "them" get away with something. The prevalence of what has come to be named "call-out culture" in contemporary social activist circles—that a "them" needs to be publicly called out for their oppressive behavior and actions—follows this logic. But I want to highlight that while it *is* critically important to name and define acts of physical and epistemic violence perpetrated by the various "them's" against the various "we's," accurately naming these practices does not for the most part change the behavior or the worldview of their perpetrators. At best the shaming aspect causes perpetrators to be silent in public and openly resentful in private; at worst it causes them to publicly double down in justifying behavior they may not even have originally been actively committed to in the first place. (By this I mean that oppressive norms are so pervasive and normalized that they are often enacted without thought or intention in a routinized manner.) The limitation of relying on we/them narratives is that through them we are *documenting* violence but not affecting the behavior of the "them." "Them" does not need to care what "we" have to say; that is within the very nature of the dichotomous construction. The documentation of violence has a powerful use in another arena, however: to enable someone within our "we" who has not themselves been subject to the specific form(s) of violence being named and articulated to apprehend it and potentially ally themselves against it. It does not make perpetrators of violence stop.

The violences that we can effectively stop are those that are employed within a "we." The existence of that "we" is necessary but not sufficient for making change—it is the ground of possibility. The concept of "we" that I am relying on here is contingent and chosen. It relies on relationality and as such is nether fixed nor essential. Everyone inhabits multiple "we's" that are shaped by both external and internal identifications. For the purposes of my analysis "we" denotes any collectivity with which we acknowledge a mutual relation, however ambivalently, contingently, or externally shaped. It must always be chosen—it is not a "we" if any of those "included" have not consented to their incorporation. That dynamic is more accurately named "appropriation."

Building our understanding of "we" is crucial because in starting with "we," our actions and analyses are not dependent on the responses of an other; we are not strategizing how to get someone else to change their thinking or behavior but analyzing how we can change ours in the service of expanding solidarity with those whose oppressions we do not share. Thinking from a "we" is necessary but not sufficient, and any "we" that we inhabit is not static and must expand.

Privileged statuses are mostly invisible to those privileged by them because forms of oppression are usually invisible to those who do not suffer from them. Their invisibility is part and parcel of their maintenance. An important goal, then, must be to become conscious of oppressions we do not ourselves suffer both for reasons of alliance and solidarity with others *not* like us, and as a means of better understanding our own privileges and oppressions. The socially produced invisibility of privileged statuses and norms requires that we actively and consciously develop strategies to make what is invisible legible to those who do not experience its oppressive force and *unconsciously* benefit from it, in simple or complex ways. (An important caveat: I am not talking here about those who deliberately shape policies and practices of inequality, but those who would be disturbed if they understood how they benefit from structures of oppression they have not been consciously aware of. The genuinely "well-intentioned," in other words, no matter if ignorant or naive.)

Straight men can choose to notice and combat sexism and homophobia; U.S. nationals can choose to notice and combat immigration abuses and deportation horror stories; non-Muslims can choose to notice and combat the Islamophobia propagated in the mainstream media and political life; non-Black people can choose to notice and combat pervasive forms of anti-Black state and interpersonal violence within white and non-Black communities of color; non-Indigenous people can choose to notice and combat the pervasive and ongoing erasure of Indigenous people, genocidal violence, and land theft; the well-housed can choose to notice and combat the conditions creating homelessness, and so on. The abuse of privilege grows out of the choice to not notice that which we are not structurally forced to reckon with, and thus it is imperative for us to develop a more nuanced discussion of privileges that are both unearned and unasked for.

Making no distinction between the inhabiting of a privileged status and the abuses that that status enables prevents many of us from carefully analyzing the privileges available to us, and what they might enable us to do in the service of solidarity and social justice. What is discouraging is the token acknowledgment often given to the concept of interlocking oppressions and intersectional analyses that in practice usually returns to a binary relation. Bernice Johnson Reagon and the phenomenal performers of "Sweet Honey in the Rock" asked the questions of complicity and responsibility in their song about the journey of an inexpensive shirt sold at J.C. Penney through its abusive and coercive multinational manufacturing process prior to their purchase of it—"Are My Hands Clean?" Our hands may not be equally dirty, but neither are they clean. The effects of our collective refusal to see our own participation in the marginalization, erasure, and dismissal of others are critical elements in the maintenance of systems of dominance. There is no one singular dominant "Them"—there is a collection of subjects whose unwillingness to understand their moments of dominance may have radically different histories, roots, and motivations depending on their various social (dis)locations, but whose effect becomes the same. It doesn't matter that the various motivations are different *if* the point of so saying is to in some way explain away or justify a refusal to understand participation in dominance. A pragmatic approach to evaluating privilege and its uses and abuses is long overdue and has to be a central element of theorizing practice. We need many different nuanced and detailed analyses about the dynamics of multiple marginalization and situational privilege to truly understand how systems of dominance operate and can be dismantled. This can accomplish two critically important things—one, to put the social power of privileged statuses in the service of opening access to others; and two, to make plain that a failure to act toward doing this is just that: a failure to *act*, which is not explainable on the grounds of identity.

BUILDING ALLIANCES IN THE HOUSE OF DIFFERENCE

The fixity of the concept of "privilege" leads to a similarly static conception of what it means to be in alliance with individuals or groups who are dealing with oppressions you do not share. I propose another moratorium on the use of "ally" as a noun, not because it has no usefulness, but because it tends to drive discussion and analysis down some well-worn and played-out paths. "Alliances," on the other hand, like "treaties" or "agreements," require at least two parties to exist, while "allying" as a verb requires taking some form of action. The idea that there are "allies" and "non-allies" that exist as identity categories in the world keeps us focused on the binary of who is and who isn't, as opposed to evaluating how various words and/or actions help, harm, or are irrelevant to the various communities involved in any specific situation. The activity of alliance building is complicated, ongoing, and relationship-based. Like identity, the activity of alliance building is processual.

We have to have diverse social networks to expand our understanding of the world, to learn from the everyday and quotidian as well as the exceptional and dramatic. The space of coexistence does not have to be a space of co-optation. The ability to learn by absorbing a very different norm than you are used to can provide a space to be exposed to differences without having to explicitly reveal your own ignorances about them. This can matter to both parties—the more informed not subject to exasperatingly naive or offensive questions and comments, and the less informed not having to apologize for ignorant words and behaviors they only come to see as such much later in their acculturation to new norms. The informal and extra-academic sites of learning are powerful and invaluable, and the segregation of schools, neighborhoods, workplaces, and recreational and friendship networks diminishes all of us while perpetuating a status quo that keeps some of us disenfranchised and dehumanized.

The very first class I taught on my own while a graduate student at Berkeley, Ethnic Studies 90: Women of Color in the United States, was an object lesson in the promise and perils of thinking through difference in relationality. The class of forty-plus students was composed of women and men, immigrant and U.S.-born, from Europe, Africa, the Caribbean, the Philippines, and Mexico. They were a joy to teach, willing to think hard about difficult political and personal issues raised in the readings. There were often moments in that classroom that teachers dream of—intense silences of reflection and recognition, then heads and hands dropping to notebooks as students furiously scrawled their own thoughts. They were able to read about and think through a wide range of issues gained from experiences they both shared and did not. But one thing became apparent in these eclectic discussions—when things got too heated in terms of thinking through "horizontal hostility" and oppressive practices between groups of different people of color, the class members (including the white students) would fall back on a "well, but the white man did x" explanation of root causes. Finally I had to say to them, yes, of course there is a larger racist structure of white supremacy operating, and I am in no way trying to deny or diminish its import, but I am asking you to focus for a moment on what gets little attention in Lorde's work—the piece of the oppressor in all of us and how this plays out among and between oppressed groups. One day I called a moratorium on anyone bringing up white people during that one single class period. And they could not do it. The bonds between these very different smart, brave, and creative students and their own identifications felt too fragile for them to sustain a deep look at complicity and complication. And these were very powerful bonds that changed and sustained different students' lives both during and after the class. Almost twenty-five years later, a blonde woman approached me in a coffee shop in Ithaca, New York, and asked if I used to live in the Bay Area. She told me she had been in that class and wanted me to know she used the things we talked about in class almost every day in her work organizing with farmworkers, and I felt tears come to my eyes.

The lateral sharing of difference within multiple consensually constructed "we's" is what moves us away from the "Two-Worlds obsession" and breaks the deadlock of refusal of empathy and relationality to those whose experiences and oppressions are not our own. The power of telling stories that recognize others and build new relationships is central to our work as scholars, artists, and activists to cocreate a better world. The life and death consequences of this are starkly highlighted in the narratives (or lack thereof) about the police murders of Black men and women; the state and community violence against women and gender-nonconforming people, igniting the founders of #BlackLivesMatter; the absence of mass media coverage of the largest Native and allied gathering of land and water protectors in decades in contrast to the minute-by-minute reports on the activities of Clive Bundy and his armed white supremacist claimants to "federal lands"; the Zionist narratives of Israel's latest assault on Gaza, with Palestinians and their allies struggling to both tell their stories and get them heard; the refugees from U.S.-backed violence across the world denied sanctuary; the undocumented surveilled and torn from family, pushed across colonially constructed borders in the ultimate hypocrisy of the settler state.

June Jordan understood this in her 1982 response to the First Intifada when she wrote, "I was born a Black woman/ and now/ I am become a Palestinian" in her poem "Moving Towards Home."[16] It was Jordan, too, in her essay "Report from the Bahamas," who noted we might not end up wanting the same things outside the context of the freedom from oppression that we seek, but we have to find a way to speak across and to our differences lest we only become unified in our shared death.[17]

Locations of experience and affiliation are locations of knowledge production—whose stories you hear; who you come to understand as related to you and how.

What were we born; what will we become; what stories are we responsible to tell?

LISA KAHALEOLE HALL is a multiracial Kānaka Maoli associate professor with a long history in community-based cultural production. Her creative and scholarly work has been published in *American Quarterly*, *Contemporary Pacific*, *Wicazo Sa Review*, *Journal of International and Intercultural Communication*, *Out/look: National Lesbian and Gay Quarterly*, *Sinister Wisdom* and various anthologies. She is currently collaborating with Scott Morgensen, A. W. Lee, and Dana Wesley on a multiyear Canadian SSHRC grant, "The AKIN Project: Documenting Queer Genealogies of Anti-Racist and Anti-Colonial Activism in Canada," and is finishing a book about women of color and queer of color ethnic studies work in the 1980s and 1990s entitled "Making Relations in the 'House of Difference.'" Her BA in women's studies and MA/PhD in ethnic studies have left her thoroughly undisciplined.

NOTES

1. Toni Cade Bambara, "Deep Sight and Rescue Missions," in *Deep Sightings and Rescue Missions*, ed. Toni Morrison (New York: Pantheon, 1996), 146–78.

2. Toni Cade Bambara, "The Education of a Storyteller," in *Deep Sightings and Rescue Missions*, 246.

3. Ibid., 249.

4. June Jordan, "Finding the Haystack in the Needle," in *Technical Difficulties: African-American Notes on the State of the Union* (New York: Pantheon, 1992), 90–91.

5. Cherríe Moraga and Gloria Anzaldúa, "Entering the Lives of Others: Theory in the Flesh," in *This Bridge Called My Back: Writings by Radical Women of Color*, ed. Cherríe Moraga and Gloria Anzaldúa (Watertown, Mass.: Persephone, 1981), 23.

6. Barbara Christian, "The Race for Theory," *Cultural Critique* 6 (1987): 51–63.

7. Rudolph Byrd, "The Feeling of Transport," in *Savoring the Salt: The Legacy of Toni Cade Bambara*, ed. Linda Holmes and Cheryl Wall (Philadelphia: Temple University Press, 2007), 170–80.

8. Video recording of 1982 reading by Toni Cade Bambara at San Francisco State University, author's personal collection.

9. Toni Cade Bambara, foreword to Moraga and Anzaldúa, *This Bridge*, viii.

10. Bambara, "Deep Sight and Rescue Missions," 160–61.

11. Ibid., 178.

12. Toni Cade Bambara, *The Seabirds Are Still Alive: Collected Stories* (New York: Random House, 1977).

13. Lisa Kahaleole Chang Hall, "Eating Salt," in *Names We Call Home: Autobiography on Racial Identity*, ed. Becky Thompson and Sangeeta Tyagi (New York: Routledge, 1995).

14. Deborah A. Miranda, *Bad Indians: A Tribal Memoir* (Berkeley, Calif.: Heyday Press, 2013), 186–90.

15. Audre Lorde, *Zami: A New Spelling of My Name* (Trumansburg, N.Y.: Crossing Press, 1982), 226.

16. June Jordan, "Moving Towards Home," in *Living Room* (New York: Persea Books, 1985) 132.

17. June Jordan, "Report from the Bahamas," in *On Call: Political Essays* (Boston: South End Press, 1985), 39–50.

American University Consensus and the Imaginative Power of Fiction

COURTNEY MOFFETT-BATEAU

Although it is commonly believed that U.S. universities are sites of social justice and inclusion, as reflected in the increasing diversification of programs and faculty and student bodies since the 1960s, the Political within U.S. institutional work has only allowed for permutations in Western social order rather than complete reform. The Political is a contained self-reflexive system that structures violence into its promise of transformation and allows struggle to represent the hope for inclusion. By turning to Mat Johnson's *Pym* and Ralph Ellison's *Invisible Man*, this essay asks what is at stake when refusing diversity. What happens when race is institutionalized as diversity—to the institution, to the individuals forced to perform diversity, and to the relationships we might hope to build with each other in and beyond the university? Faced with the paradox of participating within American consensus through the Political, critical ethnic studies intellectuals constantly come up against the self-reflexive system of the Political. Yet what does it mean to resist the promise of inclusion and its deep commitments to the renewal of race-based capitalist orders? This essay turns to literature to ask what forms of resistance are even possible when practices of exclusion are disguised as diversity and narrated through the democratic hope for inclusion. Contending that we are never *not* being made complicit in the reordering of racist capitalist order—"the work of blackness is inseparable from the violence of blackness"[1]—this essay shows how striving for the achievement of American consensus bears with it the hopeful attitude of the Political.

This essay prioritizes the disruptive power of literature to bring to life the diverse worlds in which power can be conceptualized and imagined differently. By reading Mat Johnson's *Pym* in conversation with Ralph Ellison's *Invisible Man*, this essay reflects on the capitalist modes that (1) organize social uplift and institutional affiliation and (2) encourage people of color to compete for the "democratic" hope of inclusion. According to Calvin Warren, hope structures the political project of antiblackness that governs our existence:

> The Political, we are told, provides the material or substance of our hope; it is within the Political that we are to find, if we search with vigilance and work tirelessly, the "answer" to the ontological equation—hard work, suffering, and diligence will restore the fractioned three-fifths with its alienated two-fifths and, finally, create One that we can include in our declaration that "All men are created equal." We are still awaiting this "event."[2]

If we extend Warren's concept of hope to ask what can be done about the university, it would seem that the political project of hope is key to maintaining participation within the university system. It is a faith-based system that necessitates a belief in transformation. By referring to itself as both the answer and solution, the politics of hope positions antiblack violence as a natural hurdle in the competition for inclusion. Any pain experienced within the Political is justifiable because of its promise of inclusion.

This type of analysis has its roots in the Black radical tradition. It pokes holes in theories that believe in liberation through inclusion. In 1983, Cedric Robinson wrote in his *Black Marxism: The Making of the Black Radical Tradition*, "Molded by a long and brutal experience and rooted in a specifically African development, the [Black radical] tradition will provide for no compromise between liberation and annihilation."[3] In many ways the Black radical tradition anticipates a collective pain or death in the fight for liberation through inclusion. As Robinson proposes, "The Black radical tradition suggests a more complete contradiction" rather than a neat solution.[4] In his "Black Study, Black Struggle," Robin D. G. Kelley states:

> Black studies was conceived not just outside the university but in opposition to a Eurocentric university culture with ties to corporate and military power. Having emerged from mass revolt, insurgent black studies scholars developed institutional models based in, but largely independent of, the academy. In later decades, these institutions were—with varying degrees of eagerness—incorporated into the university proper in response to pressure to embrace multiculturalism.[5]

Although the university may appropriate Black studies in hopes of disguising the Political, Black studies is not multiculturalism. It feels under no obligation to be used in the service of the university. Following Stefano Harney and Fred Moten, "the black aesthetic is not about technique, it is not a technique."[6] It is not something to be used for an end, as it refuses structural containment.

The first major rebellion in the institutional framework of U.S. universities erected itself in the early 1970s out of student-faculty activism with the institutionalization of Black studies, ethnic studies, women studies, and queer studies. Black nationalisms not only diversified literary markets, they democratized American institutions;[7] equally noteworthy is how they intervened into various scientific disciplines.

The inauguration of these programs immediately created a new set of curricula, requiring new books and textbooks, on which publishers were then quick to capitalize. A *Newsweek* story entitled "The Black Novelists: Our Turn" revealed what the article referred to as a "black revolution" in literature and described how publishers were "scrambling to add black writers to their lists." Many Black-authored texts immediately began to appear. "In 1969, at least six anthologies of slave narratives and interviews were released. In 1970, something like twenty-five Black novels were published."[8]

Authors such as "Toni Morrison, Ishmael Reed, Louise Meriweather, Alice Walker, Toni Cade [Bambara], Mari Evans, Michael Harper, Audre Lorde, and Maya Angelou each published a major work."[9] Arising out of radical traditions that wished and demanded for national and institutional recognition of their local existence, many historians of color—including Manning Marable and John Henrik Clarke—radically and dramatically changed their fields by making room for Black, brown, Indigenous, women, and queer experience(s).[10]

The 1990s witnessed the rise of many prominent scholars of color despite the many shortcomings of multiculturalism. In her "Crisis of the Negro Intellectual: A Post-Date," Hortense Spillers settles in the paradox of being complicit with a university system that appropriates radical liberation struggles to renew "liberal" permutations of race-, class-, and gender-based practices of discrimination. For many, Spillers contends, it seemed possible that "the period 1968–1970 meant, at last, the fruition of a radical and pluralistic democracy, or so it seemed."[11] Writing in 1994, Hortense Spillers appears cautious to endorse all the social achievements that multiculturalism seemed to claim—especially, but not limited to, its appropriation of 1960s/70s radical academic and social rebellion. Robin Kelley adds: "The point of liberal multiculturalism was not to address the historical legacies of racism, dispossession, and injustice but rather to bring some people into the fold of a 'society no longer seen as racially unjust.'"[12] Each defining moment of progress within the institutional history of American universities, whether celebrating the first women's or Black colleges, or even the admission of its first Black, brown, Indigenous, queer, or women students into traditionally white cis-male institutions of higher educations, has therefore been celebrated as natural progressions of American social order. Through multiculturalism, American universities perfected how to incorporate radical critique in the service of the university. Therefore, finding an escape from the Political project of inclusion cannot only be thought of in terms of the university because, as this essay shows, the power of American ideology is so strong that it absorbs critique into its very definition of self. In this way, multiculturalism gets to celebrate the plurality of diversity without taking on its burdens.

The process of institutionalizing diversity has not always been a simple translation from social struggle to institutional order. Quite the contrary, and the cultural wars of the 1980/90s are a reflection of that struggle. In his *Unmaking the Public University*, Christopher Newfield argues that the culture wars of the 1990s (which carried on into the early 2000s) were fundamentally economic—as conservatives set out to discredit the cultural nationalist legacies of civil rights and women's rights struggles, thus separating many group-membership affiliates from their traditional cultural epicenters.[13] As Newfield rightly notes, this unsaid social contract within university systems mandated that in order for them to rise within their university ranks as full elite members, they in many ways had to abandon the cultural hubs from which they came. Thus, the 1980/90s saw a new stratification among academics on how to negotiate projects of social justice. Mark McGurl accounts for this period in American institutional history as a mixture between "democratized modernism" and "elitist pluralism," because it celebrates the institutional claim of cultural distinctiveness via narratives of inclusion, while still forcing its new members to subscribe to its exclusivity (which are based on capitalist market practices of exclusion done in service of the elite institution). In this way, students, faculty, and administrators are encouraged to "savor their own open-mindedness."[14] Yet, "because universities are still a long way from offering unrestricted social access to the masses,"[15] they continue to participate in exclusionary knowledge economies that rely on culture, socioeconomic status, and access.

The departments of Black, Indigenous, gender, sexuality, and women's studies are therefore necessary constituents in the Political project of democratic modern universities, because without them (and their diverse scholars) the university system could not market themselves as American or compete competitively in global knowledge economies. They are what make the university system unique, rich, innovative, and most importantly symbolic of an overall national project of American democracy.[16] Through carefully staged engagements with critique, the university allows diversity to be performed so that it can market itself as modern, innovative, and inclusive. As follows, the university celebrates itself as culturally distinct and scholastically exceptional for *allowing* the critique to take place within its institutional confines. Sacvan Bercovitch has argued that the power of American ideology is its capacity to incorporate dissensus as fundamentally American, writing: "To criticize myth is to 'appreciate' it from within, to explicate it 'intrinsically,' in its own 'organic' terms."[17] Moten and Harney caution against the repurposing of critique to serve university interest—contending that critique is not only used for institutional transformation but is instead turned violently outward.[18] "Critique endangers the sociality it is supposed to defend, not because it might turn inward to damage politics but because it would turn to politics and then turn outward."[19] The work that is done in service of the university, in *hope* of transforming the university, can never *not* be complicit with the Political. Rather, it is this hopeful belief in the transformation of the Political that maintains the work of diversity.

Diversity work, in the university and in literature, fuses the voice into the Political project of the university. In asking what diversity means to literature, a loaded question, this essay will not claim that literature exists outside of the Political project of inclusion.[20] It rather turns to the novel to ask what happens when writing Black experience has the goal of social and institutional transformation. Madhu Dubey builds on the work of Henry Louis Gates Jr. to contend, "From its beginnings, African American literature has been fueled by an immense faith in the egalitarian promise of print modernity."[21] By remembering their experience within the Political, people of color have long documented their voices into the modern print medium as a political means for negotiating inclusion. In literature, Robert Stepto identifies "the strident, moral voice of the former slave recounting, exposing, appealing, apostrophizing, and above all *remembering* his ordeal in bondage [as] the single most impressive feature of the slave narrative."[22] Likewise, diversity work requires its practitioners to include their personal experience into traditionally white university systems in the hope of transforming U.S. institutional history. As Sara Ahmed comments, "Diversity work can take the form of description: it can describe the effects of inhabiting institutional spaces that do not give you residence."[23] Whether through policy or fiction, both modes of documenting personal experience of pain (that happens as direct result of the Political project from which they seek residence), participate in the Political promise of inclusion. While Black scholars use scholarship to seek residence from their university systems, Black novelists use *voice* to ask for inclusion within American print culture and its institutions. In both instances, Black scholars and novelists document their experiences of asking for residence or inclusion within the Political as a means of transforming Western social and/or institutional order.

Now that we have arrived at another key moment in literature and the academy—namely, that the new American novel is being consumed and produced in the university—this essay turns to the novel to ask what can be done about the Political within the university. From the vantage point of what Mark McGurl has coined *The Program Era*, contemporary authors of color are using literature to comment on university life and culture.[24] Building on McGurl's work, Ramón Saldívar claims that not only do they inhabit the university as professors of creative writing; contemporary authors of color such as Junot Díaz, Salvador Plascencia, Larissa Lai, Marta Acosta, and Percival Everett (and I would add Danzy Senna, Jacienda Townsend, and of course Mat Johnson) use their space (in American print culture and the institutions of higher education in which they operate) to create new American imaginaries for thinking about Western social order. Saldívar states,

> in the twenty-first century, the relationship between race and social justice, race and identity, and indeed, race and history requires these writers to invent a new "imaginary" for thinking about the nature of a just society and the role of race in its construction.[25]

Much of what Mat Johnson's 2011 novel *Pym* does is point out patterned structures of race-based constructs that as much divide American society and literature as they bring them together. Offering more questions than solutions, Johnson delves deep into the foremost contradictions of American society and its liberal institutions.

In the opening scenes of *Pym*, the reader witnesses Johnson's autodiegetic narrator being forced out of the university. Chris Jaynes, a professor of African American literature and self-proclaimed Americanist, is denied tenure despite the unanimous support of his faculty committee:

> Always thought if I didn't get tenure I would shoot myself or strap a bomb to my chest and walk into the faculty cafeteria, but when it happened I just got bourbon drunk and cried a lot and rolled into a ball on my office floor.[26]

Therefore, Johnson's novel begins when Jaynes's hope in the political project of the university dies. As the only Black professor at a predominantly white liberal arts college, Jaynes refuses to be the right type of image for his university, and in this way, he has stopped being useful to them.

Producing the right image for universities allows the Political to position discourses on diversity outward as necessary engines to fuel and fulfill the democratic promise of equal opportunity. Ahmed maintains, "Diversity work becomes about generating the 'right image' and correcting the wrong one."[27] Universities rely on staging the right image so as to make hypervisibile their promises of inclusion and less visible their problems with exclusion.

> "The language of diversity is today embraced as a holy mantra across different sites. We are told that diversity is good for us. It makes for an enriched multicultural society" (2004: 1). The language of diversity certainly appears in official statements (from mission statements to equality policy statements, in brochures, as taglines) and a repertoire of images (collages of smiling faces of different colors), which are easily recognizable *as* images of diversity.[28]

Hence, the *right* image allows universities to position the bodies of scholars of color outward through the Political to *represent* American universities as socially progressive, liberal institutions that grant access based on scholastic merit and distinction. In Johnson's story, Jaynes refuses to lend his body in this service.

In the wake of this devastating news, Jaynes sneaks away from his best friend Garth's care and, in an epic decision made while drunk, chooses to confront the college president. Both during his employment and unemployment from his college, Jaynes chooses to speak from institutional spaces that deter the university from "properly" using him: in his research, Jaynes abandons his work on Ralph Ellison for a fascination with Edgar Allan Poe and no longer attends the college Diversity Committee meetings—decisions that ultimately cause him to lose his job.

> "Is it because I refused to be on the Diversity Committee?" I demanded. I was loud, the halls were empty. The echo enhanced my argument. "Well, that certainly would have...," he began, but seeing that I was hearing every word, already planning my deposition for my discrimination lawsuit, he stopped himself. "Your file was examined as a whole. You were hired to teach

African American literature. Not just American literature. You fought that. Simple."[29]

In his imagined university system, Johnson withholds his narrator from speaking in the designated spaces of critique allotted to him by his university administration, which is a typical feature of the Black aesthetic. Harney and Moten contend, "The black aesthetic turns on a dialectic of luxuriant withholding."[30] Here, Johnson brings into conversation two possible ways of engaging with the Political: one can either submit to its institutional order by speaking within its predesignated spaces of critique or risk displacement by challenging when and where narratives of democratic inclusion are used within the Political. Both as an ethical obligation, and as an act of self-preservation, Jaynes refuses to be defined by institutional categorization.

Mark McGurl accounts for the institutional history of American universities by reading Clark Kerr's concept of the multiversity through cultural pluralism. Together, they are "driven by the logic of expansion and differentiation, and the continual birth of new scientific subdisciplines."[31] Negotiating cohesion—in what in its very definition of identity defies any one essential understanding of being—is a necessary institutional restraint imposed by university systems, so that they can be legible and marketable. In her essay "Home," Toni Morrison urged scholars to refuse the market practices of the university that liken them to exchangeable capital.

> Our campuses will not retain their fixed borders while tolerating travel from one kind of race-inflected community to another as interpreters, native guides. They will not remain a collection of segregated castles from whose balustrades we view—even invite—the homeless. They will not remain markets where we permit ourselves to be auctioned, bought, silenced, downsized, and vastly compromised depending on the whim of the master and the going rate. Nor will they remain oblivious to the work of conferences such as this one because they cannot enforce or afford the pariah status of race theory without forfeiting the mission of the university itself.[32]

The Political, which encourages students and faculty to submit to its exclusivity, requires gratitude for placement: "This very structural position of being the guest, or the stranger, the one who receives hospitality, allows an act of inclusion to maintain the form of exclusion."[33] It seems that in order to be "institutionally legible," scholars of color too often are forced to either translate themselves into the institutional framework of their university (through market practice) or remove themselves from their languages that defined their cultural hubs. Therefore, Jaynes's aesthetic of luxuriant withholding bears with it a rehearsed tradition of civil disobedience that refuses regulation and withholds service.

With each detail Johnson invites his readers to question the logical assumptions of departmental categorization and academic specialization. Johnson begins his novel by imagining his protagonist as becoming disposable once he refuses to be "institutionally legible" and help the university produce the *right* type of diversity image. "'So you want the black guy to just teach black books to the white kids.'"[34] To make things more complicated, Jaynes has strayed away from teaching literary fiction written by authors of African descent to teaching fiction written by authors of European descent—even offering the course "'Dancing with the Darkies: Whiteness in the Literary Mind' twice a year, regardless of enrollment."[35] When Jaynes talks about whiteness, he likens it to an untreated disease:

> Curing America's racial pathology couldn't be done with good intentions or presidential elections. Like all diseases, it had to be analyzed at a microscopic level. What I discovered during my studies in Poe's and other early Americans' texts was the intellectual source of racial Whiteness.[36]

As Sara Ahmed rightly notes, "Our talk about whiteness is read as a sign of ingratitude, of failing to be grateful for the hospitality we have received by virtue of our arrival."[37] Jaynes nevertheless tries desperately to explain the sociocultural context out of which his research stemmed, but his rationalizations go unheard. "'Please, listen to me,' I pleaded. 'My work, it's about finding the answer to why we have failed to truly become a postracial society. It's about finding the cure!'"[38] However, as Ahmed rightly maintains, "institutionalizing diversity is a goal for diversity workers, it does not necessarily mean it is an institution's goal."[39]

After Jaynes unsuccessfully confronts his university president, he heads to a local bar in his university town to further drown his sorrows. "There was one bar in town and there was a black guy siting in it."[40] However imperfect their first meeting turns out to be, Jaynes initially celebrates their academic accomplishment. He introduces himself succinctly and confidently: "'Chris Jaynes. Americanist.' And our fists bumped in blackademic bliss. Mr. Johnson was a younger man than I, in both years and manner. Dressed like he was straight out of Compton, but clearly straight out of a postdoc instead."[41] The semicasual setting, which fuses a place of leisure with one of confession, leaves room for spaces of comfort, aggression, and resolve. Although some of the dialogue can be interpreted in varying intensities, the setting reassures the reader that both men are having a good time over a few drinks, but like most dramatic American bar scenes, they ultimately end in a fight.

Both characters make themselves aware to the reader as Black male leaders. Although many of their values overlap, they diverge in important ways. Johnson uses these characters to rethink two paradigms in African American literature: "In the two most influential critical paradigms that have governed African-American literary studies—revolving around uplift and vernacular tradition—print literature is imbued with broad-based representative powers."[42] Whereas Jaynes's theoretical approaches to working within his contemporary university setting seem *reasonable*, for the young postdoc they seem too far-fetched and implausible. For Mosaic Johnson, Jaynes's new research makes him akin to a sellout, a traitor, one who wishes to be easily legible and successful within white literary criticism but nevertheless gets ousted from its elite ranks: "'Oh I get it. I get it now, why you love Poe. You two share one big thing in common. Neither one of you is a damn bit relevant anymore.'"[43] Neither in their investigation in literature nor in their placement in society are the two men able to agree on the same institutional values.

Mosaic Johnson represents what Dubey refers to as the *vernacular paradigm*: "In the vernacular paradigm, writers may speak for distinctively black communities insofar as they can inflect their texts with the accents and idioms of black oral culture."[44] The postdoc envisions his participation as active resistance in what—because of his sheer heroism and optimism—contribute to the betterment of university culture. For Mosaic, his proximity to the raw, authentic culture of inner-city life makes him more attuned to "the" social concerns of Black communities. Narrating himself as a "fighter," a person who, in comparison to Jaynes, is "not trying to run from the folks" but to deal with reality, Mosaic Johnson explicitly characterizes himself as a covert enactor of radical rebellion.

> "Man, in my work, I deal with the ghetto. The real shit, you know what I'm saying? Reality," he told me, motioning around the room with a silver-ringed hand as if our present setting was mere computer simulation. "I'm not trying to run from the folks. I want to be on [the diversity] committee. I'm a fighter. I want to be on that committee, to bring the fight here." The hand in the air formed into a fist.... If I was still here tomorrow, they would come

up to me and ask why I never raised the black power fist like the new guy. Undaunted, I continued.⁴⁵

Within African American literature, the vernacular paradigm is highly contested.⁴⁶ It requires the intellectual speaker to frame the cultural values, ambitions, and shortcomings of a specific community into an academic or bourgeois intellectual habitus. This has two effects: (1) it makes the speaker the authority, expert, or voice of a community or body of people that might not have the cultural or economic capital to speak for themselves; and (2) it also locates a group struggle in a single body.

In the context of the Political, as exhibited by Johnson in this bar scene, fighting not only for inclusion but authority on diversity drives their competition. Having embarked on their third round of drinks, it seems as if the two men are settling in nicely with one another and may have even negotiated a certain amount of trust that would allow for a more intimate conversation to inspire between what really are strangers. As a seasoned member of the university system, Jaynes attempts to offer some "fatherly" advice to Mosaic: "'Don't join the Diversity Committee,' I told him when the third round hit."⁴⁷ Likening it to a "slave hold," Jaynes discourages Mosaic from participating in the Diversity Committee: "Don't let them put you there. It's a slave hold. They'll fight you: they'll really want you on the Diversity Committee because if there aren't any minorities on the committee, the committee isn't diverse."⁴⁸ Although Jaynes's tone encourages resistance, the self-image that Jaynes tries to perform here for the young academic is not as physically forceful as his tone suggests.

If, then, Mosaic Johnson represents the first of two paradigms that Dubey outlines, namely the vernacular paradigm, then Chris Jaynes may represent the second, and equally problematic, paradigm of *uplift*: "The uplift paradigm cases the writer as an agent of social advancement and cultural improvement, thereby affirming the tangible value of print literacy for the masses."⁴⁹ Because Jaynes's approach is so theoretically based and largely perceived as nonconfrontational, Mosaic Johnson makes an implicit characterization of Jaynes, which insinuates his approach to that of an Uncle Tom. Spillers understands the uplift paradigm in three points:

(1) re-constitute a "talented tenth," which is itself the culminative position of the myth of representation (as both [W. E. B.] DuBois and [Harold] Cruse embraced it from their common historic past); (2) sustain the idea of the intellectual as a leading and heroic personality rather than a local point of

oscillation among contending conceptual claims; and (3) continue to pursue a theory and practice of intellectual or cultural work that is performative rather than, for lack of a better word, unfortunately, "scientific," or responsible to a "cognitive apparatus," or a "thought-idea."[50]

Here it is apparent that both men share what Erica Edwards has called *Charisma*. Both men, through their heroism envision themselves as the model for upward social mobility.

Instead of letting Mosaic make his own experiences within the university structure, Jaynes insists on imposing his institutional experience onto him. Here, in what can only be understood as a literary simulation of racial capitalism within a university context, the debate around inclusion does not leave room for cooperation.

> "No, you don't, and I'll tell you why. The Diversity Committee has one primary purpose: so that the school can say it has a diversity committee. . . . But none of the ideas that come out of all that committeeing will ever be implemented, see? Nothing the committee has suggested in thirty years has ever been funded. It's a gerbil wheel, meant to 'Keep this nigger boy running.'"[51]

This last intertextual reference to Ralph Ellison's *Invisible Man* is quickly spotted by Mosaic: "'Ellison.' He smiled. I knew a black author reference would get to him."[52] It reveals an eased, intentional reference to gain his attention and respect. Yet, it also works to highlight the impossibility of social uplift within the democratic hope for inclusion.

Here we might want to see Johnson's intertextual reference as a type of haunting, "in which abusive systems of power make themselves known and their impacts felt in everyday life, especially when they are supposedly over and done with (slavery, for instance) or when their oppressive nature is denied (as in free labor or national security)."[53] In this capitalist institutional setting that requires competition and antagonism to function, Johnson uses the intertextual reference of intergenerational struggle to comment on the complexity of upward social mobility within American consensus: The two academics use the intellectual space of university culture to annihilate the other and justify their single placement as the only Black male professor at this liberal college. This is the potential power of the university structure to empower and fuel competition. What first starts out as appreciation, brotherhood, and the potential for allyship quickly becomes infected with competition, opposition, and conquest. In order to comprehend this better, it is fruitful to understand American universities as being composed of different worlds—categorized and differentiated through departmentalization—that are constantly in competition and also at work with one another. Each researcher is in competition with their own local understanding (which may be based on individual experience and/or where one was institutionally trained), their regional understanding (here, not only understood as the individual but rather their departmental location in their field), and finally the national and international approach to the field into which they wish to subscribe (this can be understood in relationship to other universities, both nationally and internationally). Their proximity to the core of Black culture and the Black intellectual tradition becomes the barometer according to which they both measure their intellect, authenticity, and masculinity. Thus, coming back to Kerr's concept of the multiversity, as individual components of a more broad departmental entity, researchers are not only in competition with the university system; they are in constant negotiation with themselves.

Survival strategies to navigate institutional regulations are therefore never uniform—just as in American chattel slavery there was not an all-encompassing single approach to surviving within the institution of slavery. Instead there were overt acts of resistance, such as running away, suicide, or fighting back through coordinated acts of rebellion; however, there were daily instances of covert resistance such as singing, feigning ignorance or sickness. Similarly, in academia scholars of color negotiate resistance and institutionalization differently. This has been well documented throughout the Black intellectual and Black radical traditions. Debates on how to combat American racism—whether through overt or covert resistance (Malcolm X and Dr. Martin Luther King Jr.), university education or vocational schooling (W. E. B. Du Bois and Booker T. Washington), or the use of standard language or folk dialect (Du Bois and Alain Locke)—continue to contribute to a rich field of academic excellence and a complex American literary history.

It often requires both collective and individualized strategies for survival. Racial capitalism, often in the form of intergenerational struggle for masculinist authority, promises a renewed sense of cohesion with each competing generation. The Political within the faith-based system of hope commits itself to reordering capitalism by using competition to justify the displacement of old social orders with new ones. In his *Black Marxism*, Cedric Robinson reflects on how the 1960s New Left established itself by disavowing Richard Wright. Rising young scholars such as Harold Cruse and James Baldwin came into their symbolic intellectual maturity by the time they denounced Wright. A year after his death, James Baldwin wrote of his fallen mentor: "but when we met, I was twenty, a carnivorous age; he was then as old as I am now, thirty-six; he had been my idol since high school, and I, as the fledging Negro writer, was very shortly in the position of his protégé."[54] Therefore, his coming-into-being as a man, intellectual, and leader required that he abandon his childlike relationship to Wright and stand up to him not only through imagining new social worlds in fiction but through his political writings as well. Baldwin, of course, had already written critically in his famed essay "Everybody's Protest Novel," in which he challenged the innovation of *Native Son*. Writing "Alas Poor Richard," Baldwin critiqued Wright's "gratuitous and compulsive" use of violence. Although valid, Baldwin's critiques reveal the complex forces of capitalism—which (1) used displacement to reorganize a New Left and Black radical tradition and (2) revealed Baldwin's personal or Political willingness to overturn the legacy of his former mentor to define his own. Robinson concluded, "Perhaps, like Baldwin, Cruse had also felt the need to 'kill the father.'"[55] Here it can be seen how even the most nuanced thinkers of the new 1960s Black intelligentsia are made complicit with the capitalist forces within the Political that allow them to assume authority from their literary forefathers.

In Mosaic Johnson's understanding, Jaynes becomes symbolic of an aging academic who has lost his desire to compete in the university, and Mosaic Johnson is willing to replace him so that he can more competently fill his academic and administrative roles. "'Look, cuz, unlike you, clearly, I believe in trying to change things. Fighting against racism where I see it. I don't back down, and I don't apologize for that either. Hell yeah, I'm down for the damn committee.'"[56] For Mosaic, Jaynes's defeat is logical and well deserved. "'Man, just relax. Ain't nothing personal. Yes, I'm the new hire. Yes, it was your tenure line.'"[57] For him, Jaynes's displacement from the university is necessary for institutional reform: Because of his age, Jaynes is accused of being someone stuck in time, committed to a struggle of passive resistance that justifiably no longer has a place within the "new" university wars on race. One cannot help but remember Ellison's pessimistic vision that posited the promise of upward social mobility as an antiblack apparatus and democratic progress that was much more invested in capitalist interest than individual welfare. "Capitalism and racism, in other words did not break from the older order but rather evolved from it to produce a modern world system of 'racial capitalism' dependent on slavery, violence, imperialism, and genocide."[58] In a similar gesture to the aforementioned example concerning Baldwin, Cruse, and Wright, Johnson puts Mosaic's political values in dialectical position with

Jaynes's so as to question the "logical" assumptions attached to the Political hope for institutional reform.

The scene that Johnson creates is eerily similar to Ralph Ellison's scene in *Invisible Man* when the first-person narrator is invited to participate in a battle royal for the entertainment of the town's white elites: "They were all there—bankers, lawyers, judges, doctors, fire chiefs, teachers, merchants. Even one of the more fashionable pastors."[59] That day, the first-person narrator had given his valedictorian speech and had been invited with other boys in his school to partake in this fight. Blinded, the Black boys were dressed in fighting gloves and told to attack their classmates. As the evening progressed, fewer boys were fit to continue: "Some were still crying and in hysteria. But as we tried to leave we were stopped and ordered to get into the ring. There was nothing to do but what we were told."[60] Their self-destruction provided the entertainment. Even if they resisted so as to avoid self-harm or if they did not wish to see harm done to others, they were nonetheless required to fight, and their fear of what could be worse kept them from doing otherwise: "'See that boy over there?' one of the men said. 'I want you to run across at the bell and give it to him right in the belly. If you don't get him, I'm going to get you. I don't like his looks.' Each of us was told the same."[61] This scene shows that in the relative spectrum of potential achievement, surviving the performative scenario of white entertainment is not as easily escapable as one would hope.

When it came down to the two last fighters, one was Ellison's autodiegetic narrator: "Then on a sudden impulse I struck him lightly and as we clinched, I whispered, 'Fake like I knocked you out, you can have the prize.' 'I'll break your behind,' he whispered hoarsely. 'For them?' 'For *me*, sonofabitch!'"[62] The Invisible Man even offers him five dollars: "'Give it to your ma,' he said, ripping me beneath the heart."[63] Winning, even if through false pretenses, would be debilitating to his opponent's pride. Furthermore, the Invisible Man's deal was taken as an insult because it threatened the respectability of what this fight meant to the other man. Similarly, Mosaic is all too willing to partake in the same capitalist system that made his predecessor so disposable. Through an engagement with the grotesque, Ellison then showed how achieving upward social mobility and achievement—even on a local level—justifies the annihilation of a neighbor. In a type of literary simulation, Johnson experiments with the same scenario in a modern academic setting, imagining a similar outcome.

Johnson's scenes are provocative, humorous, and insightful. His text raises more questions than it answers, thus ultimately noting a crisis in the state of

American literature and the university systems that sustain them. In many ways, Johnson is able to comment more critically and succinctly on the problems and placements of diversity discourse than literary criticism. Although Jaynes can never leave the Political, he does leave the university. The scene ends with Jaynes losing the fight to the university as well as to the young academic. "Mosaic Johnson could definitely bring the beat. To me personally, he brought the beat down. 'Poe. Doesn't. Matter,' he said as he pummeled. I respected him for that, though."[64] He gives up his faith in the university for a new faith in himself that allows him to escape the university only to later become enslaved by a barbaric breed of white Neanderthals, the snow honkies. Although fantastic, Johnson's novel shows the difficulty of escaping Western social order and the challenges of *representing* the hope for inclusion.

This essay began by asking what forms of resistance are available to scholars of color seeking inclusion from supposedly democratic university systems. I have tried to reflect on two fictional characters who are caught in the system of the Political. Even after being denied tenure, Jaynes commits himself to critiquing the Political project of university. It is what has given him an identity for so long, but by using this situation as the novel's exposition, Johnson shows how there is life after the university (even in fantasy). As the work of Harney and Moten shows: "Uncut devotion to the critique of this illusion makes us delusional."[65] In their critiques, both characters oscillate between different modes of disillusionment. Although they take two different approaches to surviving the Political, they nevertheless both succumb to the forces of racial capitalism: instead of working together, they commit themselves to conquering the other—competing for the "democratic" hope of inclusion that is as much an illusion as it is an impossibility. Therefore, it would seem that "real" change must happen outside of the university. The Political within the universities from which we seek residence is an inescapable force that makes us complicit in the reordering of intersecting racist capitalist orders. It is this faith-based system of hope that requires our compliance with institutional measures of exclusion, even when it is disguised as diversity and narrated through inclusion.

"*We run looking for a weapon and keep running looking to drop it. And we can drop it, because however armed, however hard, the enemy we face is also illusory.*"[66]

COURTNEY MOFFETT-BATEAU is a Black woman scholar and lecturer based in Germany. She has taught at the Humboldt University in Berlin and Camp Afflerbaugh-Paige, a Los Angeles County juvenile probation camp located in La Verne, California, as well as working in cooperation with the project "Förderunterricht für Kinder mit Migrationshintergrund," which offers free tutoring for German- and non-German-identifying POC pupils. Her dissertation, "Disappearing Blackness? High Cultural Pluralist Voices of the Program Era," surveys the institutional and literary mechanisms that allow American texts to be racialized through categorization. Currently, she is the recipient of the Konrad Adenauer Foundation's scholarship for "Excellent and Talented" international students. After graduating with a dual bachelor's degree in philosophy and Black studies from Pitzer College in Claremont, California, in 2008, she completed her master's degree in national and transnational studies in 2012 at the University of Münster, Germany. She is the recipient of the University of Duisburg-Essen's 2015 award for innovative teaching and a Fulbright Grant (2008–9) and also was an urban fellow for the Center for California Cultural and Social Issues in 2007.

NOTES

I would like to extend a special thanks to the peer reviewers of *Critical Ethnic Studies* and Dr. Sebastian Weier, whose thoughtful insights brought me closer to my own arguments. Also thanks to Professor Barbara Buchenau, Professor Donald Pease, Dr. Elena Furlanetto, and Dr. Dietmar Meinel from the University of Duisburg-Essen for reading earlier versions of this paper.

1. Stefano Harney and Fred Moten, *The Undercommons: Fugitive Planning & Black Study* (New York: Minor Compositions, 2013), 50.

2. Calvin Warren, "Black Nihilism and the Politics of Hope," *CR: The New Centennial Review* 15, no. 1. (2015): 216.

3. Cedric Robinson, *Black Marxism: The Making of the Black Radical Tradition* (Chapel Hill: University of North Carolina Press, 1983), 317.

4. Ibid., 317.

5. Robin D. G. Kelley, "Black Study, Black Struggle," *Boston Review: A Political and Literary Forum*, March 7, 2016, accessed 22 August 2017, http://bostonreview.net/forum/robin-d-g-kelley-black-study-black-struggle.

6. Harney and Moten, *Undercommons*, 48.

7. Ashraf H. A. Rushdy, "The Neo-Slave Narrative," in *The Cambridge Companion to the African American Novel*, ed. Maryemma Graham (Cambridge: Cambridge University Press, 2004), 89. As Rushdy, Hortense Spillers, and James Edward Smethurst note, U.S. book market culture and print culture, as well as U.S. institutions of higher education, changed as a direct result of radical cultural nationalism of the late 1960s and early 1970s. Hortense Spillers, "Crisis of the Negro Intellectual: A Post-Date," *boundary 2* 21, no. 3 (1994): 107: "For all intents and purposes, the years immediately following the publication of [Harold Cruse's 1967] *The Crisis of the Negro Intellectual*—1968–1969—marked the inaugural years of black studies as a new institutional

site within the main-stream academy. At Brandeis University, for instance, the student occupation of Ford Hall, during eleven days in February 1969, had elaborated fourteen demands, one of which called for the creation of black studies, whose chief administrative officer would be chosen by the students them-selves"; James Smethurst, *The Black Arts Movement: Literary Nationalism in the 1960s and 1970s* (Chapel Hill: University of North Carolina Press, 2005), 1: "Indeed, many of these departments, programs, and committees (and publishers, book imprints, academic book series, art galleries, video and film production companies, and theaters) were the direct products of 1960/70s nationalism."

8. Rushdy, "Neo-Slave Narrative," 89.

9. Graham, introduction to *Cambridge Companion to the African American Novel*, 14.

10. Rushdy, "Neo-Slave Narrative," 89: Black Power intellectuals such as Sterling Stuckey, Michael Thelwell, Vinvent Harding, and John Henrik Clarke greatly impacted the works of Eugene Genovese and Martin Duberman. Also see Robinson, *Black Marxism*, 175–76: "For one, as we have seen, the history of Black peoples has been recast consistently in both naïve and perverse ways. Most particularly the memory of Black rebelliousness to slavery and other forms of oppression was systematically distorted and suppressed in the service of racialist, Eurocentric, and ruling-class historiographies. The sum total was the dehumanizing of Blacks." See also Eugene Genovese, "The Legacy of Slavery and the Roots of Black Nationalism," in *Black Liberation Politics: A Reader*, ed. Edward Greer (Boston: Allyn and Bacon, 1971), 43: "American radicals have long been imprisoned by the pernicious notion that the masses are necessarily both good and revolutionary.... This viewpoint now dominates the black liberation movement, which has been fed for decades by white radical historians who in this one respect have set the ideological pace for their liberal colleagues. It has become virtually sacrilege—or at least chauvinism—to suggest that slavery was a social system within which whites and blacks lived in harmony as well as antagonism, that there is little evidence of massive, organized opposition to the regime, that the blacks did not establish a revolutionary tradition of much significance, and that our main problem is to discover the reasons for the widespread accommodation and, perhaps more important, the long-term effects both of the accommodation and of that resistance which did occur." (cf. Robinson, 176)

11. Spillers, "Crisis of the Negro Intellectual," 68: "The period 1968–1970 meant, at last, the fruition of a radical and pluralistic democracy, or so it seemed, with, for example, comparatively larger numbers of African American students admitted to the mainstream academy and agitation for the movements in black studies and women's studies, and their far-reaching implications for a radically altered curriculum, especially in the humanities."

12. Kelley, "Black Study."

13. Christopher Newfield, *Unmaking the Public University: The Forty-Year Assault on the Middle Class* (Cambridge, Mass.: Harvard University Press, 2011), 6. "They sought to reduce the economic claims of their target group—the growing college-educated majority—by discrediting the cultural framework that had been empowering that group. This target group was to provide the postindustrial economy and

its descendant, the 'New Economy,' with the knowledge workers on which its productivity and adaptability depended. The culture wars discredited the cultural conditions of the political and economic ascent of these college-educated, middle-class workers. The culture-war strategy was a kind of intellectual neutron bomb, eroding the social and cultural foundations of a growing, politically powerful, economically entitled, and racially diversifying middle class, while leaving its technical capacities intact."

14. Mark McGurl, *The Program Era: Postwar Fiction and the Rise of Creative Writing* (Cambridge, Mass.: Harvard University Press, 2009), 58.

15. Ibid., 58.

16. Hameed Khalid Darweesh, et al., petitioners, and People of the State of New York, by Eric T. Schneiderman, Attorney General of the State of New York v. Donald Trump, President of the United States, et al. (2017): In opposition to Donald Trump's travel ban that targeted mostly Muslim countries where his personal businesses had no investments, seventeen U.S. American universities filed an amicus brief. They state: "Because amici seek to educate future leaders from nearly every continent, attract the world's best scholars, faculty and students, and work across international borders, they rely on the ability to welcome international students, faculty and scholars into their communities. The Executive Order at issue in this case threatens that ability, and creates significant hardship for amici's valued international students, faculty and scholars." The amici include Brown University, Carnegie Mellon University, University of Chicago, Columbia University, Cornell University, Dartmouth College, Duke University, Emory University, Harvard University, Johns Hopkins University, Massachusetts Institute of Technology, Northwestern University, University of Pennsylvania, Princeton University, Stanford University, Vanderbilt University, and Yale University.

17. Sacvan Bercovitch, "The Problem of Ideology in American Literary History," *Critical Inquiry* 12 (1986): 638.

18. Kelley, "Black Study": "Harney and Moten disavow the very idea that the university is, or can ever be, an enlightened place, by which I mean a place that would actively seek to disrupt the reproduction of our culture's classed, racialized, nationalized, gendered, moneyed, and militarized stratifications. Instead they argue that the university is dedicated to professionalization, order, scientific efficiency, counterinsurgency, and war—wars on terror, sovereign nations, communism, drugs, and gangs. The authors advocate refuge in and sabotage from the undercommons, a subaltern, subversive way of being in but not of the university. The undercommons is a fugitive network where a commitment to abolition and collectivity prevails over a university culture bent on creating socially isolated individuals whose academic skepticism and claims of objectivity leave the world-as-it-is intact."

19. Harney and Moten, *Undercommons*, 19.

20. Paula Moya, *The Social Imperative: Race, Close Reading, and Contemporary Literary Criticism* (Stanford: Stanford University Press, 2016), 7. "Literature is most usefully understood as a system (made up of even smaller systems) of formalized activities enabling social communication via culturally-specific forms of aesthetic expression. These activities (writing, reading, publishing, reviewing, advertising, and

discussing) operate within a field of interaction involving a variety of sentient and non-sentient 'actors' commonly associated with the literary field (Latour, Modern; Latour, Reassembling; Bourdieu). Some of these actors are the humans to whom people give the names of writer, reader, reviewer, publisher, or advertiser; others are the culturally-specific forms of aesthetic expression (novels, magazines, essays, newspapers) through which and with which these writers and readers interact." Based on my understanding of literature as a social institution, literature cannot neatly solve or escape the problematics of the Political. Instead, because the Political is so deeply entrenched in the inner doings of U.S. institutions, structural violence can very easily inform the academic consumption (how to read), production (how to write), and/or practice (how to exchange information) of literature.

21. Mahdu Dubey, *Signs and Cities: Black Literary Postmodernism* (Chicago: University of Chicago Press, 2003), 6: "As Henry Louis Gates observes, the nineteenth-century slave narratives were 'propelled by the Enlightenment demand that 'race' place itself on the Great Chain of Being primarily through the exigencies of print.' If the slave narrative equated 'the rights of man with the ability to write,' much of the subsequent African American literary tradition was galvanized by the belief that print literature could effectively press the case for full black participation in national life."

22. Robert Stepto, "Narration, Authentication, and Authorial Control in Frederick Douglass' Narrative of 1845," in *African American Autobiography: A Collection of Critical Essays*, ed. William L. Andrews (Englewood Cliffs, N.J.: Prentice Hall, 1993), 26.

23. Sara Ahmed, *On Being Included: Racism and Diversity in Institutional Life* (Durham, N.C.: Duke University Press, 2012), 176.

24. McGurl, Program Era, ix. "This book argues that the rise of the creative writing program stands as the most important event in postwar American literary history, and that paying attention to the increasingly intimate relation between literary production and the practices of higher education is the key to understanding the originality of postwar American literature."

25. Ramón Saldívar, "Historical Fantasy, Speculative Realism, and Postrace Aesthetics in Contemporary American Fiction," *Oxford Journal of American Literary History* 23, no. 3 (2011): 574.

26. Mat Johnson, *Pym* (New York: Spiegel & Grau, 2011), 7.

27. Ahmed, *On Being Included*, 34.

28. Ibid., 51–52.

29. Johnson, *Pym*, 13.

30. Harney and Moten, *Undercommons*, 48.

31. McGurl, *Program Era*, 57.

32. Toni Morrison, "Home," in *The House That Race Built: Original Essays by Toni Morrison, Angela Y. Davis, Cornel West, and Others on Black Americans and Politics in America Today*, ed. Wahneema Lubiano (New York: Pantheon Books, 1997), 11. Also see Spillers, "Crisis of the Negro Intellectual," 105: Spillers's discussion of community is also based in a concept of home: "As I understand it, community, however, is already a cross-weave—its local economisms linked into a larger network of sociopolitical/cultural relations and the messages that traverse it consequently—

that prepares its subjects to receive the supplemental. We cannot imagine learning, acquisition, the foreign language, precisely as the various pains of intrusion unless we first understand how community has intimately prepared the ground as the apparent continuing unity against which 'unhome' is measured."

33. Ahmed, *On Being Included*, 43.
34. Johnson, *Pym*, 13.
35. Ibid., 8. Also see Toni Morrison, *Playing in the Dark: Whiteness and the Literary Imagination* (New York: Vintage, 1992), 6–7. This intertextual reference to Morrison's *Playing in the Dark* is not at all discrete but a noticeable indication of Morrison's at-length criticism of American authors such as Hawthorne, Melville, and also Edgar Allan Poe: "As a disabling virus within literary discourse, Africanism has become, in the Eurocentric tradition that American education favors, both a way of talking about and a way of policing matters of class, sexual license, and repression, formations and exercises of power, and meditations on ethics and accountability.... It provides a way of contemplating chaos and civilization, desire and fear, and a mechanism for testing the problems and blessings of freedom." By blending the social critique characteristic of African American literature with the aesthetic form that traditionally exemplifies American literary history, Johnson's *Pym* showcases the power of fiction and maybe also the limits of literary criticism.
36. Johnson, *Pym*, 8.
37. Ahmed, *On Being Included*, 43.
38. Johnson, *Pym*, 14.
39. Ahmed, *On Being Included*, 22.
40. Johnson, *Pym*, 16.
41. Ibid., 17.
42. Dubey, *Signs and Cities*, 6.
43. Johnson, *Pym*, 20.
44. Dubey, *Signs and Cities*, 6.
45. Johnson, *Pym*, 18.
46. Morrison, "Home," 7. Morrison cautions against the hope of "imagining race without dominance." Insisting that her hope to "manipulate American English was not to take standard English and use vernacular to decorate it, or to add 'color' to dialogue." Finding the right *words* to describe nonbourgeois communities of color is a profoundly difficult intellectual (as well as civic) exercise with which bourgeois intellectuals must grapple. Following Morrison, those who choose to describe these communities or act as cultural interlocutors for or on behalf of communities of color should also "develop an epistemology that is neither intellectual slumming nor self-serving reification." Also see Adolph Reed, *Stirrings in the Jug: Black Politics in the Post-Segregation Era* (Minneapolis: University of Minnesota Press, 1999), 190: Referring to this relationship as the "first person—third person" relationship in his *Stirrings in the Jug*, Reed cautions intellectuals speaking within U.S. institutions on behalf of urban communities. Faced with the awkward position of "framing" discussions of poverty this "first—third" person relationship often produces intellectual speakers with a mute referent. In literature, see Dubey *Signs and Cities*, 28: "Writers of popular fiction have also actively entered the public debate about the middle class's

proper disposition toward the urban poor, with Toni Morrison cautioning against 'intellectual slumming,' James Alan McPherson lamenting the alienation of the middle class from the vernacular idioms of the people, Ishmael Reed lambasting black academics 'posing as experts on the inner city, which for them is another planet,' Toni Cade Bambara noting the linguistic gap between a 'working-class sister from the projects who ... speaks in nation-time argot' and 'more privileged sister ... who speaks the lingo of postmodern theory,' and Bebe Moore Campbell disputing Wilson's exodus thesis through her journalistic portraits of professional African-Americans who remained or returned to help the inner-city poor." Also see Stephanie Batiste, "Lens/Body: Anthropology's Methodologies and Spaces of Reflection in Dunham's Diaspora," in *Darkening Mirrors: Imperial Representation in Depression-Era African American Performance* (Durham, N.C.: Duke University Press, 2012), 190.

47. Johnson, *Pym*, 17.

48. Ibid.,, 18.

49. Dubey, *Signs and Cities*, 6.

50. Spillers, "Crisis of the Negro Intellectual," 87. Also see Erica Edwards, *Charisma and the Fictions of Black Leadership* (Minneapolis: University of Minnesota Press, 2012). Also see Robinson, *Black Marxism*, 177: Referring to C. L. R. James and W. E. B. Du Bois, Robinson states: "Their era began with the endings of slavery. They were, it might be said, the children of the slaves. The phenomenology of slavery formed and informed them. And in the vortex of its ending, more particularly in the wake of the social forces that compelled new and different situations of Blacks and others destined to serve as labor forces, these theorists discovered their shared social and intellectual location. The twentieth century was for the most part their biographical station, but merely one site in the zone of their interrogation."

51. Johnson, *Pym*, 18. Also see Ahmed, *On Being Included*, 6: Diversity documents cannot only read well, they must be effective. "I began to appreciate the importance of focusing not so much on what documents say but what they do." Ahmed gives the example of an interview with a diversity practitioner who wrote an equality policy that the woman described as "an amazing document" but got buried with a change of government. Ahmed states: "The document thus acquires no force. It ceases to have an official existence, even if it is still exists in electronic and paper form."

52. Johnson, *Pym*, 18.

53. Avery Gordon, *Ghostly Matters: Haunting and the Sociological Imagination* (Minneapolis: University of Minnesota Press, 2008), xv–xvi: "The first was how to understand modern forms of dispossession, exploitation, repression, and their concrete impacts on the people most affected by them and on our shared conditions of living. This meant trying to comprehend the terms of an always already racial capitalism and the determining role of monopolistic and militaristic state violence. In this way, the book reflects the type of Marxian inspired and inflected analysis, my intellectual training, that nonetheless has had to part company with the orthodoxies, reductions, and aggravating ongoing refusals to accept the incontrovertible facticity of racial capitalism itself."

54. James Baldwin, *Nobody Knows My Name* (New York: Dial Press, 1961), 191.

55. Robinson, *Black Marxism*, 305.

56. Johnson, *Pym*, 20.
57. Ibid., 19–20.
58. Robin D. G. Kelley, foreword to Robinson, *Black Marxism*, xiii.
59. Ellison, *Invisible*, 18.
60. Ibid., 21.
61. Ibid., 21.
62. Ibid., 24.
63. Ibid., 25.
64. Johnson, *Pym*, 21.
65. Harney and Moten, *Undercommons*, 19.
66. Ibid., 19.

The Order of Disciplinarity, the Terms of Silence

JOSHUA MYERS

Music is the silence between the notes.
—Attributed to Claude Debussy

Don't play all that bullshit, play the melody! Pat your foot and sing the melody in your head or play off the rhythm of the melody, never mind the so-called chord changes.... Don't pick up from me, I'm accompanying you! ... The *inside* of the tune [the bridge] is what makes the outside sound good.... You've got to know the importance of discrimination, also the value of what you *don't* play.... A note can be as big as a mountain, or small as pin. It only depends on a musician's imagination.
—Thelonious Monk, quoted in Robin D. G. Kelley, *Thelonious Monk: The Life and Times of an American Original*

I.

The silences make the song. They remain in place not because they are oversights. They do not exist because they are forgotten spaces. They exist to make real that which must be heard. They are not merely spaces of absence. They determine how and what we hear. And obviously what we do not. To fill those silences then is to transform the hearing of the song. To play notes in place of silences makes the song unintelligible. It is no longer familiar. It is not even the song.

II.

While the practice of exposing and addressing silences has become a significant one within the academy, and while it is how some might characterize the leading motive of Black intellectuals in the academy, it is nevertheless reductionist and misleading to conceive of the whole of Black intellectual history as a corrective to the silences that make Western knowledges. It is perhaps not ironic that the works that collect and categorize Black intellectual history and frame it as a project of addressing silences, filling lacunae, and making visible the invisible are, by their very nature, marketed as resistance to a silence. These works have mistaken their subject as *their* project. It is as if this act of addressing silences (the study of Black intellectual history) can only conceive of the silences they are addressing:

> (the subject of Black intellectual history itself) as a project aimed at addressing silences, the perennial "dilemma" of the Black scholar.[1] And yet the glaring silence—perhaps the necessary silence—in too many of these studies revolves around the challenges that Black intellectuals have made to the very epistemological "forms of producing knowledge" that their rescuers have utilized to make them heard.[2]

Here we might raise a question, one that was raised by a coterie of intellectuals whose academic credentials were either nonexistent or less important to their work, and that is whether the silences at the center of this corrective work were constitutive of the disciplines that were subject to their exposure? What does it mean to expose a silence if it was not simply overlooked, but intentionally ignored in order to advance a particular regime of truth? Put another way, given the interests that disciplines serve and the political function that the university performs both historically and currently, do the silences that we believe call for our correction actually exist for a purpose?

One is reminded of the oft-quoted disquisition on the meaning of historical silences by the anthropologist Michel-Rolph Trouillot in his *Silencing the Past*. There, Trouillot engages the necessary question of the relations between absences in the historical record and in the archive, as well as how the record and archive are located vis-à-vis power relationships in the social order, particularly those of the modern world. These locations reveal the key consideration that these absences are both logical and necessary given the importance of historical narratives and official memories of the past. Trouillot is often cited to endorse the projects that address narrative silences, that nonetheless attempt to remain *within* these official memories, neglecting a more honest insight about Western historiographical conventions, which is that Black conceptions of what it means to be human, Black "ideals of life," remain "unthinkable" in the still domineering "framework of Western thought" that guides the very need to resist silence.[3]

In a recent article on this question, Jennifer L. Morgan revealed that it was only in writing *against* the archive, and thus against the normative thrust of historiographical inquiry, that Black women's lives could be legible.[4] The writing against and writing beyond are hallmarks for radical Black intellectual inquiry, and yet how do we think of ways of replicating such forms of writing when everything that we are required to do in the academy asks us to write *within*, to correct absences rather than understand why they were constituted? What are disciplinary knowledges, that we should so desire their recognition?

Academic disciplines house Western knowledges in institutions that privilege and reward charisma, spaces, both conceptual and physical, that represent themselves as the prime locations to consider the meaning of reality: the modern research university. The conditions that exist to produce and make known facts about the world dictate that contributing to such projects requires the evocation of "new" knowledge. That is, one's contribution rests on the assumption that what has been said has never before been said.[5] This conception of intellectual work naturally inculcates an impulse to challenge silences, to add sound to compositions that we imagine to be incomplete, to say something *new*. These corrections produce fascinating interventions that we argue reveal insights theretofore hidden. Our conceptual world expands. We believe ourselves to have contributed to our disciplines when those silences no longer exist.

Yet, if regimes of race construct the known world from a set and range of "admissible and possible knowledges," then this means that they necessarily impute silences.[6] The question of Black intellectual history, inasmuch as it revolves around how to imagine a world that disrupts those regimes, makes it an *inadmissible* product within the very regime that needs and requires race—as well as "normative" constructions of gender and sexuality.[7] This is a regime that includes the university and thus requires its forms of producing knowledge: disciplinarity. And herein lies the paradox for the production of knowledge within the university. Whereas work that might not challenge normative terms of knowledge can easily be folded into the interstices of academic disciplines, perhaps advancing their range and scope, it has been the case that work that necessarily challenges the foundations of racial capitalism, the work that considers and imagines "alternative, oppositional, or simply different relations of power," when it has emerged from sites within the university, has meet a consistent refusal to be acknowledged—and where it has been acknowledged, it has met disavowal.[8]

III.

The ways that disciplines have responded to their exposures perhaps is a first step to understanding their sense of what the silences mean to their project. The ways that disciplines routinely contain and marginalize them reveal that much like other regimes of truth, disciplinary traditions are "unrelentingly hostile" to the "exhibition" of their purposeful erasures. Following the late Cedric Robinson, who applies this analysis to theater and film, a "discoverable history" of the racial terms of disciplinary and Western knowledges "is incompatible" and "threatens their authority" and "claims of naturalism."[9]

Mentions that replace silences are structurally cacophonous to compositions already imagined as coherent. These interventions then are silenced, producing a double silencing: the underlying silence plus the attempt to reveal it. This returns us to the same normative conclusions that required an intervention. They are updated, perhaps adapted, but they are ultimately reinforced rather than fully abandoned. Trouillot's example of the historiography of the Haitian Revolution is instructive. He argues that these historical interventions "were made to enter into narratives that made sense to a majority of Western observers and readers ... the narratives they build around these facts are strikingly similar to the narratives produced by individuals who thought that such a revolution was impossible."[10] Further, and perhaps most importantly, he states:

> Effective silencing does not require a conspiracy, not even a political consensus. Its roots are structural. Beyond a stated—and most often sincere—political generosity, best described in U.S. parlance within a liberal continuum, the narrative structures of Western historiography have not broken with the ontological order of the Renaissance. This exercise of power is much more important than the alleged conservative or liberal adherence of the historians involved.[11]

Of course, the same could be said about attempts to expose the racial orders inherent to disciplines. Another example of this structural hostility (but also much more) can be found at the intersection of history and economics. Black thinkers have argued for years that slavery provided the foundation for capitalist development. Works from such thinkers as Eric Williams, C. L. R. James, and W. E. B. Du Bois, who shared diverse origins but found themselves drawn to what Cedric Robinson calls the "renegade Black intelligentsia," were not necessarily concerned with making a historical claim as they were about making a political one.¹² In some ways they ended up doing both, but their historical claims were silenced if not occluded, less for reasons of historiography—even though they did challenge many theoretical and conceptual norms of the craft—than for reasons of their political stance. According to Peter James Hudson, the recent attempts to update and revise some of the central claims about the link between slavery and capitalism reveal inquiries that disavow the radical scholarship that originated them, a tradition "that derives historical questions as much from political commitments as from academic concerns." The radical intelligentsia that drew the linkages, in other words, shared a central interest: "the modern project of emancipation."¹³

A few generations later, historians and economists not sharing that political posture (or "racial" consciousness) have emerged with new studies drawing connections between slavery and capitalism without these explicit political commitments, which has required that they be feted as innovators in the field. This has not come without pushback. The economists that have responded, however, have been more keen to attack the data that supports these claims, in order to, it seems, free capitalism from the taint of an association with enslavement. The debate, which has prominently centered on Edward Baptist's *The Half Has Never Been Told*, has focused on questions of cottonseed variety and the efficiency of coercion and force to produce a certain level of production and not the moral questions at the center of the very idea of capitalism and the resistance to the social structures it has engendered.¹⁴ Even as these structures are ever-present and the underlying concern, the debates about the new histories rarely target capitalism for condemnation and destruction. What has happened is that the exposure of a silence—the idea that slavery generated modern capitalism—was greeted with disdain, only to be embraced generations later, often cleaved of the ideological stance of those earlier adherents, in order to advance a disciplinary regime of truth, a project of historiography rather than human liberation. The new sounds were imagined as complementary to the old; a new chord was produced, leaving the original silences intact. The result has been the further erasure of Black thought and its complex approaches to understanding the world. Disciplinary regimes were (and are) required to be hostile to Williams, James, and Du Bois, yet flexible enough to embrace this "new history of capitalism" within its complex of knowledge.¹⁵

From a different angle, we might see the desires to project W. E. B. Du Bois as a founder of modern "American sociology" as an attempt to address a silence that is at the heart of that academic discipline: the foundation of

American society as a racialized system of order. And just as much, the ways that this has been resisted is evidence of a more sinister prospect: that American sociology as a knowledge project endorses that very order. For Aldon Morris, whose *The Scholar Denied* is the most representative of this trend, Du Bois's alternative "school" of sociology at Atlanta University both preceded in time and challenged the most-cited founding "school" at the University of Chicago, which housed a Social Darwinist approach to the question of race relations led by Robert Park. Morris argues that Du Bois challenges these foundations by asserting a social constructionist view of race, but also by clearly viewing his project as an attempt to liberate African Americans by way of clarifying and arguing for the destruction of the structural relationships that underpinned both American and global caste systems. In this reading, Du Bois's social science was so far removed from the "mainstream," because it was imagined to break with the racial capitalism that the latter was created to manage and discipline.[16]

While perhaps necessary to recover Du Bois and the structures that opposed him, Morris and others have nevertheless occluded the more pertinent consideration, which is, at root, an epistemological one. If Du Bois attempted to utilize science to undermine a racial regime and generations of sociologists, including those practicing the craft today who continue to maintain it, how is it possible that they are practicing the same "discipline"? If Du Bois challenged sociology's pretense toward valorizing innate racial differences and its desire to elevate them into scientific law, would not the subsequent adoption by American sociology of the very ideas Du Bois stood against mark his project as different than theirs? If so, which one was "sociology"?[17] It is difficult to imagine the depth of Du Bois's oeuvre, so aptly explored in *The Scholar Denied*, as simply another subdiscipline of American sociology. This is especially the case when one reads "Sociology Hesitant," Du Bois's early twentieth-century argument against the idea that human action could be measured by tools derived from the natural sciences.[18] One reads Du Bois's studies as necessarily grappling with the tensions between scientific methodologies and disciplinary conventions. Ultimately, however, Du Bois's "multimethod" approach intentionally flouts the logics of disciplinarity in order to more effectively wield knowledge as a cudgel in the pursuit of both a political and epistemological space *beyond* the constrictions of the disciplines. Again, the recovery of Du Bois's praxis is a necessary one, and that this effort has met a significant amount of resistance *and* incorporation thus far might lead us to ask about the possibilities of doing something other than folding Du Bois's insights into the interstices of any single discipline and perhaps finding a space beyond all of them where we do not *have* to acknowledge his relevance, a space where the "liberation capital" of his work is assumed.[19]

While the impulse to correct the record is understandable, much of the work of addressing silences remains wedded to disciplinary practices that reveal their decadence. When we consider the questions of inclusion and rethinking discussed above and how they have been debated and discussed in the disciplines of history and sociology, we see the ways that disciplines are decaying, and their pretensions to certainty have led to conditions where they assert themselves as "ontological."[20] Lewis Gordon makes the argument that at this point, disciplines become "self-circumscribed" systems operating under the delusion that they are "*the world*" rather than "efforts to understand the world."[21] Knowledges and knowing that emerge outside such conceptual systems, such political boundaries, such theoretical norms are not properly that discipline's knowledge or—and here Gordon is most prescient—become the evidence of the need for the underlying knowledge to be more disciplinary. That is, it must conform to how that discipline has already constituted its world.[22]

We can stipulate that some of the appeal in addressing silences rests in identifying exemplars that shared our ideas, our political sensibilities, our shared racial struggles, which we imagine would then signify that we belong, that the disciplines are redeemable, or, even more naively, that the silences were just accidental omissions. But again, the naïveté is structural. We should heed Vincent Harding's statement about the meaning of vocation and its relationship to disciplinarity and ponder why it still resonates for many of us:

> Our truth demands that we reject the artificial barriers of the academic disciplines to seek the human unity which underlies the experience of our people. Just as the best of the anti-colonial revolutionary leaders reject the national political, economic, and social systems created by the colonizers, so do we deny a priori validity of methodological disciplines, concepts, and "fields" which have been established without our participation, and which have often worked against the best intellectual and political interests of the African peoples.[23]

Given what we know about the academic disciplines' capacity to retain their ontologies, despite these critical interventions, we might ask what other intellectual projects might emanate from sites within the academy. While it is the case that ethnic studies projects necessarily engage and grapple with the past, with social reality, and with the meaning of art, does that mean that they must necessarily intervene in the project of constructing new histories, new theories, and new criticist projects and folding them into the existing disciplinary traditions that silenced them in the first place? If it is true that disciplines are decaying, what does choosing "wisely from among the dying" look like for those who view knowledge as inherently emancipatory?[24]

IV.

The project of Black studies serves as a pathway to the resolution of this question. It was a project that was not simply about corrective measures or a pivot toward inclusion, but one understood as a "critique of Western civilization," of the very grounding assumptions that guided how disciplines approached reality.[25] In that same vein, the discipline (perhaps more appropriately the "antidiscipline") was conceived as a reconstruction project.[26] But the idea was not to reconstruct or repair the West, which seemed to be the project of those using Black studies as a mechanism to diversify the university; a project of diversity rooted in the denial of its political foundations that resisted the liberal assumptions of the academy.[27] Black studies stood on a different foundation.

In the aforementioned essay, Harding argues that Black intellectuals such as C. L. R. James and others situated in university spaces during the founding eras of Black studies had "moved continuously beyond, and sometimes against, the disciplines assigned to them by the university. Instead they have allowed the experience of our people to become the organizing reality."[28] This seems to run counter to claims that today seek to brand Black studies and other ethnic studies projects as "inherently interdisciplinary," an approach that obscures the reality that this often presupposes a form of disciplinarity that is not necessarily "shaped by the truth of the black community, especially its struggles."[29] The struggle of transformation must prefigure claims to disciplinary traditions. We might remind ourselves that what we are reconstructing is not a project from which we were excluded, but our memories of what existed before, our understanding of what exists now, our knowledge of ways of being and existing and producing knowledge about the world that cannot produce the silences that negated them.[30] Emancipatory work requires new compositions, with musical notes that are not crying out to be heard because they can only be heard; compositions that only contain radical silences that reproduce familiar, melodic sounds rather than the cacophony of noise; those that contain space-clearing, discriminatory silences that produce harmony, rhythm, and balance rather than music we do not recognize as such.

Antidisciplinarity, counterdisciplinarity, or undisciplinarity, however one crafts alternatives to and of the disciplinary projects of the academy—such alternatives then are not evasions of the necessity of knowing. Rather, they are the abandonment of the desire to be included in spaces that can only marginalize. But going further than opposition, these maroon spaces created to think differently also privilege other ways of knowing that emanate from different political projects than those that guaranteed the primacy of the disciplines we engage (and embrace). It is not an accident that the disciplines of knowledge grew up and affirmed the liberal-democratic projects of Western society and began to fracture into countertraditions as the grounding assumptions of this order came under attack from anti-imperial, anti-colonial, and broader Leftist formations in the twentieth century.[31] If the arrival of the postmodern moment mirrored the questioning of the regimes of late capitalism, then the reappearance of fixed disciplinarities in the modern academy mirrors the neoliberal hegemony that has wrested conceptual ground from the Left.[32] Thankfully, this has not erased those earlier countertraditions completely, but it appears they are becoming less and less visible and appropriated to other apolitical projects. What role have disciplines played in this new dispensation? It would appear that they continue to carry political commitments that cannot be disconnected from the knowledge claims that they support and that are considered possible under their aegis.[33]

In a 2015 talk at Princeton University, entitled "Mike Brown's Body," Robin D. G. Kelley asserted that his goal in undertaking a historical autopsy of the killing of Michael Brown was not to make a "historiographical contribution, but a political intervention."[34] The work to be done required more than simply making one's contribution to the "necessary" historiographical silences that have produced suffering—a deeper knowing also required an understanding that a critical lens from within these disciplinary matrices was not enough. Part of this approach seeks to reveal the facile process of rewriting liberal historiographies as contributing to the as yet unimagined freedoms that liberal narratives promise—and the freedoms stemming from other sources that these liberal narratives conceal.[35] Perhaps this sensibility can be traced to Kelley's mentor, Cedric Robinson, who more than most was able to exemplify what it meant to critically engage the disciplines of knowledge, exposing both their complicity in the modern world and imagining ways of thinking about that very world as well as past and future worlds without reinscribing the orders of knowledge that made it—and that "made" us, African people, into Negroes.[36] Like Kelley, Robinson, and others such as Sylvia Wynter, the question for us is not *whether* we should attempt this sort of fugitive Black study; the question is if we *can* in the places we inhabit.

For Robinson, this was the only alternative.

V.

New compositions, rather than additional notes. This is how we might characterize Cedric Robinson's thought. His recent transition afforded the opportunity for many thinkers attached to similar academic and critical projects to reflect anew on this work. The chords of this work resounded for us because it showed us possibilities for freedom and for the expression of the depth of Black humanity that had been so constricted, and necessarily so, by the thinking traditions that define the academy. We hold on to the Black radical tradition as a conceptual path back to ourselves. It is a resolution to and a refuge from the alienation that is a product of academic disciplinarity.

Robinson's *Black Marxism* is the text that is most commented upon, for it is the work where he clearly distills the logical and spiritual foundations of Black radicalism, doing so in ways that were misunderstood by the few honest interlocutors that seriously engaged the work. But for those for whom this work resonated, admittedly a growing number, it has fundamentally shaped engagements with the meaning of modernity and Black life, but also the meaning of African spiritual traditions, and the political traditions they created and continue to create, and the ways that this has and continues to be captured by the radical intelligentsia.[37] One simply does not read and understand this work without experiencing a deep transformation in their conception of how the modern world should be conceived and reckoned with. And yet the work continues to be misunderstood, particularly by those more concerned with disaggregating certain components of the text, rather than seeing them holistically. This misunderstanding, perhaps, issues from a desire to take elements of *Black Marxism* and to discipline them—that is, fold them into the projects that guide how disciplinarily oriented interpreters imagine and order reality, rather than how Robinson charted that path. Historians of enslavement seek the text to contribute to their understanding of the lives and contexts of the enslaved. Intellectual historians grapple with the chapters on Du Bois, James, and Wright as well as, not surprisingly, the silences of these chapters. Sociologists interpret the question of class in parts one and three, attempting to reckon with the unorthodox ways

Robinson interprets its historical development. And Marxists of various disciplinary commitments assume the text is about—well, Marxism. The text—too often, and to our detriment—becomes disciplined, a practice that could be read as a disavowal of the intent and the tradition of struggle in which it was grounded.

No one has done more to interpret the conditions of Robinson's arrival than Robin D. G. Kelley. By arrival what is meant is not simply his physical location in the world of academe, but how he came to inhabit the conceptual space he did. In the days after his transition, Kelley penned "Cedric J. Robinson: The Making of a Black Radical Intellectual," which provided the biographical details to the familiar refrain, for Robinson readers, that his work was, at its base, both a critical and reconstruction project. Robinson *was* Black studies. Here is Kelley:

> Cedric Robinson was a wholly original thinker whose five books and dozens of essays challenged liberal and Marxist theories of political change, exposed the racial character of capitalism, unearthed a Black Radical Tradition and examined its social, political, cultural, and intellectual bases, interrogated the role of theater and film in forming ideologies of race and class, and overturned standard historical interpretations of the last millennia. Like W.E.B. Du Bois, Michel Foucault, Sylvia Wynter, and Edward Said, Robinson was that rare polymath capable of seeing the whole—its genesis as well as its possible future. No discipline could contain him. No geography or era was beyond his reach. He was equally adept at discussing Ancient Greece, England's Middle Ages, plantations in Cyprus or South Carolina, anticolonial rebellions in Africa or Asia, as well as contemporary politics of Iran and Vietnam, El Salvador and the Philippines. No thinker—not Hegel, not Hannah Arendt, not even Frantz Fanon—was above criticism. We can see why academia basically ignored his writings until recently: he threw down the gauntlet before the altar of "Social Sciences," and challenged Black Studies to embrace its radical mission, which he once described as "a critique of Western Civilization."[38]

Kelley is correct to assert that no discipline could contain them, that his thought was uncontainable. We might extend the point by going back to Trouillot's insights above; Cedric Robinson's thought was *unthinkable*. It is in his unthinking of the thinking traditions of Western order where we find a viable location to ponder the doings of the academy, and the possible undoings of its imperial logics and how they structure how we think of ourselves and others. As Kelley states, Robinson was ignored, but he was ignored by people who could not afford to listen. But we who believe in freedom cannot afford to close our ears. His silencing should reveal to us not only different sounds, but new ways of hearing.

VI.

While Robinson's aforementioned magnum opus, *Black Marxism*, contains the kernel of this methodological unthinking and has received a fair amount of attention for those seeking to unthink Western radicalism and its necessary silences, the most unthinkable of Robinson's work might be the text that preceded it by three years, the recently republished *Terms of Order*.

A place to begin to unwrap the complex arguments of *Terms of Order* is the brilliant foreword to the reissue composed by Erica R. Edwards. Along with clearly stating the main arguments of the text, she pointedly connects the work to Robinson's larger conceptual project, particularly as it connects to the more familiar *Black Marxism* and *Forgeries of Memory and Meaning and Meaning*. In Edwards's view, *Terms of Order* is consonant with Robinson's method, a consistent critique of Western knowledge systems, in order to "carefully excavate the mechanisms of power."[39] At the core of these mechanisms, as has been argued by many thinkers, was "the whole of Western social science."[40] The task of the scholar, she reminds us, was for Robinson the dismantling of "the assumptions that found political science, Western statecraft, and the very idea of the political" rather than "Black scholasticism."[41] This characterization is drawn from Robinson's critique of George Shepperson and liberal historiography and is interesting because it mirrors much of the argument above about historical silencing and the subsequent co-opting of historical corrections, and because it does for history, albeit in a shorter work, what *Terms of Order* sought to accomplish for political science.

In, "Notes Toward a 'Native' Theory of History," Robinson characterized scholasticism as the "the addition of 'new' facts or the challenge to old ones" as "insufficient in itself."[42] A "native" theory of history would address itself to the idea of Africans "as producers of material and cultural wealth, as producers of ideologies and epistemologies, as producers of history," a historiographical project requiring resetting the terms under which liberal traditions were founded.[43] Edwards's invocation of this article is a reminder of the fact that *Terms of Order*, and Robinson's thought, was not simply a critique of political science, or the narrow question of leadership—it encompassed those and much more.

Robinson's "vantage point" for the discussion of his subject was that it was "inherited from a people only marginally integrated into Western institutions and intellectual streams."[44] And that secured for him the possibilities of excavating the meaning of what he called "the political" or "the order of politicality" in ways that were decidedly unthinkable. For it demonstrated that if political order, and the forms of leadership and authority that existed to enact it, were in fact mythologies, then it would stand to reason that they were, as he concludes, a "temporarily convenient, illusion."[45] Interestingly enough, one of the key features of this argument was that arrival to it was closed off from the very discipline that made the political its focus. For as Robinson demonstrates, the political was justified by the disciplinary practice of political science. And as such the only possible conclusion to be gained from contributing to this discipline would be perhaps the restructuring of order—which is necessarily structured by market justifications for violence and coercion—and not its dismantling. In fact, not only could one not understand how to resist the political from within political science, but one would not even be able to see how its foundations itself were constructed.[46]

To complete this task, Robinson employs "instruments, approaches which have a marginal relationship to the 'world hypothesis' of political order—approaches which convene critically if not exactly with what Michel Foucault called the 'Counter-Sciences' to construct a 'mixed paradigm,'" which conceives of the rational elements of the political together with their irrational foundations in order to demonstrate the ways in which the former appropriated the latter to render the world more orderly.[47] With the countersciences of structural linguistics, analytical mythology, and philosophy of history, among others, Robinson unpacks the Greek origins of order and the Judeo-Christian attempts to contain charisma. In engaging Max Weber's understanding of the meaning of charisma and the political, Robinson is able to pinpoint his error:

> Weber recognized the primitive and irrational elements associated with eschatological ideologies, whether Christian or Marxist, but in reversing these historicisms his theory of history remained no less primitive and irrational. His charismatic legitimation of authority was no less mythological than the traditions upon which it too rested. The mixed paradigm of charisma was ideological, epistemological, and archaic.[48]

This inability extended to the antipolitical traditions that emerged in the West. In the final chapter of the text, Robinson demonstrates how anarchism as a conceptual and revolutionary tradition could not effectively escape the episteme of the political. While anarchists opposed the ravages of the political, and while they resented its imposition on their lives, they did not oppose order. While theirs was an attempt to remap the various traditions of Western life along different paths than the *current* order—it was not a rejection of the *idea* of Western order.[49]

The next task then became the fulfillment of the other portion of Edwards's characterization of Robinson's method, that of detailing "the radical epistemologies and ontologies that those mechanisms [of power] have been erected to restrain."[50] In the Ila-tonga, Robinson sought a continuous and transferable example of a conception of order that remarkably did not require forms of hierarchy and violence that had marked Western conceptions of the idea. While the tools for excavating this example—functional anthropology—were just as compromised, Robinson's analysis was able to avoid the assumption that the absence of order necessarily produced chaos; or what anthropologists labeled "primitive society."[51] In the Tonga, Robinson found a society that found ways of resolving human problems from first-order premises that did not rely on violence and coercion, but on the notion that humans were not indivisible from their own (the Tonga's *mukowa*) and from every other "thing" in the universe.[52] This required other forms of authority based on kinship. And it is this that remains unthinkable on spectrums of the political, both left and right.

The Terms of Order is one of a growing number of interventions that reveal what Western disciplinarities have necessarily silenced. And in the case of the other ways of knowing that Robinson has excavated for us—in this example the Tonga, and in his other texts, a range of different peoples and traditions—are those conceptions of reality that require different interpretive compositions to be heard. On those terms, to follow Robinson, must we resist and "subvert" the political—and other disciplinary traditions—as *the* way "of realizing ourselves"?[53]

VII.

While Robinson's thought demonstrates that there are more productive ways to construct emancipatory knowledge systems, ones that do not revolve around disciplined categories for knowing the world, there is still more to be said about why the latter resonate: They are recognizable. We are all trained to think and categorize reality in this way. Breaking up is hard to do. But there is more, even for those committed to unthinking. There is the methodological concern that these projects by constructing different ways of knowing, if approached haphazardly, could end up replicating other forms of silence. How do we imagine, as Hortense Spillers does, the kinds of instruments we might use to "play" these sorts of tunes?[54]

First, we might address other attempts to play. Many Black studies compositions have been uncommitted to the playing of instruments imagined as necessary by Spillers and others and have thus been insufficiently attuned to the ways that racial subjectivities necessarily incorporated sexual ones, to the detriment of truly liberatory sounds. Not only were these initial compositions insufficient, but they also misread the Black radical tradition through a particularly Western "bodily" framing—ones that reified male identity as normative. Black thought in its most freeing manifestations might create a model that undoes projects of race, undoes projects of gender, so that what Wynter called "the human" might emerge. [55]

There, too, is the conceptual concern that revolves around how expansive these models might be and/or how closed they should be. Does antidisciplinary work require permeable boundaries, and if so, where would we mark their conceptual limits?

These are critical issues to be resolved. As a consequence, Black studies—insofar as it seeks to claim for itself the goal of emancipation—remains undone, unfinished. And depending on how one resolves the above concerns, it might be conceived as perpetually incomplete, if the task is to consistently comprehend the real. What remains to be seen is whether we can take the energies consumed by projects of inclusion and diversity and the impulse to frame intellectual work as contributing to silences at the core of Western traditions of knowledge, and replace them with a project that does not require such silencing, even as it engages these knowledges, à la Robinson. Part of that requires unearthing the deep philosophical basis of the need to respond to silences. Lewis Gordon writes of African philosophers and their approach to the question of erasure, not as a project of addressing silences, but from a deeper need to address the "disappearance" of ancestors who must remain in view, as they must inhabit our present as much as our past:

> For the African philosopher and intellectual historian, the narrative is about ancestors and their deeds and thoughts and their suffering. If part of their suffering was their "disappearance," which may be in effect similar to the wrong of an improper burial, then the act of getting the past right is also a corrective act of justice through the resources of truth. It makes the role of the African philosopher, whether that philosopher likes it or not, more than

secular notions of method and procedure, and it poses a challenge that transcends aspirations enmeshed in the dialectics of professional recognition.[56]

The way from here to there is less a question of intellectual capacity than it is one portending other kinds of concerns. Creating proper ways of correcting centuries of Africans subjected to "improper burials" has been sacrificed at the behest of the "academic" concern of professional viability. Disciplines have made "realizing ourselves" a professional liability. And thus the kind of reimagining that Gordon, Robinson, Wynter, and others suggest is deeply political and vivifying them requires resistance.[57] The tools necessary for this reimagining require different kinds of training and modes of knowledge that resist the formations in which we find ourselves. As Lisa Lowe suggests, and as responses to our often misplaced desire to address silences reveal, there are many "matters absent, entangled, and unavailable" to practices founded under the rubric of formations devoted to academic study.[58]

One possibility for another formation comes from the oft-cited work of Stefano Harney and Fred Moten. In their reading, those committed to Black radical praxis should take our locations in the academy and convert them into "the undercommons." Harney and Moten's framing of fugitive Black study resonates as a place committed to the unthinkable and to the unthinking of disciplinary silences that, absent an undoing, will perpetuate the role they have played in the power structures that enslave us. It is only by creating refuge for those whose life was "stolen by the Enlightenment"—by creating a space to think that is free of the academic and disciplinary justifications for that Enlightenment knowledge project—that we can develop a sort of foundation to think anew.[59] This must become the only meaning, the only relations of our presence in the university. The academy is nothing to us if not a site to perpetuate the tradition of spaces like the Communiversity, the Centre for Black Education, the New School of Afro-American Thought, and other, more recent formations.[60] Yet it must be remembered that there is a danger to institutionalizing the undercommons. The undercommons is the space for thinking about the formation and connecting to existing spaces that animate other ways of being and existing; it is not *the* formation. *The* formation requires a different world.

VIII.

We do not simply oppose the silences. We recognize they constitute a reality. A reality we would like to change. But we do not need to address these silences, on terms set by the silencers, to change our realities. A new reality only requires us to take what was never here, in those silences, to enliven what is always there, in *our* consciousness of what is possible; our song.

JOSHUA MYERS teaches Africana studies at Howard University, where he works on the convergence between Black thought and the ways in which it engages the worlds of modernity and the institutional locations that structure knowledge production. He is currently working on a manuscript that examines Africana studies and disciplinarity as well as a history of the 1989 student protest at Howard University, tentatively titled, *We Are Worth Fighting For*. In addition, he works with the SNCC Legacy Project's DC Black Power Chronicles, which is currently building an oral history and archive on the Black Power Movement in Washington, D.C.

NOTES

1. Works that describe Black intellectual history in this manner or draw attention to this particular dynamic include, for instance, John Hope Franklin, "The Dilemma of the American Negro Scholar," in *Soon, One Morning*, ed. Herbert Hill (New York: Alfred A. Knopf, 1963), 60–76; Jonathan Scott Holloway and Ben Keppel, "Introduction: Segregated Social Science and Its Legacy," in *Black Scholars on the Line: Race, Social Science, and American Thought in the Twentieth Century*, ed. Jonathan Scott Holloway and Ben Keppel (Notre Dame, Ind.: University of Notre Dame Press, 2007), 1–37; Mia Bay, Farah J. Griffin, Martha S. Jones, and Barbara D. Savage, "Introduction: Toward an Intellectual History of Black Women," in *Toward an Intellectual History of Black Women*, ed. Bay et al. (Chapel Hill: University of North Carolina Press, 2015), 1–14; Kevin Gaines, "African-American History," in *American History Now*, ed. Eric Foner and Lisa McGirr (Philadelphia: Temple University Press, 2011), 400; and Mamadou Diouf and Jinny Prais, "Casting the Badge of Inferiority beneath Black Peoples' Feet": Archiving and Reading the African Past, Present, and Future in World History," in *Global Intellectual History*, ed. Samuel Moyn and Andrew Sartori (New York: Columbia University Press, 2013), 205–27.

2. Ellen Messer-Davidow, David R. Shumway, and David J. Sylvan, "Introduction: Disciplinary Ways of Knowing," in *Knowledges: Historical and Critical Studies in Disciplinarity*, ed. Ellen Messer-Davidow, David R. Shumway, and David J. Sylvan (Charlottesville: University of Virginia Press, 1993), 1.

3. "Ideals of life" is from W. E. B. Du Bois, "The Conservation of Races," in *African-American Social and Political Thought, 1850–1920*, ed. Howard Brotz (New Brunswick, N.J.: Transaction, 2008), 485. "Unthinkable" and "framework of Western thought" are from Michel-Rolph Trouillot, *Silencing the Past: Power and the Production of History* (Boston: Beacon Press, 1995), 82.

4. Jennifer L. Morgan, "Archives and Histories of Racial Capitalism: An Afterword," *Social Text* 125 (December 2015): 153–61.

5. See William Clark, *Academic Charisma and the Origins of the Research University* (Chicago: University of Chicago Press, 2006); Andrew Abbott, *Chaos of Disciplines* (Chicago: University of Chicago Press, 2001); and Tony Becher, *Academic Tribes and Territories: Intellectual Enquiry and the Cultures of Disciplines* (Bristol, Pa.: Society for Research into Higher Education and Open University Press, 1989).

6. "Admissible and possible knowledges" is from Cedric Robinson, *Forgeries of Memory and Meaning: Blacks and the Regimes of Race in American Theater and Film before World War II* (Chapel Hill: University of North Carolina Press, 2007), xi.

7. In discussing these issues, Jonathan Scott Holloway's intellectual histories of Black thinkers during the Jim Crow era consistently frame race as an ever-present limit on their social and scholarly advancement, while concluding at the same time that racial discrimination in the imagination of these scholars was not necessarily the product of the philosophical foundations of Western knowledge. It appears that in his framing, Western knowledges possessed the potential to be made race-neutral and that Black scholars did not conceive of this complex of knowledge as inherently racial, but understood their mission as a concerted attempt to achieve recognition or make a contribution to their discipline in spite of their race and in most cases to bring an analysis of race discrimination to bear within these disciplines. Interestingly, Black studies is also projected as an extension of the tension between traditional Western knowledges and the desire for advocacy. See, particularly, Holloway and Keppel, "Introduction"; Jonathan Scott Holloway, *Confronting the Veil: Abram Harris Jr., E. Franklin Frazier, and Ralph Bunche, 1919–1941* (Chapel Hill: University of North Carolina Press, 2002); and Holloway, *Jim Crow Wisdom: Memory and Identity in Black America since 1940* (Chapel Hill: University of North Carolina Press, 2013).

8. Robinson, *Forgeries of Memory and Meaning*, xi. Following Neil Roberts's insights, the refusal of acknowledgment is less concerning than disavowal, for the latter requires "a simultaneous *double* movement: an acknowledgement *and* a denial. By simultaneously acknowledging and denying an event, one does not silence its existence. Rather, one strategically locates an event and then rejects its relevance, knowing full well that it occurred." Neil Roberts, *Freedom as Marronage* (Chicago: University of Chicago Press, 2015), 29.

9. Robinson, *Forgeries of Memory and Meaning*, xii–xiii.

10. Trouillot, *Silencing the Past*, 96.

11. Ibid, 106.

12. Cedric Robinson, *Black Marxism: The Making of the Black Radical Tradition* (Chapel Hill: University of North Carolina Press, 2000), 181–84. These works included Eric Williams, *Capitalism and Slavery* (Chapel Hill: University of North Carolina Press, 1944); C. L. R. James, *The Black Jacobins: Toussaint L'Ouverture and the San Domingo Revolution* (London: Secker and Warburg, 1938); W. E. B. Du Bois, *The Suppression of the African Slave-Trade to the United States of America, 1638–1870* (New York: Longmans, Green, 1896); Du Bois, *Black Reconstruction: An Essay toward a History of the Part Which Black Folk Played in the Attempt to Reconstruct Democracy in America, 1860–1880* (New York: Russel and Russel, 1935).

13. Peter James Hudson, "The Racist Dawn of Capitalism," *Boston Review*, March–April 2016, 42.

14. On this debate, see Marc Parry, "Shackles and Dollars," *Chronicle of Higher Education*, December 8, 2016, http://www.chronicle.com/article/ShacklesDollars/238598. While Baptist and Sven Beckerts's work do not deny the political saliency of their subject, they both tend to assume and realize the question of emancipation in liberal cloaks, which ultimately dismiss how racial slavery was rearticulated in the forms of exploitation that define the liberal traditions that followed it. Another contributor to the new histories, Walter Johnson, has discussed this question, as has Lisa Lowe. See Walter Johnson, "To Remake the World: Slavery, Capitalism, and Justice," *Boston Review Forum 1: Race Capitalism Justice*, 2016, 11–31; Lisa Lowe, "History Hesitant," *Social Text* 125 (December 2015): 85–107; Lowe, *The Intimacies of Four Continents* (Durham, N.C.: Duke University Press, 2015), 3–12, 135–75. The texts that have been most consistently constituted as "the new history of capitalism" include Edward E. Baptist, *The Half Has Never Been Told: Slavery and the Making of American Capitalism* (New York: Basic Books, 2014); Sven Beckert, *Empire of Cotton: A Global History* (New York: Alfred A. Knopf, 2014); and Walter Johnson, *River of Dark Dreams: Slavery and Empire in the Cotton Kingdom* (Cambridge, Mass.: Harvard University Press, 2013).

15. Importantly, this hostility was described as a tendency in liberal historiography by Cedric Robinson forty years after Eric Williams's *Slavery and Capitalism*: "The impulse which is adumbrated in the varied critical reactions to *Capitalism and Slavery* is not (as Curtin, Davis and O'Brien have suggested) 'guilt'. It concerns the ideological imperatives of the present historical moment, rather than any obligation to the past. It has to do with the constructions of an acceptable discursive reality for a world-system in which the relationship between the Western metropoles and non-Western peoples is one of continuing a deepening exploitation. The 'urgency' of the matter has to do with the necessity of *reconstituting* the rationale of an increasingly brutal and visible domination in a post-imperialist era. This has required both a reconceptualization of the character of capitalist society and of the identity of non-Western peoples" (italics in the original). Cedric J. Robinson, "Capitalism, Slavery, and Bourgeois Historiography," *History Workshop Journal* 23, no. 1 (1987): 135. Arguably this discursive project continues, with historians offering challenges to the interpretation of the new history of capitalism that both resituates Williams and seeks to undermine the strength of the thesis advanced by the newer approaches. See James Oakes, "Capitalism and Slavery and the Civil War," *International Labor and Working-Class History* 89 (Spring 2016): 195–220.

16. Aldon D. Morris, *The Scholar Denied: W. E. B. Du Bois and the Birth of Modern Sociology* (Berkeley: University of California Press, 2015), 3–4.

17. Morris's analysis deftly underscores Du Bois's challenge to normative considerations of race then present in America. While he argues that his "constructionist" approach has roots in his training in Berlin with the German school of historical economics, he never truly explains how both Du Bois's and the American approach could constitute founding traditions in the discipline, even as he details the eventual impact the former would have upon the sociology of race (a "subdiscipline" that emerged much later). See Morris, *Scholar Denied*, 19–54. Julian Go's review of Morris's work appears to suggest that the ultimate conclusion one could draw is that the

discipline of sociology might rewrite its founding not simply to include Du Bois as an ethical correction, but as an epistemological one. Sociology must be crafted upon an entirely different episteme. Du Bois's school must replace Park's in the conception of the discipline. This call, a radical one indeed, would if enacted fundamentally shape the discipline to render it unintelligible to its other founders and adherents. If successful, would it still be appropriate to call the project by the same name? Does the rejection of a founding tradition and articulation of a new episteme require the creation of a new discipline? See Julian Go, "The Case for Scholarly Reparations," *Berkeley Journal of Sociology*, January 11, 2016, http://berkeleyjournal.org/2016/01/the-case-for-scholarly-reparations/, as well as Reiland Rabaka, *Against Epistemic Apartheid: W. E. B. Du Bois and the Disciplinary Decadence of Sociology* (Lanham, Md.: Lexington Books, 2010). Patricia Hill Collins's critique of Morris's project originates from a slightly different concern, arguing that Du Bois's ostracization from the sociological fraternity was necessary to advance his intellectual work. Her perspective suggests, quite convincingly, that Du Bois's acceptance within that field might have required his acquiescence to its norms rather than the radical project he ended up developing. See Patricia Hill Collins, "Du Bois's Contested Legacy," *Ethnic and Racial Studies Review* 39 (2016): 1398–406.

18. Written in 1905, the essay argues that the search for natural laws in sociology buried the reality that human movements are often products of "Chance." Morris explores this essay and ultimately concludes that it preceded the challenge of Robert Merton, who, in 1949, sought to build social reality on theories of "the middle range" between abstraction and empirical certainty. See Morris, *Scholar Denied,* 29; Robert Merton, *Social Theory and Social Structure* (New York: Free Press, 1949). This conclusion, however, does not convince us that it could constitute the founding logic of sociology. In fact, it proves the opposite. On empiricism in sociology amid the shifts to which Merton contributed, see Roger Bannister, "Sociology," in *The Modern Social Sciences*, ed. Theodore Porter and Dorothy Ross (Cambridge: Cambridge University Press, 2003), 329–53; Lynn McDonald, *The Early Origins of the Social Sciences* (Montreal: McGill-Queen's University Press, 1993). These foundations and origins prompt us to consider whether sociology as presently constituted is capable of recentering itself upon Du Bois's approach to the study of social problems demonstrated in "Sociology Hesitant" as well as in his "The Study of Negro Problems" written seven years earlier. We might ask what connections exist between Du Bois's theoretical ruminations and his insistence that social knowledge be framed to advance a concept of political liberation. But just as well, we might ask what its limits were in producing that very possibility. See W. E. B. Du Bois, "Sociology Hesitant," *boundary 2* 27, no. 3 (Fall 2000): 37–44; Du Bois, "The Study of Negro Problems," *Annals of the American Academy of Political Science* 2 (January 1898): 1–23.

19. The resistance to Morris's work revolves around many tensions, not least the inability to see Du Bois as a theorist, which ironically is what inspired Morris to write the book after a conversation with Lewis Coser while still a graduate student. See Morris, *Scholar Denied,* xv. For other examples of this resistance see Go, "Case for Scholarly Reparations"; Martin Bulmer, "A Singular Scholar and Writer in a Profoundly Racist World," *Ethnic and Racial Studies* 39 (2016): 1385–90. On "liberation

capital," see Morris, *Scholar Denied*, 187–94. It is important to connect Du Bois's relationship to the advancement of knowledge to the sites of its production as well as its political inspirations. Du Bois consistently saw HBCUs (historically black colleges and universities) as a site of such work, despite their many challenges. See Du Bois, "Study of Negro Problems," 22–23, and his discussion of his project in *The Autobiography of W. E. B. Du Bois: A Soliloquy on Viewing My Life from the Last Decade of Its First Century* (New York: International, 1968), 308–21.

20. Lewis R. Gordon, *Disciplinary Decadence: Living Thought in Trying Times* (Boulder, Colo.: Paradigm, 2006), 8.

21. Ibid. (italics in the original).

22. Here are Gordon's ideas quoted at length: "Disciplinary decadence, as we have seen, is the process of critical decay within a field or discipline. In such instances, the proponent ontologizes his disciplines far beyond its scope. Thus, a decadent scientist criticizes the humanities for not being scientific; a decadent literary scholar criticizes scientists and social scientists for not being literary or textual; a decadent social scientist sins in two directions—by criticizing either the humanities for not being social scientific or social science for not being scientific in accord with, say, physics, or biology. And, of course, the decadent historian criticizes all for not being historical; the decadent philosopher criticizes all for not being philosophical. The public dimension of evidence is here subordinated by the discipline or fields functioning, literally, as the world. Thus, although another discipline or field may offer evidence to the contrary, it could, literally, be ignored simply on the basis of not being the point of view of one's discipline or field." Ibid., 33.

23. Vincent Harding, "The Vocation of the Black Scholar and the Struggles of the Black Community," in *Education and Black Struggle: Notes from the Colonized World*, ed. Institute of the Black World (Cambridge, Mass.: Harvard Educational Review, 1974), 24.

24. Robinson, *Black Marxism*, 316.

25. Chuck Morse, "Capitalism, Marxism, and the Black Radical Tradition: An Interview with Cedric Robinson," *Perspectives on Anarchist Theory* 3 (Spring 1999): 8.

26. James E. Turner, in calling Black studies "reconstructive," meant that "Black Studies represents a disillusionment and critique of 'certified knowledge,' and the historical currents of disillusionment with the mainstream are also a current of progressive contribution towards a more adequate social analysis and public policy.... If the reconstruction method, is itself, a workable procedure we have in Black Studies a way of arriving at new theory. Black Studies is a conceptual paradigm that principally tells us, like other academic discourse, what counts as a fact and what problems of explanation exist." Elsewhere in this article, Turner argues that Black studies through reconstruction is fundamentally about renaming the world. See James E. Turner, "Foreword: Africana Studies and Epistemology: A Discourse in the Sociology of Knowledge," in *The Next Decade: Theoretical and Research Issues in Africana Studies*, ed. Turner (Ithaca, N.Y.: Africana Studies and Research Center, 1984), xvii–xviii; for renaming, see ibid., xi.

27. See, for instance, Roderick A. Ferguson, *The Reorder of Things: The University and Its Pedagogies of Minority Difference* (Minneapolis: University of Minnesota Press, 2012), 180–208.

28. Harding, "Vocation of the Black Scholar," 24.

29. Ibid. On the question of interdisciplinarity and Black studies, see James Stewart, "Riddles, Rhythms, and Rhymes: Toward an Understanding of Methodological Issues and Possibilities in Black/Africana Studies," in *Ethnic Studies Research: Approaches and Perspectives*, ed. Timothy Fong (Lanham, M.D.: AltaMira Press, 2008), 179–217, and his seminal "Reaching for Higher Ground: Toward an Understanding of Black/Africana Studies," in *The African American Studies Reader*, ed. Nathaniel Norment Jr. (Durham, N.C.: Carolina Academic Press, 2007), 420–37. On the disciplinarity of interdisciplinarity, see Abbott, *Chaos of Disciplines*, 131–36.

30. On this conception of Black studies, see Greg Carr, "Toward an Intellectual History of Africana Studies: Genealogy and Normative Theory," in Norment, *African American Studies Reader*, 438–52; Carr, "What Black Studies Is Not: Moving from Crisis to Liberation in Africana Intellectual Work," *Socialism and Democracy* 25 (March 2011): 178–91.

31. See the contributions to Messer-Davidow, Shumway, and Sylvan, *Knowledges*.

32. Jean-Francois Lyotard, *The Postmodern Condition: A Report on Knowledge* (Minneapolis: University of Minnesota Press, 1984); Henry A. Giroux, *Neoliberalism's War on Higher Education* (Chicago: Haymarket Books, 2014); Wendy Brown, *Undoing the Demos: Neoliberalism's Stealth Revolution* (Chicago: Zone Books, 2015), 175–200.

33. Gordon, *Disciplinary Decadence*, 1–12.

34. Robin D. G. Kelley, "Lecture One: Mike Brown's Body: Meditations on Race, and Democracy," (Lecture, Toni Morrison Lectures, Princeton University, April 13, 2015), https://www.youtube.com/watch?v=1obMkRRWeHE&t=2012s.

35. On this question, see Lowe, "History Hesitant," 89–91; Lowe, *Intimacies of Four Continents*, 40–41.

36. "The African became the more enduring 'domestic enemy,' and consequently the object around which a more specific, particular, and exclusive conception of humanity was molded. The 'Negro,' that is the color black, was both a negation of African and a unity of opposition to white. The construct of Negro, unlike the terms 'African,' 'Moor,' or 'Ethiope' suggested no situatedness in time, that is history, or space, that is ethno- or politico-geography." Robinson, *Black Marxism*, 81.

37. See Robin D. G. Kelley, foreword to Robinson, *Black Marxism*, xi–xxvi, and the recent *Black Perspectives* roundtable on the text, ed. Paul C. Hebert, 2016, http://www.aaihs.org/tag/black-marxism/.

38. Robin D. G. Kelley, "Cedric J. Robinson: The Making of a Black Radical Intellectual," *Counterpunch*, June 17, 2016, par. 1, https:www.counterpunch.org/author/robin-kelley. See also Darryl C. Thomas, "The Black Radical Tradition—Theory and Practice: Black Studies and the Scholarship of Cedric Robinson," *Race and Class* 47 (October 2005): 1–22.

39. Erica R. Edwards, foreword to *The Terms of Order: Political Science and the Myth of Leadership*, by Cedric J. Robinson (Chapel Hill: University of North Carolina Press, 2016), xix.

40. Ibid., xvii.

41. Ibid.

42. Cedric Robinson, "Notes Toward a 'Native' Theory of History," *Review* 4 (Summer 1980): 46.
43. Ibid., 48.
44. Edwards, foreword, xxx.
45. Robinson, *Terms of Order*, 215.
46. See ibid., 9–26.
47. Ibid., 6.
48. Ibid., 155.
49. Ibid., 184–85.
50. Edwards, foreword, xix.
51. Robinson, *Terms of Order*, 188–89.
52. Ibid., 197–98.
53. Ibid., 215.
54. "The black creative intellectual does not make music, as it were, and should not try, but he/she can 'play.' What, then, is his/her 'instrument'?" Hortense Spillers, "The Crisis of the Negro Intellectual: A Post-Date," *boundary 2* 21 (Fall 1994): 94.
55. Ibid., 114; Sylvia Wynter, "Black Studies Manifesto," *Forum N.H.I.* 1 (Fall 1994): 3–11. On the question of the exclusions and silences of Black studies and of gender, body politics, and the production of knowledge, see inter alia, Ferguson, *Reorder of Things*, 110–31; Vivian Gordon, *Black Women, Feminism, and Black Liberation: Which Way?* (Chicago: Third World Press, 1991); Oyeronke Oyewumi, *The Invention of Women: Making an African Sense of Gender Discourses* (Minneapolis: University of Minnesota Press, 1997).
56. Gordon, *Disciplinary Decadence*, 73.
57. Carr, "Toward an Intellectual Genealogy," 439–40.
58. Lowe, *Intimacies of Four Continents*, 41.
59. Stefano Harney and Fred Moten, *The Undercommons: Fugitive Planning and Black Study* (Brooklyn, N.Y.: Minor Compositions, 2013), 28.
60. See Robin D. G. Kelley, "Black Study, Black Struggle," *Boston Review* 42 (March–April 2016), 17, for more recent examples of undercommons spaces.

Higher Education and the Im/possibility of Transformative Justice

SHARON STEIN

It has become commonplace to lament that many U.S. scholars and students work and study in neoliberal universities. Other terms have also been employed to characterize the shifts in U.S. higher education over the past forty years—privatization, commercialization, financialization, corporatization, marketization. These descriptors have important differences, and some may be more precise than others, but in general they are all intended to account for declining public funds, growing use of corporate management techniques, and the intensification of institutional practices that directly support capital accumulation. In this moment, there is a strong sense of dissatisfaction about where we are (the present) and where we appear to be headed (the future), particularly in relation to where we have been (the past). The connections we construct among past, present, and future affect how we understand the problems at hand and, therefore, our horizon of imagined possible responses.[1] Thus, it is necessary to trace the narrative emplotments that undergird our critiques of the contemporary university.

Many critical accounts of the neoliberalization of higher education in the United States are organized by a demand that the state make good on its post–World War II liberal promises of distributed affluence, inclusion, and social mobility. Even as some admit that access to higher education alone is not enough to address growing inequality and diminishing employment prospects, most remain deeply invested in ensuring that higher education can fulfill earlier commitments to the public good by balancing civic, humanistic, and economic development.[2] Such narratives tend to elide at least four important considerations that would challenge their internal logics. The first is that neoliberalism did not emerge out of nowhere but is rather the latest iteration of capitalism's *longue durée*.[3] The second is that capitalism is, at its core, a racialized and colonial process and set of social relations. That is, "capitalism has lived off—always backed by the colonial and national state's means of death—of colonial/racial expropriation"; this includes the capitalism of the liberal welfare state.[4] The third consideration is that the state has always been imbricated with both the accumulation and securitization of capital and, thus, has always been implicated in the violence of racialization and colonization.[5] The fourth and final consideration is that although many ultimately think of the university as a benevolent and autonomous institution, in the U.S. context its ethical-political possibilities are consistently (re)shaped by its structural entanglements with state power, the imperatives of capital accumulation, and their ordering logics of racialized de/valuation.[6] As such, the institution has adjusted over time to remain aligned with, and to help manage, shifting priorities of the state-capital articulation—as indeed it has done with the most recent shifts.

These four elements point to the possibility that current crises of the U.S. university are not entirely the result of novel transformations or the betrayal of its underlying values, but rather their fulfillment. In other words, and following the analyses of prison abolitionists and others working against state violence, the university is not broken—it was built this way.[7] This also means that without diminishing the importance of what happens within the institution itself, any radical transformation of the university is unlikely to happen without the accompanying radical transformation (dismantling) of the state and capital that serve as its material base. However, few of the most commonly used analytical tools and practical strategies for contesting the contemporary configuration of the university have the conceptual capacity to situate the present within this larger context of racial and colonial violence.[8] Why this violence remains largely unthought in critical higher education scholarship, and how we might reorient critical conversations to attend to it both ethically and politically, are the orienting concerns of this essay.

I begin by noting the colonial elisions in accounts of the neoliberal present that rest on nostalgia for a prior commitment to higher education as a state-sponsored means of educating enlightened citizens and ensuring social mobility. Next, I review the critiques of the modern subject offered by Sylvia Wynter and Denise Ferreira da Silva. I then contrast this subject's violently enforced separability, and denial of relationality, to our actual collective condition of entanglement and consider the ethical and political obligations that follow from this entanglement. I argue that the protagonist of mainstream critical accounts of the neoliberal university is this very modern subject, and ask what is overlooked when we overrepresent this subject and take for granted the cruel conditions of his existence.[9] I suggest the need to look outside of liberal notions of justice in the university toward transformative praxis, drawing on Wynter and Silva as well as the work of those who have sought to create and regenerate justice outside of the state's racial and colonial frames. Finally, after considering how transformative justice might inform our approaches to the study and practice of higher education, I briefly address some of the potential circularities that result from romanticizing our own efforts to disassemble the violence of the modern subject and the architectures that hold him up.

COLONIAL ELISIONS IN CRITIQUES OF THE NEOLIBERAL UNIVERSITY

The contemporary neoliberal university is often compared to the liberal welfare state model that was hegemonic from after World War II until the 1970s. According to Jeffrey J. Williams, "the welfare state university held a substantial role in redistribution; the post-welfare state university holds a lesser role in redistribution and a more substantial role in private accumulation."[10] In many critical accounts of the contemporary university, the state is no longer adequately committed to funding education as a means of preparing individuals for the practice of citizenship and freedom—as it is perceived to have done in the postwar social contract. For instance, Henry Giroux argues, "the obligations of citizenship have been replaced by the demands of consumerism, education has been reduced to another market-driven sphere, pedagogy has been instrumentalized, and public values have been transformed into private interests."[11] Christopher Newfield laments the lost opportunity for a more inclusive and racially diverse formation of national citizenship, a would-be multiracial mass middle class.[12] Wendy Brown also suggests that the extension of access to liberal arts education during this era was a means for non-elites to "become potentially eligible for the life of freedom long reserved for the few," and argues that today universities overemphasize human capital accumulation at the expense of "producing a public readied for participation in popular sovereignty."[13] The idea of education for citizenship was not novel after World War II; however, it took on a new significance, and higher education specifically was believed to be important for guaranteeing a free and democratic society, ensuring the opportunity for class mobility, and fending off perceived threats like that of recently defeated fascisms and ongoing specters of communism.[14]

Few contemporary accounts of the postwar era are entirely romanticized, however. Brown qualifies her analysis: "This is not to say that higher education in this period realized perfection or was absent the usual cruel exclusions from Western humanism, only that its values and practices were vastly superior to those preceding and succeeding it,"[15] while Sheila Slaughter and Gary Rhoades attest, "Ironically, the 'social contract' between university science and society, of which research was the cornerstone, was built on military funding that flowed from the cold war."[16] It is not clear where the irony lies, however, as indeed the U.S. was effectively a "welfare-warfare" state during this era.[17] In fact, since at least the 1862 Morrill Act, which funded public land-grant universities with the scrip of stolen Indigenous lands that had been accumulated through war and other violent means, the U.S. state has often funded "public goods" by way of acquisitive militarism. This suggests that racial and colonial violence are not primarily an effect of "cruel exclusions from Western humanism," but rather precisely what creates the conditions for such a humanism to exist. Furthermore, although human capital development has increasingly been perceived as the responsibility of the individual rather than the state, the notion of preparing skilled and productive workers in the service of capital accumulation was also central to postwar higher education policy. In fact, some have argued that conditional racial inclusion during this era was in part a calculated move to shield U.S. global hegemony and racial capitalism from critique.[18] Thus, rather than afterthoughts, I treat these qualifiers as the starting point for formulating the questions that guide this essay. Namely, what does it mean for universities to educate for "citizenship" within an anti-Black, settler colonial, and imperial capitalist nation-state? And who is the imagined "public" of a nation-state ordered by the racial, heteropatriarchical, and ecocidal logics of personhood and property?

I suggest that, despite significant differences between the postwar (liberal) model of *students as engaged and productive citizens* and the current (neoliberal) model of *students as customers and entrepreneurs*, both models are rooted in the same template, or what Sylvia Wynter calls "genre," of the human.[19] That is, they are different versions of the same base modern subject, who is educated to rationally pursue affluence, maximize utility, and enact seamless progress and development through the supposedly universal governing architectures of the nation-state and global capital.[20] This, in turn, is thought to prepare students to efficiently manage so-called resources (both natural and human), foresee and forestall risks, and engineer consensual societies and solutions to social problems. Though generally elided, racial capitalism, white supremacy, and heteropatriarchy underlie this framing of education: the imperatives of rational planning, risk assessment, and asset protection are all mobilized to justify the sacrifice of some peoples' well-being (up to and including their lives) for the benefit of others.

Racial and colonial violence are therefore not products of ignorance, as many would have it, but rather of an apparatus of racial knowledge that naturalizes Indigenous disappearance, Black death, and imperial occupation. In other words, this violence is a product of what Christina Sharpe describes as a "death-dealing episteme" and its accompanying material apparatus.[21] Thus, until more people are willing to ask, as Wynter does, "What is wrong with our education?," efforts to reimagine the university will fail to identify, let alone disrupt, the patterns of violence that run deeper than the neoliberal present—that is, they will fail "to imagine possibilities for the politics of opposition against both neoliberalism and postcolonial empire."[22]

In this essay, I reframe and refocus Wynter's question slightly (although still in the spirit of her critique), to ask, and begin to answer: What is wrong with the modern subject (who is also the presumed subject of U.S. higher education)? This is a necessary reversal of the damage-centered research that often takes Black and Indigenous communities as its object.[23] Ultimately, however, the task is to undo the modern categories that determine the subject, object, and their violent relation, rather than to have the racial other/object occupy the position of the subject.

THE MODERN SUBJECT

In this section I review accounts of the modern subject that trace the concepts, categories, desires, and frames of reference that reproduce his onto-epistemological assemblage and therefore, necessarily, also reproduce the racial and colonial matrix of our "modern/colonial world system."[24] Through extended engagements with the work of Wynter and Silva, I trace how the material architectures and conceptual grammar of colonial expropriation and racial subjugation naturalize a particular figure of humanity and violently refuse other possibilities for knowing, being, and relating.[25]

The Overrepresentation of Man

By offering a genealogy of "our present ethnoclass (i.e., white, Western, bourgeois) conception of the human, Man," Wynter traces how "Man" overrepresents himself as the only legitimate embodiment of humanity.[26] The effect is that all others—Indigenous, Black, other racialized peoples, as well as the unemployed, the incarcerated, the homeless, the poor, and those otherwise deemed "underdeveloped"—are measured against him and deemed to be less human than he, which is to say, less than human.[27] Katherine McKittrick argues that today, "the human [is] understood as a purely biological mechanism that is subordinated to a teleological economic script ... whose macro-origin story calcifies the *hero figure* of *homo oeconomicus*, who practices, indeed normalizes, accumulation in the name of (economic) freedom."[28] While this narrow script of existence is clearly evident in the ideology and manifestations of neoliberalism, beyond these more recent and immediate effects the violence of nearly six centuries of Man's dominance threatens to destroy, through ecological catastrophe, countless more human and other-than-human lives than those that have already been taken (including Man's own).

In order to understand what enabled Man to reach his current claim to represent the pinnacle of humanity, Wynter carefully traces the transformations that led from a shift in the dominance of the "True Christian Self" before the Renaissance to the dominance of the "[Secular] Rational Self" by the end of the Enlightenment.[29] This transformation came about in large part through the attempted conquest of Indigenous peoples of the Americas and enslavement of peoples of Africa starting in the fifteenth century, which provided the economic and epistemological conditions of possibility for Europe's ontological emergence. It was through these violent processes that Man constructed an "irrational/subrational Human Other to [his] civic-humanist, rational self-conception" and established the global architectures of capital and of nation-states to represent and serve his interests, thereby externalizing the costs of his own reproduction.[30]

Today, this onto-epistemological assemblage not only "governs our global well-being/ill-being," but Man's genre of being human has also been "projected onto, and incorporates" not just those who are deemed to legitimately embody this subject position (that is, middle-/upper-class white males), but the entirety of the globe.[31] Though never fully admissible to his ranks, those who Man deems to be his others are nonetheless judged and held to account according to his norms and scripts, and some have adopted for themselves his asserted hierarchy of humanity and narrative of human progress. For instance, Wynter notes the push in the mid-twentieth century by newly decolonized nations to "modernize" following in the path of the West. This push was and continues to be contested with alternative visions and demands, just as alternatives were and are still envisioned and demanded within the West itself. Yet even those who contest Man's dominance and create and keep alive other possibilities for existence are often compelled to at least partially adhere to his scripts in order to ensure immediate survival.[32]

In addition to the power and resources under Man's control, Wynter notes that built into Man's self-conception of universality is the repression of his actual particularity as only one "genre" of humanity among many. What Wynter therefore puts forth is "the possibility of undoing and unsettling—*not replacing or occupying*—Western conceptions of what it means to be human."[33] Further, because the coherence of our currently dominant episteme is dependent on Man's specious claim to universalism, Wynter argues that escaping his dominance would require that we "collectively undertake a rewriting of knowledge as we know it ... without falling into the traps laid down by our present system of knowledge."[34] For Silva, the role of knowledge is also central. As such, the "ethico-political question becomes whether or not justice can be imagined from within the available modalities of knowledge."[35] In the following section, I explore her insights about what and how these modalities of knowledge produce modern existence, and what makes them so violent, and so difficult to dismantle. Although Silva and Wynter differ in their understanding of the possibilities and conditions for enacting existence otherwise, their critiques of Man, or what Silva calls the modern subject, can be complementary.[36]

The Modern Subject and His Affectable Other

Silva's work is largely driven by the argument that racial and colonial violence is not ancillary to modern society and its subjects, but rather productive of them in all spheres of modern life: economic, juridical, and ethical.[37] The modern subject understands himself as transparently operating according to universal reason and, therefore, rightfully enacting his self-determined will on the world through the instrumental application of knowledge, mediated by commodities, concepts, and categories determined by linear causality.[38] Following Descartes and Kant, the modern subject's existence is defined by interior thought, and, following Hegel, his European origins assure him that he is the height of a linear, teleological history of human progress. In order to claim this self-determinedness, interiority, and transparency, however, modern man must deny that his existence was actually only made possible in exteriority, that is, through the relations of violence enacted through slavery and colonialism and the still ongoing racial and colonial difference they instituted.[39] In turn, racial and Indigenous subjects are imagined to be outer-determined, as both their minds and bodies are thought to be shaped by their inferior geographic origins and a lower evolutionary location along the purportedly linear development of humanity (often as signified and read through the tools of scientific racism).

Thus, Silva argues that the rational, self-determined, universal character of the modern subject is necessarily produced not only in contrast to but through the construction of the irrational, outer-determined character of the racial and colonial other (or object). According to Silva, this relation of raciality is built into the grammar of the founding discourses of Western knowledge and, thus, into the "modern conditions of existence."[40] Both symbolically and materially there would be no modern subject without racial and colonial violence. Accordingly, modern reason both requires and is threatened by the very racial and colonial difference it produces: universality and interiority can only be assured in comparison to particularity and exteriority, which in turn always threatens to reveal the fact that the modern subject, too, is determined in exteriority—by his racial and colonial others.[41] Because of this threat, the spatial/geographic and temporal separation of the modern subject (as the always here and now) and those he deems his others (as the always there and then) is continually asserted and policed. This separation and its effects are then justified and explained by the argument that "the causes of the subordination of the others of Europe reside in their physical and mental (moral and intellectual) characteristics."[42] In other words: they are to blame for their own subjugation.

The co-constitutive modern categories of the universal and the particular create a double bind for resistance to racial and colonial subjugation. To be legible and legitimized within modern horizons of political possibility, those not deemed to be modern subjects must assert themselves as self-determining masters of universal reason. If they do not, they are understood not as proper political subjects but rather as improper embodiments of difference.[43] The available choices are stark: be engulfed into "universal reason" or have one's difference rewritten yet again as an object of that universal reason, which justifies continued racial and colonial violence.[44] Yet the former choice (that is, inclusion into universal humanity as defined by Man) is also illusory, because critiques that frame racism or colonialism as a matter of exclusion from universality (rather than productive of it) fail to recognize that the modern subject's claim to universality is itself already premised on and requires racial and colonial difference.[45] Thus, even strict adherence to Man's norms do not guarantee the nonviolability of racialized and Indigenous persons, whose irreducible difference is ascribed within Man's governing biopolitical logics of coloniality and raciality.[46] Efforts to interrupt these logics that are oriented by the imperative to "include" racial and Indigenous others within existing frames and institutions are therefore inadequate/impossible to the task of disassembling the modern subject and the conceptual and material regimes that guarantee his existence.

Rather than rearrange the borders of modern social categories, Silva therefore considers the possibility of "dismantling the existing strategies for knowing and opening the way for another figuring of existence without the grips of the tools of scientific reason."[47] Silva prefigures possibilities for existence that attend to "affectability (relationality, contingency, immediacy)" and that refuse to rely on "the separation and determination of efficient causality and its categories/forms."[48] It is the process of an "unknowing and undoing of the World that reaches its core"—or, "the End of the World as we know it"—that might offer a means to dismantle the modern subject, his institutions, and the set of relationships they instantiate, and to establish "juridico-economic architectures of redress" for racial and colonial violence.[49]

THE MODERN SUBJECT OF HIGHER EDUCATION

As U.S. higher education remains a significant site in which people invest their desires, some have referred to this investment as an example of the "cruel optimism" described by Lauren Berlant. For Berlant, "a relation of cruel optimism exists when something you desire is actually an obstacle to your flourishing ... when the object that draws your attachment actively impedes the aim that brought you to it initially."[50] Described here is the cruelty of the fact that the object of one's desire—in this case, higher education—fails to deliver on its promised outcomes. Berlant asks: "Why do people stay attached to conventional good-life fantasies ... when the evidence of their instability, fragility, and dear cost abounds?"[51] Yet, when Berlant describes the "cost" of conventional good-life fantasies, she emphasizes the price of unfulfilled promises to the fantasy-haver.[52] If we emphasize only this dimension of cruelty, we lose sight of the kinds of questions that drive this essay: who is the presumed subject of that "good-life" fantasy, who defines what is "good," and at what and whose expense is this fantasy fulfilled? Derived from the critical insights of Wynter, Silva, and many others, the answers are most commonly: the "good-life" is for the modern subject, as defined by the modern subject, at the expense of those he deems his racial and colonial others. Of course, the latter includes many who labor and study in the university—as students, service workers, and faculty—and many who do not, but regardless, they are rarely the addressees of the analytic of the cruel university.

As David Lloyd and Patrick Wolfe suggest, the "public patrimonies of the modern liberal state that emerged from an earlier moment of enclosure and dispossession represent vast storehouses of capital, resources, services and infrastructure."[53] If neoliberalism has largely been an effort to redirect those public resources into private (wealthy, mostly white) hands, it must be remembered that, in the U.S. context, these resources were in the first instance largely accumulated through early processes of racial-colonial capitalism—namely, slavery and colonization. Thus, not only do public goods remain under perpetual threat of privatization under the imperatives of capital accumulation, but regimes of both public *and* private property are premised on the continued occupation of Indigenous lands and subjugation of Black lives. As the public goods disproportionately enjoyed by the white U.S. middle class (modern subjects) increasingly become the target of privatization, this population is subject to some of the methods and rationales of accumulation that were previously reserved for Black, Indigenous, and other racialized populations. Yet, even as the impacts of dispossession are more widely felt, they still most acutely affect those populations who were subject to the initial round of dispossessions. That is, each new regime of capital accumulation does not replace but rather adds new dimensions to the historical and ongoing violence that has yet to be redressed.

Thus, what appear to be novel cruelties of the contemporary configurations of higher education, the nation-state, and global capital often have precedents that are invisibilized because they have affected and continue to most significantly affect populations who were/are deemed to fall outside of the realm of Man's ethical obligation and political rights. As higher education increasingly becomes itself a target of accumulation, there is both an ethical imperative and a political opportunity to imagine futures that do not depend on dispossession. But this remains unthinkable for those who continue to center the modern subject as their primary concern.

Although I argue that the U.S. university has been held up by the same conceptual, material, and affective architectures that reproduce the modern subject, it is not my intention to suggest that these formations have remained unchanged, either in the transition between the postwar and the present, or for the country's four hundred years of higher education history. Though racial subjugation and colonial expropriation repeat the same basic grammar on loop, the vocabularies through which they are expressed are contingent, often shifting with new formations of the nation-state and global capital, as well as the dynamics that arise in efforts to resist their violence, and efforts in turn to co-opt and contain that resistance. While this essay offers neither a full account of the colonial history of higher education nor a fully developed alternative account of neoliberalization to the mainstream (liberal) account reviewed above, anticolonial, race-centered histories of the political present remain important and are thankfully being undertaken by various radical historians and critical ethnic studies scholars.[54]

"DIFFERENCE WITHOUT SEPARABILITY"

How might we not only decenter the modern subject from critical analyses of the university, but also ultimately dismantle him and the material and epistemological architectures that uphold his existence? If the production of modern subjects is premised on what M. Jacqui Alexander describes as the collective but unevenly distributed condition of "fragmentation and dismemberment at both the material and psychic levels," what kinds of ethical and political practice would not presume his reproduction?[55] In Silva's speculative insights, derived from what she calls the practice of Black Feminist Poethics, she suggests that any effort to examine the limits of what it is possible to know through the modern subject's supposedly universal knowledge must denaturalize "all the effects and implications as well as the presuppositions informing our accounts of existing with/in one another."[56] Having done so, it might be possible to engage and encounter a radically different kind of knowing, and possibilities for existence in excess of that which can be neatly measured or mediated by modern ways of knowing.

Fred Moten engages with Silva in conjunction with his work on "black study."[57] In particular he suggests that the modern subject's desire for self-determination is connected to claims of self-possession, both of which are more fantasies than facts. They are fantasies because, Moten suggests, we exist in a condition of "difference without separability." We are, he argues, "entangled, vulnerable, open, non-full, more than and less than [ourselves]."[58] Entanglement signals a condition of enmeshment and an accompanying ethical and political responsibility before/beyond will, which could not be further from the liberal notion of ethical/legal relationships between separate, individuated beings that are instituted by free will through the rational calculation of utility maximization and shared self-interest. In a condition of difference without separability, entanglement is impervious to common or divergent values or interests; it is not premised on universalism, transparency, consensus, or harmony, but rather includes the full range of possibilities, including violence, pain, joy, conflict, creativity, and community.

Also in contrast to the liberal humanist impulse is the fact that entanglement refers not anthropocentrically to the condition of all humans in relation to other humans, but rather to the entanglement of *everything with everything else*. This seriously challenges the notion of the supposedly self-determined and autonomous modern subject of interior reason by suggesting that he is in fact just as outer-determined and affectable as supposedly inferior racialized and Indigenous others.[59] The condition of entanglement is ours whether or not we agree to it, and persists even when we disavow it. Why does this matter? Because denial of affectability and assertion of independence (and thus, separation) is what allows for the violence of capitalism and racism to continue without generating an ethico-political crisis.[60] The imperative is thus to grapple with and unmake/reverse the ongoing effects of the violent colonial architectures and patterns of relation that presume separation and autonomy, and deny obligation.[61]

The possibilities signaled by recognition of entangled existence also shift dominant ideas of solidarity. The condition of entanglement suggests that the modern architecture of existence is violent for everyone (because there is no separation), even as its psychic, material, and symbolic harms are distributed in highly uneven ways (because there is difference). This being the case, speaking about the possibility of building coalition with those who consider themselves privileged, Moten suggests, "I don't need your help. I just need you to recognize that this shit is killing you, too, however much more softly, you stupid motherfucker, you know?"[62] Because difference shapes individuals' particular positioning within collective political interventions, we each must take account of (and be accountable for) our specific locations within modern matrices of power and, at the same time, be answerable to the fact of our entanglement. While indeed "decolonization is a project for *all*," as is abolition, it demands very different things of us.[63]

The above authors are only a handful of the many scholars and activists who have engaged in a critique and refusal of the modern subject, and specifically his production through racial and colonial violence. This includes others writing as part of the Black diaspora, particularly in the traditions of Black feminist and Black radical thought, as well as Indigenous scholars who have long critiqued the modern subject's epistemological, ontological, and metaphysical violence as central to settler colonization, emphasizing the denial of entanglement with and obligation to the earth itself as a precondition for its objectification, commodification, and extraction. These scholars not only offer distinct, and at times incommensurable though often complementary, analyses of modernity's constitutive violences but also gesture elsewhere, to possibilities that offer something other than merely a revised and expanded regime of Man.

Thus, if on the one hand these critiques point to and denaturalize the persistent dominance of the modern subject and the violence that is required for his self-realization, they also remind us that other possibilities have always existed and continue to exist. The question then becomes, "what cultural and aesthetic resources are available to us that would make it more possible to claim, rather than to disavow, this condition [of entanglement and affectability] which is already ours, irreducibly, in a way that we cannot avoid?"[64] If indeed we are concerned to affirm this condition, to remember our boundless responsibility to everyone and everything (before will), to un-numb suppressed senses, to unlearn our investments in presumed supremacies and entitlements, and to practice other modes of sociality, then this question is only one of the many that must be asked. In the case of the neoliberal university, we are pushed to ask about the pasts, presents, and futures that have been imagined and built for higher education, and the desires and material forms that (falsely) foreclose the possibility of collectively imagining and enacting something different. As Alexander suggests, "our task is to reexamine and transform inherited practices that stand in the way of justice."[65] That is, to study, unmake, and reconfigure the relations of power and knowledge that produce the university "as we know it."

TOWARD TRANSFORMATIVE JUSTICE

Within the predominant imaginary of higher education that is premised on liberal ideas of justice that presume *in*justice is rooted in a betrayal of, and/or denial of inclusion into, the economic, juridical, and ethical regimes of Man, critiques and visions for change will tend to reproduce the racial and colonial violence that underwrites these regimes. Liberal frames of justice—whether premised on representation, recognition, redistribution, or otherwise—have no mechanism by which to substantively redress the population-level epistemological and material violences that are instituted by the supposedly universal architectures of modern existence (i.e., nation-state, capital, Enlightenment knowledge) that are its own conditions of possibility.[66] Self-preservingly, liberal justice can only address violence that is legible within its frame, which means it cannot comprehend, let alone redress, the violence that is instituted by that very frame. We therefore need another kind of justice, one that targets the frame itself.[67]

A transformative justice praxis that both confronts and cracks open the bounds of liberal justice would necessarily entail denaturalizing the violence that is required to reproduce the (material and epistemological) forms of the modern subject and his institutions, dismantling those forms, and experimenting with what else is possible at/with/beyond the determinations and separations they impose.[68] While it is impossible to know in advance "the aftermath of decolonization or what the world will have become after it has been known anew," transformative justice movements that seek to create or regenerate alternative systems of justice against and beyond the liberal justice administered by the state might be instructive for those committed to undertaking this task in the context of higher education.[69]

generationFiVE, which seeks "to end the sexual abuse of children within five generations," is one such group.[70] For generationFiVE, transformative justice requires frameworks and subsequent actions that bring together "social analysis and critique of 'power-over' dynamics and relationships; community education regarding dynamics of violence; understandings of trauma and healing; community-based interventions; community organizing to change social and political institutions, norms, and access to resources."[71] The ultimate goals of these analyses and actions are "survivor safety, healing and agency; accountability and transformation of those who abuse; community response and accountability; and transformation of the community and social conditions that create and perpetuate violence."[72]

Importantly, a transformative justice approach is not premised on romanticizing those who are most affected by racial and colonial violence, nor does it presume to assess whether they are "deserving" of solidarity, as this would only serve to reproduce liberal forms of justice premised on the impossible task of proving one's "innocence" within a fundamentally unjust system.[73] This approach also does not consider those most affected by violence to be responsible for "saving" the rest of humanity, including their abusers, which would rather absurdly task the most vulnerable populations with the intellectual and affective labor and material risks of educating and transforming those who subjugate them.[74]

Nearly every issue of concern in higher education today could be addressed through a transformative approach. However, translating transformative justice to higher education is not straightforward. For instance, would it seek to abolish the university in the same way that many transformative justice advocates seek to abolish prisons? We cannot in good faith claim that the university is equivalent to the prison, even as they are hardly opposites.[75] On the other hand, if abolition means not simply the abolition of prisons but rather "the abolition of a society that could have prisons, that could have slavery, that could have the wage," then any university in the *after* of such abolition would be radically transformed, if not unrecognizable.[76] Indeed there are many who have "hacked" the colonial structure of the university from within in order to work toward that very end, guided by the idea that it is necessary to work ourselves out of a job, just as there are those who focus their efforts on building something different.[77] Both are important.

Apart from questions of analytical transferability, as with all contexts, the higher education setting presents particular challenges. For instance, consider one of the primary goals outlined by generationFiVE: "accountability and transformation of those who abuse." In the case of the university, it is not only individual students and faculty, but also the institution itself that has perpetuated abusive relations. Are institutions that are premised, above all, on ensuring their own preservation open to being held accountable and transformed? Responses to recent antiracist student protests and demands, and indeed the entire history of institutional suppression and/or strategic instrumentalization of such demands, suggest not. Recent university apologies for participation in Black enslavement (such as those offered by Harvard, Brown, the University of Virginia, and Georgetown) and, more rarely, Indigenous genocide (at Northwestern and the University of Denver), signal a tentative openness to accountability. Yet, the almost total absence of subsequent actions taken by these institutions to enact redress by returning lands, resources, or other institutional wealth that was generated through this violence, or by addressing *ongoing* material and epistemological violence against communities of color and Indigenous communities on and around campus, signals a firm limitation to universities' conceptualization of accountability and to the possibility of transforming the institutional conditions and logics that produce(d) that violence in the first place.[78] These institutional responses also signal the difficulty of achieving another transformative goal outlined by generationFiVE: "survivor safety, healing and agency," which in the case of the university would include not just those within its walls, but also the kin (both human and other-than-human) of those whom it has subjugated and exploited throughout its history and the local communities that are deeply affected by its presence. How is healing possible when the abuse remains ongoing, and when critiques are only acknowledged if they can be reduced to a demand for difference that makes no real difference?[79]

Even as we grapple with these difficult questions, we can consider that transformative justice is not only a process of undoing harm but also of making space for regenerating and being taught by systems of justice rooted in different epistemologies and ontologies than those of the racial and colonial state. For instance, Sarah Hunt argues that Indigenous legal systems offer frameworks of justice that uphold Indigenous self-determination and refuse state justice systems that overwhelmingly reproduce rather than interrupt colonial relations.[80] Hunt also prompts us to ask what it might look like if universities were held accountable to the ceremonial and legal practices of the Indigenous peoples whose lands they occupy.[81] She illustrates this imperative of accountability in arguing that deepened understanding of the gendered nature of colonial violence must be central to any transformative effort to address campus sexual violence. Given that bodily dispossession and the dispossession of lands are intimately linked, Hunt suggests, "if we do not apply a decolonial lens to our understanding of sexual violence on the UBC [University of British Columbia] campus, and on campuses all across North America, the roots of rape culture will remain intact."[82]

To continue with this example, what might it look like to apply a transformative, or decolonial, lens to campus sexual violence? Here I offer some general possibilities, while also recognizing that place-based knowledges, practices, and relationships should significantly inform any actual interventions. Applying such a lens would require looking elsewhere than the state to deliver justice for survivors of campus sexual assaults, for instance, by ceasing to presume that justice is delivered within colonial courts, and by discontinuing reliance on campus or local law enforcement to ensure safety on campus, in particular the safety of Indigenous and racialized students, faculty, staff, and guests whom are often targeted by those very same officers. A transformative approach would ask why the assaults reported by racialized and Indigenous peoples are often received through gendered racial and colonial administrative frames that presume the survivor's inherent sexual violability—and thus, that they either wanted or deserved to be assaulted. This approach would also not frame those who commit sexual violence through liberal narratives of exceptional bad actors and instead would consider the larger set of colonial logics, social norms, and material structures into which assaulters were educated. Sexual violence is not only perpetrated and experienced unevenly across populations, but it is also embedded within a system that occupies Indigenous lands without consent, polices the bodies of nonwhite, female, trans*, Two-Spirit, and nonbinary people (i.e., those who do not qualify as "modern subjects"), and systemically produces and transmits knowledge and professional practices that rationalize this violence for (the modern subject's) profit, pleasure, and, yes, education.

To recognize that U.S. higher education has always been violent, and that its imagined student has tended to be the modern subject, even as the particulars have shifted over time, does not require that we immediately give up on the university, nor dismiss the possibility of situated, strategic actions within it. Just as making demands on the state does not necessarily signal confidence in its ability or intention to deliver justice, making demands in/of the university does not necessarily signal earnest belief or investment in the possibility of its reform, nor a desire for its restoration to an earlier form.[83] Is it possible to resist the continuing tide of university privatization without employing the foil of a benevolent state, or an innocent public? Benevolent or not, it is difficult to turn away from the state as a preferred source of material support for the foreseeable future, given the available alternatives (onerous student loans or suspect private donors). Even if so, we can nonetheless signal that these are contingent, harm reduction strategies, rather than the ultimate ends of transformation. As Tiffany Lethabo King argues, "temporarily resuscitating the subject, specifically within the context of the neoliberal university, may be necessary even to those interrogating the very terms and existence of the subject," for instance, to ensure that demands are legible to administrators in the context of organized labor campaigns.[84] Yet, she also suggests, even as this "important strategizing is occurring, having the capacity to move in, between, through, and outside of subject formations is essential."[85]

CODA

Even for those who are agnostic about whether the university can ever be "made just," as long as these institutions are in place there remains a responsibility to make them more accessible and livable for the most marginalized within them and to also mitigate the violence that the institutions affect beyond their walls. Whether that work ultimately leads to transformation, or what the *after* of transformation will look like, cannot be determined in advance, particularly if transformative justice ultimately requires the end of the university/the world as we know it, and the creation and/or regeneration of something different that would not repeat the same mistakes.[86] Whatever happens, it is inevitable that we will make new and different mistakes as part of this process. Even as we remain answerable to those mistakes, humility is crucial, as is an attentiveness to the complexities and contradictions of doing this work. The risks of romanticism are not reserved for those steeped in liberal nostalgia about the past; we must also consider that we are prone to romanticism about our own efforts to enact transformation in the present. Thus, I conclude by attending to some of the circularities that arise in efforts to do this kind of work, which must be addressed alongside efforts to defend the most vulnerable from the violent backlash of a modern subject who will resist his own dismantling.

First, too often stated commitments are equated with actually doing the difficult work of unlearning separability, unraveling material domination, and enacting relationships that affirm our entanglement with and responsibility to one another in everyday practice.[87] For instance, by offering a critique of the neoliberal university, we may position ourselves outside of it, where we and those who join us can "come to know and reaffirm what is right and what is wrong through the conduct of the critique."[88] The fact that we might benefit from some elements of neoliberalism at the same time as we are harmed by it is then suppressed by the dubious conviction that speaking out against something will spell its end.[89] More generally, there is a reluctance to admit that many of us remain (even if reluctantly) invested—and thus, implicated—in the very institutions that we critique, and so we fail to substantively consider how these conflicted investments might have contradictory effects on the work that we do toward transformation.[90] That is, we cannot always be certain whether our desire to transform the university is ultimately rooted in a desire to create something entirely otherwise or to preserve it.

Another common circularity is that in efforts to engage the "cultural and aesthetic resources" that provide glimpses of otherwise ways of knowing and being, these resources are imported, or grafted, back into the same supposedly universal matrix of intelligibility and value that previously denied them legitimacy.[91] Any effort whose end is to simply include difference in the world of the modern subject, rather than to dismantle that world, will always be conditional—for instance, by including only that which is not disruptive, and/or translating it into colonial categories of meaning and capital in the process of institutionalization. Regardless of intention, selective inclusion of non-Western knowledges can proliferate colonial claims to ownership of non-Western knowledge, thereby re-silencing possibilities and peoples that exceed the bounds of what can be neatly classified and contained by modern frames.[92]

These possible pitfalls point to the difficulty of transformative work, or some might conclude, its impossibility. Yet, instead of a dead end, perhaps exhausting all imaginable possibilities is precisely where the potential for something else becomes viable. While political imagination is important, transformative justice cannot be determined in advance of its doing, as "[a]bove all, we need to learn how to *practice* justice, for it is through practice that we come to envision new modes of living and new modes of being that support these visions."[93]

SHARON STEIN is interested in examining and being taught by the edges of what it is possible to do and imagine within inherited institutions of (higher) education. She is also committed to collectively creating alternative educational futures and frameworks of justice that do not presume the continuation of the nation-state, Euro-humanism, or global capital.

NOTES

This paper was originally presented at the Cultural, Social and Political Thought Graduate Student Conference at the University of Victoria in 2015. It has since been significantly improved through subsequent conversations with Denise Ferreira da Silva and Vanessa Andreotti, as well as thorough the editorial suggestions of Dallas Hunt, and the generous critiques and guidance of the *Critical Ethnic Studies* editors and anonymous reviewers.

   1. David Scott, *Conscripts of Modernity: The Tragedy of Colonial Enlightenment* (Durham, N.C.: Duke University Press, 2004), 1–6, 32.
   2. Sara Goldrick-Rab, *Paying the Price: College Costs, Financial Aid, and the Betrayal of the American Dream* (Chicago: University of Chicago Press, 2016), 20.
   3. Giovanni Arrighi, *The Long Twentieth Century: Money, Power, and the Origins of Our Times* (New York: Verso, 1994); Jamie Peck, "Geography and Public Policy: Constructions of Neoliberalism," *Progress in Human Geography* 28, no. 3 (2004): 392–405.
   4. Paula Chakravartty and Denise Ferreira da Silva, "Accumulation, Dispossession, and Debt: The Racial Logic of Global Capitalism—An Introduction," *American Quarterly* 64, no. 3 (2012): 368.
   5. Ibid; Maile Arvin, Eve Tuck, and Angie Morrill, "Decolonizing Feminism: Challenging Connections between Settler Colonialism and Heteropatriarchy," *Feminist Formations* 25, no. 1 (2013): 8–34; Jodi A. Byrd, *The Transit of Empire: Indigenous Critiques of Colonialism* (Minneapolis: University of Minnesota Press, 2011); Glen Coulthard, *Red Skin, White Masks: Rejecting the Colonial Politics of Recognition* (Minneapolis: University of Minnesota Press, 2014); Denise Ferreira da Silva, "Toward a Black Feminist Poethics: The Quest(ion) of Blackness toward the End of the World," *Black Scholar* 44, no. 2 (2014): 81–97.
   6. Ananya Roy, "Praxis in the Time of Empire," *Planning Theory* 5, no. 1 (2006): 7–29; Lori Patton, "Disrupting Postsecondary Prose: Toward a Critical Race Theory of Higher Education," *Urban Education* 51, no. 3 (2016): 315–42; Craig Steven Wilder, *Ebony and Ivy: Race, Slavery, and the Troubled History of America's Universities* (New York: Bloomsbury, 2014).
   7. Nick Mitchell, Twitter post, October 27, 2016, 3:25pm, https://twitter.com/touch faith/status/791767914630098944; see also Eli Meyerhoff, "Prisons and Universities Are Two Sides of the Same Coin," *Abolition Journal Blog*, July 24, 2015, https://aboli

tionjournal.org/eli-meyerhoff-abolitionist-study-against-and-beyond-higher-education/; Fred Moten and Stefano Harney, "The University and the Undercommons: Seven Theses," *Social Text* 79 22, no. 2 (2004): 114–15; Dylan Rodríguez, "Racial/Colonial Genocide and the 'Neoliberal Academy': In Excess of a Problematic," *American Quarterly* 64, no. 4 (2012): 809–13.

8. Rodríguez, "Racial/Colonial Genocide."

9. I use male pronouns here and throughout the text advisedly, in recognition of the fact that the normative modern subject is not only White/European, middle/upper class, able-bodied, and highly educated, but also (cisgender) male.

10. Jeffery J. Williams, "The Post-Welfare State University," *American Literary History* 18, no. 1 (2006): 198.

11. Henry Giroux, "Once More, with Conviction: Defending Higher Education as a Public Good," *Qui Parle: Critical Humanities and Social Sciences* 20, no. 1 (2011): 123.

12. Christopher Newfield, *Unmaking the Public University: The Forty-Year Assault on the Middle Class* (Cambridge, Mass.: Harvard University Press, 2008), 91.

13. Wendy Brown, *Undoing the Demos: Neoliberalism's Stealth Revolution* (Cambridge, Mass.: MIT Press, 2015), 184.

14. Julie A. Reuben and Linda Perkins, "Introduction: Commemorating the Sixtieth Anniversary of the President's Commission Report, Higher Education for Democracy," *History of Education Quarterly* 47, no. 3 (2007): 265.

15. Ibid., 180.

16. Sheila Slaughter and Gary Rhoades, *Academic Capitalism and the New Economy: Markets, State, and Higher Education* (Baltimore: Johns Hopkins University Press, 2004), 47.

17. Ruthie Wilson Gilmore, "Globalisation and U.S. Prison Growth: From Military Keynesianism to Post-Keynesian Militarism," *Race & Class* 2/3 (1999): 177.

18. Roderick Ferguson, *The Reorder of Things: The University and Its Pedagogies of Minority Difference* (Minneapolis: University of Minnesota Press, 2012); Jodi Melamed, "The Spirit of Neoliberalism: From Racial Liberalism to Neoliberal Multiculturalism," *Social Text* 24, no. 4 (2006): 1–24; Nick Mitchell, "(Critical Ethnic Studies) Intellectual," *Critical Ethnic Studies* 1, no. 1 (2015): 85–88.

19. Sylvia Wynter, "Unsettling the Coloniality of Being/Power/Truth/Freedom: Towards the Human, after Man, Its Overrepresentation—An Argument," *CR: The New Centennial Review* 3, no. 3 (2003): 257–337.

20. Cash Ahenakew, Vanessa de Oliveira Andreotti, Garrick Cooper, and Hemi Hireme, "Beyond Epistemic Provincialism: De-Provincializing Indigenous Resistance," *AlterNative: An International Journal of Indigenous Peoples* 10, no. 3 (2014): 216–30.

21. Christina Sharpe, "Black Studies: In the Wake," *Black Scholar* 44, no. 2 (2014): 61.

22. Sylvia Wynter, "No Humans Involved: An Open Letter to My Colleagues," *Forum N.H.I.: Knowledge for the 21st Century* 1, no. 1 (1994): 59; Chakravartty and Silva, "Accumulation, Dispossession, and Debt," 379.

23. Eve Tuck, "Suspending Damage: A Letter to Communities," *Harvard Educational Review* 79, no. 3 (2009): 409–28.

24. Chakravartty and Silva, "Accumulation, Dispossession, and Debt," 364.

25. Denise Ferreira da Silva, "The Racial Limits of Social Justice: The Ruse of Equality of Opportunity and the Global Affirmative Action Mandate," *Critical Ethnic Studies* 2, no. 2 (2016): 184–209.

26. Wynter, "Unsettling the Coloniality," 260.

27. Ibid., 261, 317–27; Sylvia Wynter and Katherine McKittrick, "Unparalleled Catastrophe for Our Species? Or, to Give Humanness a Different Future: Conversations," in *Sylvia Wynter: On Being Human as Praxis*, ed. Katherine McKittrick (Durham, N.C.: Duke University Press, 2015): 20–24.

28. McKittrick in Wynter and McKittrick, "Unparalleled Catastrophe," 10.

29. Wynter, "Unsettling the Coloniality," 265–66.

30. Ibid., 281–82.

31. McKittrick in Wynter and McKittrick, "Unparalleled Catastrophe," 10, 19.

32. Ahenakew et al., "Beyond Epistemic Provincialism."

33. Katherine McKittrick, "Yours in the Intellectual Struggle: Sylvia Wynter and the Realization of the Living," in McKittrick, *Sylvia Wynter*, 2.

34. Wynter in Wynter and McKittrick, "Unparalleled Catastrophe," 18.

35. Denise Ferreira da Silva, "Before *Man*: Sylvia Wynter's Rewriting of the Modern Episteme," in McKittrick, *Sylvia Wynter*, 103.

36. Ibid., 101–4.

37. Denise Ferreira da Silva, "To Be Announced: Radical Praxis or Knowing (at) the Limits of Justice," *Social Text* 31, no. 1 (2013): 114.

38. Silva, "Toward a Black Feminist Poethics."

39. Ibid.

40. Denise Ferreira da Silva, "Notes for a Critique of the 'Metaphysics of Race,'" *Theory, Culture & Society* 28, no. 1 (2011): 140.

41. Denise Ferreira da Silva, "An Outline of a Global Political Subject: Reading Evo Morales's Election as a (Post-) Colonial Event," *Seattle Journal of Social Justice* 8 (2009).

42. Silva, *Toward a Global Idea of Race*, xiii.

43. Silva, "Outline of a Global Political Subject."

44. Silva, *Toward a Global Idea of Race*.

45. Silva, "Outline of a Global Political Subject."

46. Silva, "Notes for a Critique," 144–47.

47. Silva, "Toward a Black Feminist Poethics," 82.

48. Ibid., 81, 92.

49. Ibid., 85. Although "the End of the World as we know it" comes from Silva, it echoes Aimé Césaire's words in *Notebook of a Return to the Native Land* (1947; Middletown, Conn.: Wesleyan University Press, 2001), 22: "What can I do? One must begin somewhere. Begin what? The only thing in the world worth beginning: The End of the world of course."

50. Lauren Berlant, *Cruel Optimism* (Durham, N.C.: Duke University Press, 2011), 1.

51. Ibid., 2.

52. Byrd, *Transit of Empire*, 34–37.

53. David Lloyd and Patrick Wolfe, "Settler Colonial Logics and the Neoliberal Regime," *Settler Colonial Studies* 6, no. 2 (2016): 109.

54. This includes Roderick Ferguson, rosalind hampton, Kristi Carey, Nick Mitchell, Sheeva Sabati, Zach Schwartz-Weinstein, and Abbie Boggs, among others.

55. M. Jacqui Alexander, *Pedagogies of Crossing: Meditations on Feminism, Sexual Politics, Memory, and the Sacred* (Durham, N.C.: Duke University Press, 2005), 281.

56. Silva, "To Be Announced," 44.

57. See Fred Moten, "Blackness and Nothingness (Mysticism in the Flesh)," *South Atlantic Quarterly* 112, no. 4 (2013): 737–79; Fred Moten, "The Subprime and the Beautiful," *African Identities* 11, no. 2 (2013), 237–45; Fred Moten, "Performance and Blackness" (video file), https://vimeo.com/100330139. What Moten describes as "black study" predates and exceeds what has been institutionalized as "Black Studies" within the university.

58. Moten, "Performance and Blackness."

59. Silva, "To Be Announced," 49.

60. Silva, *Toward a Global Idea of Race*; Moten, "Performance and Blackness."

61. Alexander, *Pedagogies of Crossing*, 281–82; Denise Ferreira da Silva, "Speculations on a Transformative Theory of Justice," *Hearings: The Online Journal of Contour Biennale*, April 11, 2017, http://hearings.contour8.be/2017/04/11/speculations-transformative-theory-justice/.

62. Stefano Harney and Fred Moten, *The Undercommons: Fugitive Planning & Black Study* (New York: Minor Compositions, 2013), 140–41.

63. Alexander, *Pedagogies of Crossing*, 272 (emphasis in the original).

64. Moten, "Performance and Blackness."

65. Alexander, *Pedagogies of Crossing*, 92–93.

66. See Justin Leroy, "Black History in Occupied Territory: On the Entanglements of Slavery and Settler Colonialism," *Theory & Event*, 19, no. 4. (2016); Lisa Lowe, "History Hesitant," *Social Text*, 33, no. 4 (2015): 85–107; Silva, "Speculations on a Transformative Theory," Silva, "To Be Announced."

67. Silva, "Speculations on a Transformative Theory."

68. Ibid.

69. Ibid.

70. generationFive, "About Us," http://www.generationfive.org/about-us/; other instructive movements and organizations include Critical Resistance, INCITE! Women, Gender Non-Conforming, and Trans people of Color* Against Violence, and Project NIA.

71. generationFive, "Ending Child Sexual Abuse: A Transformative Justice Handbook," 2017, 37.

72. Ibid., 45.

73. Zoé Samudzi, "Dehumanization by Deification: On Kamala Harris and 'Black Women Will Save Us,'" *Verso Books Blog*, August 5, 2017, https://www.versobooks.com/blogs/3344-dehumanization-by-deification-on-kamala-harris-and-black-women-will-save-us.

74. Jackie Wang, "Against Innocence: Race, Gender, and the Politics of Safety," *LIES: A Journal of Materialist Feminism* 1 (2012): 145–71.

75. Moten and Harney, "University and the Undercommons," 114.

76. Ibid.

77. Vanessa de Oliveira Andreotti, Sharon Stein, Cash Ahenakew, and Dallas Hunt, "Mapping Interpretations of Decolonization in the Context of Higher Education," *Decolonization: Indigeneity, Education & Society* 4, no. 1 (2015): 27; Ilan Kapoor, "Hyper-Self-Reflexive Development? Spivak on Representing the Third World 'Other,'" *Third World Quarterly* 25, no. 4 (2004): 644; Riyad A. Shahjahan, Gerardo Blanco Ramirez, and Vanessa de Oliveira Andreotti, "Attempting to Imagine the Unimaginable: A Decolonial Reading of Global University Rankings," *Comparative Education Review* 61, no. S1 (2017): S51-S73. There is a long tradition of deinstitutionalized education, recent examples being the Dechinta Centre for Research and Learning in Canada, or Freedom University in Georgia.

78. See Tressie McMillan Cottom, "Georgetown's Slavery Announcement Is Remarkable. But It's Not Reparations," *Vox*, September 2, 2016, www.vox.com/2016/9/2/12773110/georgetown-slavery-admission-reparations; Sharon Stein, "Universities, Slavery, and the Unthought of Anti-Blackness," *Cultural Dynamics* 28, no. 2 (2016): 169–87.

79. See Leanne Simpson's reflections, in *Dancing on Our Turtle's Back: Stories of Nishnaabeg Re-Creation, Resurgence, and a New Emergence* (Winnipeg: Arbeiter Ring, 2011), about how reconciliation practices in Canada mirror an abusive relationship in which the abuser "doesn't want to change. In fact, all through the process he continues to physically, emotionally, spiritually and mentally abuse his partner. He just wants to say sorry so he can feel less guilty about his behaviour. He just wants to adjust the ways he is abusing; he doesn't want to stop the abuse" (21–22).

80. Sarah Hunt, "Representing Colonial Violence: Trafficking, Sex Work, and the Violence of Law," *Atlantis: Critical Studies in Gender, Culture & Social Justice* 37, no. 2 (2016): 25–39; Sarah Hunt, "Violence, Law and the Everyday Politics of Recognition" (presentation at the Annual Meeting of the Native American and Indigenous Studies Association [NAISA], Washington, D.C., June 6, 2015).

81. Sarah Hunt, "Decolonizing the Roots of Rape Culture: Reflections on Consent, Sexual Violence and University Campuses" (presentation at The Power of Our Collective Voices: Changing the Conversation on Sexual Violence at Post-Secondary Institutions, Musqueam Territories, September 30, 2016).

82. Ibid.

83. Jared Sexton, "The Vel of Slavery: Tracking the Figure of the Unsovereign," *Critical Sociology* 42, no. 4-5 (2016): 589.

84. Tiffany Lethabo King, "Post-Identitarian and Post-Intersectional Anxiety in the Neoliberal Corporate University," *Feminist Formations* 27, no. 3 (2015): 134–35.

85. Ibid., 134.

86. Silva, "Toward a Black Feminist Poethics," 84.

87. Hunt, "Violence, Law and the Everyday Politics."

88. Andrew Whelan, "Academic Critique of Neoliberal Academia," *Sites: New Series* 12, no. 1 (2015): 13.

89. Mitchell, "(Critical Ethnic Studies) Intellectual," 90, 92.

90. Ibid., 92.

91. Cash Ahenakew, "Grafting Indigenous Ways of Knowing onto Non-Indigenous Ways of Being," *International Review of Qualitative Research* 9, no. 3 (2016): 323–40.

92. Eve Tuck and Rubén A. Gaztambide-Fernández, "Curriculum, Replacement, and Settler Futurity," *Journal of Curriculum Theorizing* 29, no. 1 (2013): 72–89; Sara Ahmed, *On Being Included: Racism and Diversity in Institutional Life* (Durham, N.C.: Duke University Press, 2012); Rauna Kuokkanen, "What Is Hospitality in the Academy? Epistemic Ignorance and the (Im)possible Gift," *Review of Education, Pedagogy, and Cultural Studies* 30, no. 1 (2008).

93. Alexander, *Pedagogies of Crossing*, 92–93.

Robin D. G. Kelley and Fred Moten in Conversation

Moderated by Afua Cooper and Rinaldo Walcott

CRAFTED TRANSCRIPT CREATED BY LEKEISHA HUGHES

This conversation took place as part of a public lecture series at the University of Toronto on April 3, 2017. We are grateful to be able to include a crafted transcription of this discussion between U.S. and Canadian scholars that asks us to consider what it has meant for Black studies, as a "transformative project" that "has earned the right to look out for itself" to take place in the university and beyond it. Robin Kelley, Fred Moten, Afua Cooper, and Rinaldo Walcott point us to the future and present concerns of Black studies by considering the politics and movements that have produced and continually produce it. *Critical Ethnic Studies* managing editor LeKeisha Hughes has crafted this transcript to assist in the ebb and flow of the discussion, but the ethic is to share things as closely as possible to how they happened in Tkaronto.

RINALDO WALCOTT: I thought that we might begin by asking you to offer us a kind of meditation on the contemporary relationship between Black studies and Black politics—to think aloud what the current urgencies inside Black studies and Black politics might be. In part, this question is motivated by a series of articles that Robin Kelley has been writing in the *Boston Review* just prior to and then after the 2015 U.S. presidential election, in particular the dossier on Black studies.[1]

I am also thinking about a couple of interviews that Fred Moten has done recently in *Lit Hub* in which you've really worked across questions of literature and theory and music and personal memory. You offer us a kind of rethinking of what is at stake for Black people in this moment in terms of how we write and think and maneuver.[2] Maybe we can begin there for meditation on the relationship between Black studies and Black politics.

AFUA COOPER: I am thinking of how at Dalhousie University, we launched a Black studies minor this year. We want it to be a major, and we have big ambitions eventually for it to become a department.

The thing is that I am an endowed chair. It is a Black studies chair. It is the only one in Canada. But being an endowed Black studies chair is a paradoxical situation in that there was no Black studies anything. So setting up the Black studies minor had a lot of challenges. Suffice to say we came through.

I know across Canada there are schools and departments that do teach a variety of courses that pertain to the Black experience, and we thought it would be in this moment in the Ebony Tower that it's about time we have something like that in Canada. In the United States they have this long history of Black studies, and I'm thinking that knowledge about Black people is a form of reparation. Because oftentimes when we think about reparations, people, especially white people, run for cover because they think that all of us are going to march and ask for checks, which I don't have any problems with. I know a lot of Black people are saying it doesn't only have to be checks. I don't have a problem with the checks. Write me my check. I'm ready to get it. But I think knowledge is a form of reparation.

So it's important for all of us, everybody, to have this knowledge about Black people globally, but I think it's especially pertinent for Black people, for Black students, for Black kids that they know this thing about themselves. It's probably the most ultimate form of reparation.

That's one of my objectives. We do have an objective, we do have an agenda to interrupt the curriculum. It's about time that the white-centric curriculum be interrupted or thrown out of the window. And so that was also another one of my motivations—that we just have to interrupt the curriculum.

And I'm urging people, those of you who teach in colleges and universities, if there is a critical mass of you—and not just Black people, because we know it is just not Black people teaching about Black people; if there are people who are willing to come together and set this up, that's fantastic. When I went to Dalhousie, in every single faculty there is a Black body, and that person is tenured. You have the usual people who are doing the sessionals, and that's another story because they're the overworked, underpaid people. But there is always a critical mass of *us* at any given institution. So I'm urging people to bring together that critical mass and establish this curriculum. It is critical.

FRED MOTEN: I tend to think of Black studies not so much as an academic discipline or confluence of disciplines but as the atmosphere in which I grew up. And I love that atmosphere. I love the way that it felt, and I love the way that it smelled, and I love the flavors, and I love the sounds, and I love the movements.

So it is again something that I think has a certain place maybe in the university, and what it has meant for Black studies to take that place in the university has been both good and bad. I think it's probably done much more for the university than it has done for Black studies, and that's something worth thinking about. I don't say that because I'm trying to advocate some withdrawal of Black studies from the university, but I'm thinking that at this stage of the game, in having done the work of attempting to actually bring the university into some sense of what ought to be its own intellectual mission, Black studies has the right to look out for itself now for a little bit, and I think it's worth it to do that.

Insofar as Black studies has earned the right to look out for itself, what that really means is that Black studies has earned the right to try again to take its fundamental responsibility, which is to be a place where we can look out for the Earth. I think that Black studies has on a fundamental level a specific, though not necessarily exclusive, mission to try to save the Earth, and on a secondary level, to try to save the possibility of human existence on Earth. That's a big statement, but I think maybe it is important to just leave that big statement out there for a minute and just make sure you know that I knew that I said it when I said it.

ROBIN D. G. KELLEY: Let me just begin by saying that one of the pieces that Rinaldo was referring to was an essay I wrote called "Black Study, Black Struggle," which was entirely inspired by Fred Moten and Stefano Harney's book, *The Undercommons*.[3] It was a way of applying the notion of Undercommons to understanding what was happening at that moment, which in the fall of 2015 there was an explosion of Black protests on campus. I won't repeat what's in the article, but it is not an accident that some of those struggles were products of what was happening in the streets.

In other words, what happened in Ferguson and Baltimore, what happened all over the country, and what happened in places like here in Toronto were the catalysts for a kind of explosion on campuses where students were trying to figure out their place in university. They're dealing with racism and micro aggressions on university campuses. They're dealing with a kind of deracinated curriculum where ethnic studies in some places wasn't what it was in its inception.

We were also dealing with a culture of, and I hate to put it this way, anti-intellectualism. I mean universities are often anti-intellectual in that they actually disavow certain forms of knowledge and put other knowledges above that, which is an anti-intellectual position by the way. But when you're assaulted by that all the time, you end up mirroring that culture and saying, "well, I'm not going to read this, I'm not going to read that" because so and so wrote it as opposed to saying that there's nothing off the table in Black studies since Black studies is a critique of Western civilization.[4] And if that is the case, then the task is both to dismantle Western civilization, recognizing the weak edifice upon which it's built, but also to know everything that's happening within it.

So there are three points I want to make in reference to the opening question. One is that social movements have always been the catalyst for Black studies. When Fred was talking about Black studies as kind of a way of life, as an atmosphere in which he grew up and which I grew up and many of us grew up, I never thought of it that way, but that is so true. In fact, if anything, Black studies is not a multidiscipline but a project, a project for liberation, whatever that means, and liberation is an ongoing project.

Ruthie Gilmore, who was at the University of Southern California with me and Fred, had come up with this idea of renaming ethnic studies "Liberation Studies." We were serious about that as a reminder that it's not about a body. It's not about bodies. It's about ideas and about the future. It's about recognizing the past and the construction of a new future. So I think in that respect, in order to understand the future of Black studies, we have to understand the movements that produce it, the movement for Black lives, *We Charge Genocide,* and *Black Youth Project 100,* all these struggles that erupted have, in fact, pointed the way for Black studies. The problem is that what gets constituted as the institutional space "Black studies" in many cases isn't really that. There are a lot of departments that I wouldn't call Black Studies Departments that have that name. There's scholarship that goes on that has no relationship at all to the project of transformation or to actual people in the community.

One of the important things to always remember is that we wouldn't have Black studies in the United States if it wasn't for Watts or Detroit in '67, if it wasn't for those kinds of urban rebellions, if it wasn't for the struggles in the South. That's where Black studies comes from. So it moves into the university as a transformative project. That's why I think there's a disconnect between some of the protests and what was happening in the academy.

Finally, there's this question of ethnic studies as versus, against, for, within, or bedded in Black studies. One of the things that I think a lot of us are trying to figure out is to deepen the relationship between Indigenous studies and Black studies, to understand that what I call Second Wave Ethnic Studies in the 1990s, which was itself a project that was a response to neoliberalism. We don't always see that because we tend to read backwards in the 1980s and 1990s ethnic studies as identity politics in the narrowest sense of the word. That somehow this was about producing a sense of pride and a sense of identity devoid of the question of power. But if we actually look at the struggles for ethnic studies in the '80s and '90s, it was all about power. What we think of as comparative or critical ethnic studies wasn't about the celebration of difference. It wasn't liberal multiculturalism. It was an assault on a neoliberal term. We sometimes forget that and then rewrite history. That is something to remember because right now if we don't have Black studies as a critique in response to a neoliberal, neofascist turn, then it becomes sort of worthless. It's going to continue to exist, maybe not in the academy though.

WALCOTT: This is a good segue into getting both of you to talk about the work that you've been doing around questions of Palestinian struggle and freedom—Fred, the tremendous work that you did in the American Studies Association (ASA), for which the association is still living true, and Robin, the work that you continue to do with Faculty for Palestine. I'm thinking of Fred's provocation here. If Black studies is indeed about saving the Earth, it allows us to think about this relationship between the struggle and freedom of Palestine and the relationship between ongoing settler colonialisms globally. It seems to me one of the most powerful things that Black studies has done on the ground recently is to make those kinds of concerns present. Black Lives Matter visits to Palestine, Black Lives Matter in Toronto—always making sure that the invocation of the politics of settler colonialism is a part of the political organizing, fostering intimate relations with Indigenous communities.

So maybe this is a way for us to begin to talk about what's really at stake in this contemporary political moment where a radical politics, a politics that wants to think a different kind of future formation, is grappling with settler colonialism in various kinds of ways, but with Palestine being central to that, given that we know often in these universities senior administrators have an entirely different relationship to the question of freedom for Palestine.

MOTEN: Well, the work I did around the ASA's decision to endorse the academic and cultural boycott of Israel was really minimal and minor compared to a lot of other people who are really upfront and have been working tirelessly for that for many, many years. I think my contribution was more or less rhetorical in many ways and maybe theoretical only in the most minimal sense in the sense that what I wanted to do is a couple things. First, to recognize that the fundamental condition that makes up what people call modernity or global modernity is settler colonialism. And it is important we talk about settler colonialism in ways that are broader than the normal way in which we usually think: as a set of violent and brutal relations between Europe and the rest of the world.

Again, our mutual friend and mentor Cedric Robinson pointed this out emphatically and in brilliant ways early on: that settler colonialism is also an intra-European affair. It's important to understand this historic relationship between settler colonialism and the enclosure of the commons, which is part of the origins of what we now know or understand as capitalism. But if we understand that settler colonialism, the transatlantic slave trade, and the emergence of philosophical formulations that essentially provide some modern conception of Self that has as its basis a kind of possessive heteronormative patriarchal individuation—that that's what it is to be a self on the most fundamental level. If you ask anybody in the philosophy department, they'll tell you that that's true and they won't be joking, that these constitute the basis of our modernity. But for most of the people who live in the world—actually, for everybody who lives in the world, although many are not able to both recognize and say this—most people know that this modernity is a social and ecological disaster that we live, that we attempt to survive.

If we take that up, then a part of what's at stake is that we recognize that feminist and queer interventions against heteronormative patriarchy, that Black interventions against the theory and practice of slavery, which is ongoing, that Indigenous interventions against settler colonialism constitute both the practical and intellectual bases for not only our attempts to survive, but also our attempts to, as I said before, save the Earth. Putting it in the words of the great poet Ed Roberson, it is not just to save the Earth but to see the Earth before the end of the world.[5] This is an emergency that we're in now, and it's urgent. And I believe that there's a specific convergence of Black thought and Indigenous thought that situates itself precisely in relation to and is articulated through the interventions of queer thought and feminist thought that we want to take up, and it strikes me as, for me at least, a way of taking up and of imagining how we might be able to walk more lightly on the Earth, to honor the Earth as we walk on it, as we stand on it, to not stomp on it, to not stomp all over it where every step you take is a claim of ownership. One way to put it would be to not so presumptuously imagine that the Earth can be reduced to something so paltry and so viciously understood as what we usually call home.

This is part of the reason why the queer and the feminist critique is so important. It's a critique of a general problematic notion of domesticity. It presents another way of being on the Earth that doesn't allow you in some vicious and brutal way to claim that it is yours. This is important. Often the methods that we use to claim the Earth as ours involve fences, borders. This manifests itself on a private level from household to household, but it also manifests itself on a national level and at the level of the nation-state. It's not an accident that settler colonial states take it upon themselves to imagine themselves to be the living embodiment of the legitimacy of the nation-state as a political and social form.

For me, there are two reasons to be in solidarity with the people of Palestine. One is because they're human beings, and they're being treated with absolute brutality. But the other is the specific resistance to Israel as a nation-state. And for my money, to be perfectly clear about this, I believe that this nation-state of Israel is itself an artifact of anti-Semitism. What if we thought about Israel and Zionism not just as a form of racism that results in the displacement of Palestinians, but as artifacts of the historic displacement of Jews from Europe in the same way that we might think of, let's say, Sierra Leone or Liberia as artifacts of racist displacement? What if we think about it that way? The reason I'm saying this is just to make sure that you know that there's a possible argument against the formulation that criticism of Israel is anti-Semitic when we know that Donald Trump is a staunch supporter of Israel. If we know that people like Pat Robertson in the United States are staunch supporters of Israel, that ought to hint to us the fact that you can be deeply anti-Semitic and also support the State of Israel. These things go together. They're not antithetical to one another.

So then it becomes important for us to be able to suggest that resistance to the State of Israel is also resistance to the idea of the legitimacy of the nation-state. When the defense of Israel manifests itself as a defense of its right to exist, it's a defense not just of Israel's right to exist, but of the nation state as a political form's right to exist. And nation-states don't have rights. What they're supposed to be are mechanisms to protect the rights of the people who live in them, and that has almost never been the case. And to the extent that they do protect the rights of the people who live with them, it's at the expense of the people who don't.

So part of what's at stake, and one of the reasons why it's important to pay particular attention to this issue, why we ought to resist the ridiculous formulation that singling out Israel at this moment is anti-Semitic, is because it's important to recognize that Israel is a state for reasons that are totally bound up with anti-Semitism. Israel is the state that, insofar as it makes the claim about its right to exist, it is also making the claim about the nation-state's right to exist as such. It's that same kind of formulation that people often make about Black people or Indigenous people as if they were the essence of the human. So that every time Black people or Indigenous people do something that supposedly we're not supposed to do, it constitutes a violation to the very idea of the human because somehow as a function of the nobility of our suffering, we constitute the very idea of humanity. And there's nothing more brutal, nothing more vicious than having been consigned to that position.

Similarly, Israel as a function of anti-Semitism has not been placed in the position of protecting the very idea of the nation-state. So for me, first and foremost, it's important to have solidarity with the Palestinian people. But second of all, it's important to actually have some solidarity with the Jewish people insofar as they can and must be separated from the Israeli state, because ultimately, the fate of the Jewish people, if it is tied to the nation state of Israel, will be more brutal than anything that has yet been done or can be imagined. I mean everything that you think I mean when I say that.

KELLEY: Before I respond I want to acknowledge the tremendous work that the students and faculty here in Toronto are doing around the question of Palestine. I had a great lunch with members of Coalition Against Israeli Apartheid (CAIA) and the Faculty for Palestine at various institutions here, and it is just incredible.

What is incredible about that work is how much pushback everyone is getting, and, of course, this is evidence that those who are defending the State of Israel and its policies are on the defensive and actually losing legitimacy.

But let me come back to what Fred was saying, which I think is really a brilliant formulation. There's an interesting corollary that I heard from Judith Butler. She was on a plenary session, if you haven't seen, for the

Jewish Voice for Peace on Friday, and she gave a stunning talk about why it is that Netanyahu and the official Israeli State could give Steve Bannon a pass and say that he's okay because he's for Israel.[6] And remember anti-Semitism is being deployed against whom? Against supporters of BDS. Anti-Semitism as an attack is being deployed against those who are critical of Israel. In the state of California they're trying desperately to pass this bill in the assembly and trying to impose certain rules in the University of California system that would declare—and they've already done this in the U.S. senate and congress—that would declare any criticism of Israel anti-Semitic hate speech. However, actual anti-Semites who have long histories in the alt-right are getting a pass. Why? Because they are *all for* the defense of Israel.

As Judith Butler elaborated, and I don't want to put words in her mouth, but I would suggest you go back and look at it—but what she elaborated was that what they have in common is that if you look at the policies of Israel with respect to the kind of occupation and even forms of apartheid that operate within the '48 borders, that's a white supremacist state. What they have in common is white supremacy. That ultimately, that is a fundamental thing—and that's why the Steve Bannons and the Donald Trumps of the world could get a pass while someone like Omar Barghouti is being persecuted.

So that said, just a couple of things on the question of solidarity. Angela Davis made a really important point in her most recent book that looks at the recent struggles around Ferguson and Palestine. She points out that 2014 was really a turning point where you have the death of Michael Brown and the protests in Ferguson simultaneous with the assault on Gaza. The connection between these events created a space and possibility for deepening a solidarity that has been ongoing.[7]

It's been interesting because on one side, it creates some opportunities for linking these struggles, looking at the Israeli security apparatus and its relationship to the U.S. police state. On the other side it's also opened up really difficult conversations about anti-Blackness and Islamophobia, in that you have examples of Black Islamophobia and Palestinian anti-Blackness.

Instead of seeing that as a problem for solidarity, it becomes an opportunity to work through questions of our histories, our relationships, and seeing a different kind of future, one in which what appears to be parochial struggles or local struggles, even national ones, can begin to think beyond their own location, opening up the doors for delegations to Palestine.

There are, for example, groups like Black4Palestine, led by people like Kristian Davis Bailey, who have really been at the forefront of this exciting moment to think about settler colonialism.[8]

One last thing I want to add going back to the larger question of settler colonialism, not just Palestine, is that I just wrote this piece that discusses how contemporary discussions of settler colonialism don't address settler colonialism in Africa.[9] It is as if Africa doesn't exist in these analyses. For example, for some reason, the late Patrick Wolfe, as much as I loved his work, didn't engage settler colonialism in Africa. For me, critiques of settler colonialism in South Africa are where the critiques of settler colonialism really began. I want to sort of make a plea for why is it that South Africa is one of the staunchest supporters of Palestine and Palestinian liberation and what does it mean for the ongoing apartheid system in South Africa, the ongoing systems of settler colonialism in Southern Africa and also elsewhere. To consider that is also part of the conversation that Black studies needs to come to terms with.

COOPER: Thank you, both of you, for those responses. I just want us to pause for a moment and reflect that we are on the eve of the anniversary of the death of Dr. Martin Luther King forty-nine years ago tomorrow, April 4th, 1968. That was a momentous time in global history. It's still a momentous time.

I've been thinking about what happened in April throughout time, and April 8th, 1760, was the beginning of the Tacky Rebellion in Jamaica. That day was when the first initiative of the rebellion burst out in St. Mary parish. Since we're talking about liberation, we're talking about Black liberation, we're talking about breaking down the whole thing and starting from scratch, which was what Tacky and his cohort wanted to do in Jamaica in 1760. It engulfed the entire island. They wanted to overthrow slavery, overthrow white supremacy, and start again. It was the most important rebellion, revolt bursting out before the Haitian Revolution thirty years in the future.

I want to ask our two professors to reflect on this moment of global anti-Black racism, because even in the majority Black countries you have anti-Black racism. It sounds like a paradox but it's true. In terms of our bodies, in terms of Black people occupying certain spaces. One of the things I was reflecting on, coming from Nova Scotia, one of the first policies of getting Black people out of certain spaces in Canada happened around 1785 in Shelburne, Nova Scotia, when the whites of the community passed a bylaw banning "Negro frolics." It was said the Black people were having too many parties. They were dancing, they were singing, they were making noise, and so there was a bylaw that banned "Negro frolics" in Shelburne in 1785. And later on in the year, the whites attacked the Black communities, beat them up, burnt down their houses, chased people into the swamps. We call it Canada's first anti-Black race riot.

I think of this in relation to Toronto's rules regarding Afrofest, which are strikingly similar to the Sundown laws which were put into place all over Canada. Sundown laws meant that Black people had to clear out of presumably white towns at a certain time of day. So I'd like for you to share with us some reflections on the meanings of Black geographies.

KELLEY: Katherine McKittrick is here, who is a person who writes so meaningfully about Black geographies. I would love to hear from her on this question!

[Interlude of a brief exchange. The audience was so lucky!]

MOTEN: Well, it's funny. I mean I feel like the kind of Black geography that Katherine McKittrick just mentioned is kind of like what's happening right now, right here. I've been thinking about a couple of things. When you mentioned the Sundown laws, Afua, I kept thinking that there's a deep structure for these kinds of laws.

I remember when I was reading Du Bois's *Philadelphia Negro*, there's an appendix at the end of the book in which he actually lists and gives short descriptions of the laws in the Commonwealth of Pennsylvania that specifically pertain to and had an impact on Black life, and one of them was a law I think from 1732 called an Anti-Tumult Law, which outlawed the tumultuous gathering of two or more Blacks in the public square on Sundays.[10] And I remember reading it, and I kept thinking to myself, *Why? Why would you do that?* And one way to think of it, first of all is, *What is that? What would it mean to outlaw a gathering of two or more Black people?* I think one could argue that it is literally to make Blackness against the law. Which is to say, insofar as being Black is a thing that you can only do with others, I don't know that it's possible to be Black by oneself. So insofar as being Black or Black being is a necessarily irreducibly social thing, to outlaw gatherings of two or more is to simply outlaw Blackness.

Now why? Why would you outlaw Blackness? Well, because two or more gathering together, the tumultuous gathering of two or more in a public square, literally it was as if they were outlawing the weekly formation of a study group. Because what would two or more Black people be doing in Philadelphia in public in 1732 other than thinking about how to get free? That wouldn't be nothing other than the weekly meeting of a liberation study group.

But it's more than that. There's an interesting formulation in Kant's critique of judgment, in what he identifies as the regulation of a certain kind of tumultuousness. That's what he calls the "tumultuous derangements" of the imagination. This outlawing of tumult is nothing but the attempt to form a very specific and very restricted understanding of what it is to be a person. This restriction of the imagination has to occur because the imagination is itself always involved in this project of liberation.

This is about a very specific mode of world-making. We want to make a world in which this particular modality of social existence is outlawed. Let's say that we could call that certain kind of a normative geography ... I've been trying to study maps even though I can't really do it for a long time. And I met this really interesting, great Colombian mathematician named Fernando Zalamea who's written some really interesting books about topology, where a general kind of definition of topology would be along the lines of how space is preserved under duress, how space is preserved under conditions of folding and crumpling and incursion.[11]

So let's say that there's a kind of Black topological existence, which is all about the making and the preservation of space under duress. And I think maybe that's something kind of like what Katherine was talking about [a few moments ago] with regard to Black geography, and the thing about it is it's a practice of joy, which is at the same time all about the mobilization of joy in the interest of its own self-protection. The only way to protect joy is by practicing it. I think these are fundamental hallmarks of Black social life, and they manifest themselves in ways that would link up to Indigenous forms of life when it's really all about, again, trying to figure out a way to walk lightly on the Earth.

KELLEY: I think that's actually key, and I hope Rinaldo would also answer this question too because you know a lot about this. But the key word I took from Katherine's sort of interrogation is "joy." And it's interesting because historically, so many uprisings have been, even if they're planned or not planned, centered around a moment of collective joy, a moment of seizing public space as a social fact, as an insurgency, not for the sake of bringing down an order, but for the sake of claiming that space that you're talking about. I did this research a long time ago about resistance on buses in Birmingham. On the bus, we know stories about how people just simply refused to give up their seat as if it's sort of a question of the defense of their dignity. That's true. That happened. But oftentimes, it was people being arrested for being boisterous, and being boisterous basically meant that you're cutting up in the back of the bus, you're making all this noise, you're basically seizing the space because all the placards of segregation cannot stop your voice, cannot stop your sound, cannot stop the way that Black people are occupying the buses. And for the sake of joy. They weren't back there giving dissertations. They were back there playing the dozens usually on white people who are in the front of the bus.

So there's those moments of danger, and I think that's the system surveillance, whether it's slavery or postslavery, we're always actively surveilling Black and brown and Indigenous bodies and even, let's be honest, white working-class bodies as well. People like George Rudé and others talk about the kind of insurgencies of the night of working people, that there's something about the control of the body and joy, surveilling it in women's bodies in particular.[12] You can't express that joy collectively. Otherwise, you have surveillance and state repression. So I think that's all there whether we want it or not.

WALCOTT: Well, I think Katherine invoked the notion of Black joy, and Fred invoked that law against tumultuous meetings. One thing about the ways in which this question on mapping works is how Black people territorialize their own bodies. So if you think about that law of tumultuousness, its trajectories, histories, and laws, like bylaws in school where kids can't wear a baseball cap a certain way, or the ways in which various cities pass ordinances against Black men wearing their pants sagging. That's because they want to interject into Black joy and freedom, into Black people mapping their bodies in the way that they would like to map them.

So what we see is that there are these kinds of unruly geographies that Black people write onto their bodies in a whole range of ways that really disturb the meta project of the nation-state. That the nation-state's most insidious and violent relationships to Black people have been when Black people say we own our bodies. This is how we're going to shape it. This is how we're going to put it out into other spaces.

So the kinds of conversations that you all just invoked make those things deeply present. Contemporary Black youth politics like Black Lives Matter across North America have put those things on the map in really forceful ways. It reminds us that this struggle for freedom is really about a certain kind of sovereignty of the Black body over the bodies that are not white or marked as not white.

COOPER: When Dudley Laws from Black Action Defense Committee was alive—Dudley Laws was one of the leaders in the community, and he was very much involved in antipolicing and incarceration issues—we used to go to federal prisons in Kingston, Ontario, and one I went to with them was the Joyceville Penitentiary. Sometimes it was relatively easy. We could have discussions with some of the men. There was a men's prison. One of the men that we were talking to, he was on the verge of tears. He said the saddest day of his life was to see his son entering the same prison he was in. So we had two generations of men in that prison, and he said he couldn't remain sad for too long because he had to show his son the ropes. So we looked at these two generations of men, looked at the women, the wives, the mothers, the girlfriends, and so on who were left behind to carry on.

We're experiencing some real life-crushing situations. So hold that thought and the thought of liberation and joy. My question is, professors, grasping this great vision in terms of liberation, who do we grasp? With whom do we hold on to this great vision of liberation? What does it mean? What does it look like? Because we have to break through this. So provide us, all of us here, with tools. When Kwame Ture was asked this question in a different way he said, "organize, organize, organize." So you guys have the floor. Grasping the great vision.

MOTEN: I'm not trying to sidestep the question or not answer the question, but the first stage of the answer or response to that question, to that provocation, is to say I don't know. But I think I do know a little something. I'm beginning to think maybe I got a little bit of an idea about how we might come to know.

I was talking with some of the students here today in the seminar about a really good friend and mentor of mine whose name is Manolo Callahan. He teaches at San Jose State University in California, but he also has been working for a long time as part of a series of sort of interlocking organizations, the Universidad de la Tierra, University of the Earth, which is a kind of mobile, multiple-sited university in let's say what we could call greater Latin America independent of the border between Mexico and the United States, and he has been working in particular with people in the Zapatista Movement and Mexican intellectuals, in particular Mexican philosopher Gustavo Esteva.

The work that they've been doing could boil down to a couple of phrases, a couple formulations. One is they talk about the importance of what they call "convivial research," which is not just research that's about a certain kind of let's say local or working-class community, but it's research that's grounded in that community in the interest of the preservation and survival of that community.[13] But it is also research that's predicated on the notion that knowledge already exists within that community, and it's about trying to figure out exactly how to understand and to honor that knowledge. And that knowledge could take the form of intimate understandings of the techniques and strategies of the police, for instance, but that knowledge also could take the form of how to put on a barbecue. And that's important too, insofar as it's a mechanism for the ongoing production and preservation of our modalities of joy. How to cook the meat, how to make the fire, how to take care of the kids, how to make sure that the elders are taken care of and properly respected, all of those things go into what it is for community itself to be actively and constantly engaged in this process of research where research is inseparable from conviviality, from what it is to live together.

But the other formulation that they have, which is equally important and connected to it, is something that Manolo talks about under the rubric of the necessity of renewing our habits of assembly. Like we have to learn, we have to do a better job with regard to the theory and practice of getting together, of being together. And it's beautiful to be in such a large group, and it's such a full room with all of you all, and everybody looks good. I've just been kind of marveling in the back of my head literally. I'm not even joking about the tremendous infinite variety and glory of Black women's hair. I can't believe I'm seeing so many [here today in the audience].

But maybe this renewal of our habits of assembly is something that occurs on small scales. This reminds me of something I was telling students about. One time I remember I asked Robin this question, like how did the Civil Rights Movement actually happen? And one of the things he said is a beautiful moment. He said well, first of all, the Civil Rights Movement was not a mass movement.

This is tremendously important. I don't think scale is our friend. I think scale is our enemy. In order to renew our habits of assembly, we do so in small scale with hopefully infinite proliferation. And we have to learn how to get together with one another on a small scale with a kind of patience, with ethical regard for one another in ways that I think could be proliferative, could spread as fast as that fire that they said Angélique tried to start.[14] And part of what happens is, you get together with a few folks, and then we ask ourselves this question of how we proceed, of what our tools should be.

KELLEY: To live together and renewing the habits of assembly are really critical. It's true, we had this conversation about the Civil Rights Movement, and I totally agree that we assume that somehow mass movements are sources of power, and I think we misunderstand power. I was trying to talk about this on Saturday night, and there was a quote from Dr. King that I was paraphrasing, but I wanted to pull up here, which I think is really, really important, where he talks about why we shouldn't be afraid of power. He says, "You see, what happened is that some of our philosophers got off base. And one of the great problems of history is that the concepts of love and power have usually been contrasted as opposites, polar opposites, so that love is identified with a resignation of power, and power with a denial of love. Now, we got to get this thing right. What is needed is a realization of power without love is reckless and abusive, and that love without power is sentimental and anemic. Yes, power at its best, power at its best is love ... implementing the demands of justice, and justice at its best is love correcting everything that stands against love."[15]

So think about the importance of love as a center for renewing our habits of assembly, number one, and recognizing that taking power, building power is not something that we should resist but that we should claim. We often are on the other side of power. We see power as something we resist rather than something we take. I want to say that because the other person who was sort of a huge influence on many of us is Grace Lee Boggs, and one of the things that she and Jimmy Boggs were working on was they argued that dialectical materialism, as we knew it, was an epoch that was over, and to replace dialectical materialism, they argued for dialectical humanism.[16] That the fundamental struggle is not the class struggle between proletarian capitalist, especially in an age when automation and other forms are sort of transforming the proletariat, but rather our struggle to become more human, and we can debate over whatever that means, but the struggle to become more human. And to become more human is to basically recognize what it means to live with, to live for and about, with love, to build community where there's no outside. What does that mean? What does that require of us?

And we cannot build or embrace a new humanity for the future without actually acknowledging what Fred began with, and that is that our planet is in peril. To love the planet and to love each other and to love life is not a sentimental love, but agape. That is: love where there's no outside, where you're constantly building community, which is filled with tension to do that. It's a struggle to do that. But that, to me, is the only way we could build the kind of future that you're talking about. We can't have a future that's based on false utopia. That is a land of milk and honey. Our future is actually here. We're already in the future. The question is how do we hold on to that vision, that through power and love we can produce a world in which we're not shaming each other, we're not beating each other down, we're not afraid of each other, we're not vested in economies that are based on both scale and profit, where we're not trying to make new entrepreneurship as the future, that that's the only future available, that we're not reduced to human capital but human beings, whatever that means. That to me is really the essence of how to build a new future.

[The evening closed with discussion in response to several questions from the audience, which we have decided not to reproduce here. This is in part because we weren't able to seek permission from the people who posed questions to be able to include their words here. Perhaps more importantly, we do not share that portion of the discussion because of the intimacy that emerges over the course of a conversation for which everyone in the room was terrifically present.]

ROBIN D. G. KELLEY is Distinguished Professor and Gary B. Nash Endowed Chair in History at the University of California, Los Angeles. He is a historian of social movements in the United States, the African Diaspora and Africa, Black intellectuals, music, visual culture, and contemporary urban studies, among other things. His work has been featured in a variety of professional journals and publications, and he is the author of numerous books including, *Hammer and Hoe: Alabama Communists during the Great Depression* (1990), *Race Rebels: Culture, Politics, and the Black Working Class* (1996), *Freedom Dreams: The Black Radical Imagination* (2002), and *Africa Speaks, America Answers: Modern Jazz in Revolutionary Times* (2012).

FRED MOTEN teaches and conducts research in Black studies, performance studies, and poetics. He is author of *In the Break: The Aesthetics of the Black Radical Tradition* (2003), *Hughson's Tavern* (2008), *B. Jenkins* (2010), *The Feel Trio* (2014), *The Little Edges* (2015), *The Service Porch* (2016), and *Black and Blur: consent not to be a single being* (2017), and coauthor, with Stefano Harney, of *The Undercommons: Fugitive Planning and Black Study* (2013), and *A Poetics of the Undercommons* (2016) and, with Wu Tsang, of *Who Touched Me?* (2015). Moten works in the department of performance studies at New York University.

AFUA COOPER is the current James Robinson Johnston Chair in Black Canadian studies at Dalhousie University. She holds a PhD in Black Canadian studies from the University of Toronto. A multidisciplinary scholar and artist, her expertise includes African Canadian culture, gender, slavery, abolition, and freedom, Black orature, education, and Black agency and political consciousness. She has conducted research on Black life and culture all across Canada and internationally. Her coauthored publication *We're Rooted Here and They Can't Pull Us Up: Essays in African Canadian Women's History* (1994) won the Joseph Brant prize for the best history book. Her groundbreaking book on Canadian slavery, *The Hanging of Angelique: The Untold Story of Slavery in Canada and the Burning of Old Montreal* (2014), was nominated for the Governor General's award. She also received the Harry Jerome Award for Professional excellence, and was featured on SSHRC's website for her work on African Canadian history. Afua is also an accomplished poet and novelist. She has published five books of poetry, including the critically acclaimed *Copper Woman and Other Poems* (2007), and two historical novels. Her creative work has been recognized with national and international awards.

RINALDO WALCOTT is a professor in the Department of Social Justice Education at the Ontario Institute for Studies in Education (OISE) and director of the Women and Gender Studies Institute at the University of Toronto. His work is concerned with the ways in which coloniality shapes human relations across social and cultural time with a focus on Black cultural politics, histories of colonialism in the Americas, citizenship, and diaspora, gender and sexuality, and social, cultural, and public policy. He is the author of *Black Like Who: Writing Black Canada* (1997), editor of *Rude: Contemporary Black Canadian Cultural Criticism* (2000), and the coeditor, with Roy Moodley, of *Counseling across and beyond Cultures: Exploring the Work of Clemment E. Vontress in Clinical Practice* (2010).

NOTES

1. Robin D. G. Kelley, "Trump Says Go Back, We Say Fight Back," *Boston Review*, November 15, 2016, http://bostonreview.net/forum/after-trump/robin-d-g-kelley-trump-says-go-back-we-say-fight-back; Robin D. G. Kelley, "Black Study, Black Struggle," *Boston Review*, March 7, 2016, http://bostonreview.net/forum/robin-d-g-kelley-black-study-black-struggle.

2. Adam Fitzgerald, "An Interview with Fred Moten, Part I: In Praise of Harold Bloom, Collaboration and Book Fetishes," Literary Hub, August 5, 2017, http://lithub.com/an-interview-with-fred-moten-pt-i/; Fitzgerald, "An Interview with Fred Moten, Part II: On Radical Indistinctness and Thought Flavor à la Derrida," Literary Hub, August 6, 2015, http://lithub.com/an-interview-with-fred-moten-pt-ii/.

3. Stefano Harney and Fred Moten, *The Undercommons: Fugitive Planning & Black Study* (New York: Minor Compositions, 2013).

4. Cedric J. Robinson, *Black Marxism: The Making of the Black Radical Tradition* (1983; rpt., Chapel Hill: University of North Carolina Press, 2000). Cedric Robinson draws from C. L. R. James's work to emphasize this point.

5. Ed Roberson, *To See the Earth before the End of the World* (Middletown, Conn.: Wesleyan University Press, 2010).

6. Judith Butler, "Ready to Fight: This Political Moment and JVP's Role" (Jewish Voice for Peace 2017 National Member Meeting, Plenary Session with Rebecca Vilkomerson, Fadi Quran, Robin D. G. Kelley, and Judith Butler, Chicago, March 31, 2017).

7. Angela Y. Davis, *Freedom Is a Constant Struggle: Ferguson, Palestine, and the Foundations of a Movement* (Chicago: Haymarket Books, 2016).

8. See Black4Palestine, "2015 Black Solidarity Statement with Palestine," http://www.blackforpalestine.com/.

9. Robin D. G. Kelley, "The Rest of Us: Rethinking Settler and Native," *American Quarterly* 69 no. 2 (June 2017): 267–76.

10. W. E. B. Du Bois, *The Philadelphia Negro* (Philadelphia: University of Pennsylvania Press, 1889), 414.

11. See, for instance, Fernando Zalamea, *Synthetic Philosophy of Contemporary Mathematics*, trans. Zachary Luke Fraser (New York: Urbanomic/Sequence Press, 2012).

12. Eric Hobsbawm and George Rudé, *Captain Swing: A Social History of the Great English Agricultural Uprising of 1830* (1969; rpt., Brooklyn: Verso, 2014).

13. Manuel "Manolo" Callahan, "In Defense of Conviviality and the Collective Subject," *Polis* 11, no. 33 (2012): 51–90. For more on convivial research, see http://cril.mitotedigital.org/.

14. Afua Cooper, *The Hanging of Angélique: The Untold Story of Canadian Slavery and the Burning of Old Montréal* (Athens: University of Georgia Press, 2007).

15. Martin Luther King Jr., "Where Do We Go from Here?" (speech delivered at the 11th Annual Convention of the Southern Christian Leadership Conference, Atlanta, August 16, 1967), http://www.stanford.edu/group/King/publications/speeches/Where_do_we_go_from_here.html.

16. Grace Lee Boggs, "Neither White nor Black—But Revolutionary," *Correspondence,* June 1963; James Boggs, *Racism and Class Struggle: Further Pages from a Black Worker's Notebook* (New York: Monthly Review Press, 1970).

REVIEWS

Letters in Black, Care of Christina Sharpe
Book Review of *In The Wake: On Blackness and Being*

CORNEL GREY

To be in the wake is to be in ceremony with Black life. Such a state demands that we be in reverent conversation and involved in the care of and for Black people the world over. Christina Sharpe's latest book, *In the Wake: On Blackness and Being*, is an opus to Black life in four parts. This text offers a different way for us to write and think blackness.[1] Sharpe apprehends and confronts the disavowal of Black beings in the spatiotemporal moment that is the "past that is not yet past,"[2] the condition of epistemological and ontological rupture brought on by the transatlantic slave trade and its attendant mechanisms. In this New World, Black life appears as that which is outside the realm of the human.[3] At best, Black beings are fleeting punctuations in history; we appear as ellipses, asterisks, hanging apostrophes possessed as property. Sharpe illustrates what it means for Black beings to live in the wake. She makes visible the ongoing operating logics of the ship, provides a lens through which we may conceive Black life despite and in excess of the hold. Sharpe maps out the dimensions of Black life as it persists under (and despite) the weather. The culmination of this mindful labor is a work that seeks to "sound an ordinary note of care" for Black folks both dead and alive. This is what Sharpe has articulated as "wake work."[4]

As an intellectual intervention, *In the Wake* draws on a body of work grounded in Black feminist theorizing. The theoretical and poetic writings of Saidiya Hartman and Dionne Brand may be regarded as the most foundational elements of this text. Sharpe takes up Hartman's "scenes of subjection" and thinks through what it means to tell a story without replaying the violence. We encounter Venus by another name, and we sit with, at length, the condition of Black life in the moment of slavery's afterlives.[5] In this respect, Sharpe is a student of Hartman's work. Brand, on the other hand, is more aptly described as a guide. The poet-writer's oeuvre offers a map, vocabulary, and lens that Sharpe employs to "think 'the wake' as a problem of and for thought ... [and] to think 'care' as a problem for thought."[6] Politically, "care" in this work takes on multiple meanings. Sharpe is concerned with the embodied well-being of Black folks living in the wake, but she is also rethinking what it might look like to write *care*-fully about blackness and Black people in a way that does not maintain colonial ontologies of objecthood and death.

In *In the Wake*, Sharpe outlines for us the multiple registers of the wake, referencing personal, public, and historical events as a way of illustrating the intimacies of pain and joy as part of Black being-in-the-world. It is here that the stakes are set. It is only in grappling with these multiple and interconnected meanings throughout the text that we can fully appreciate the work that Sharpe is doing. The reader-audience is asked to grapple with these simultaneously operative and shifting meanings. In doing so, Sharpe erases hard distinctions between past and present, life and death, joy and pain. In sum, to be in the wake is an extended condition, a state of *being*. In other words, the operating motif of the wake is a way of marking the spatial, temporal, embodied, and political junctures of Black being in the afterlife of slavery. Chapters titled "The Ship" and "The Hold" are reflections on Black life amid processes of objectification. "The Ship," of course, refers to the slave ship and serves as the visual and figurative anchor of the work. As a method of travel, it gestures to transatlantic slavery, the Middle Passage, migration, and exile. In terms of its construction, the ship directs our attention to processes of human degradation, capital accumulation and fungibility, containment, and surveillance. Sharpe uses the documentary *The Forgotten Space*, specifically its concern with the effects of globalization and capitalism, to consider the ongoing effects of the Middle Passage but also to consider how the economics of transatlantic slavery have informed the way capital is organized in our present moment. "The Hold" refers to a ship's hold, a structure below deck meant for the storage of cargo. This chapter offers several vignettes of Black people who are effectively held by dehumanizing mechanisms of the slave ship, who live in the wake of ongoing anti-Black violence. The author makes clear, however, that the hold is not an overdetermining force in the lives of Black people. Black life persists within, through, and outside of these sites.

Sharpe discusses the ways the logic of the slave ship continues to secure the realm of the human against blackness. The result is a set of racializing codes and frameworks where Black people appear as nonpersons, essential to the operating mechanisms of modernity but always under limited conditions.

Such are the circumstances that allow for a Black woman's experience of state violence in the film *The Forgotten Space*.[7] Sharpe encounters Aereile Jackson, a Black woman whose children are removed from her care and who is conscripted to evidence, enacting the ongoing violence of capital by assigning her the title of "former mother" in the end credits.[8] Elsewhere, the screams of survivors of the Lampedusa shipwreck are misheard as the screeching of seagulls. The author speaks back to these violent encounters from this position of the wake. The chapter titled "The Weather" serves as the space in which the author names those forces, processes, and ideologies that attempt to suspend Black life and the practice by which Black folks live despite these circumstances. For Sharpe, "the weather is the totality of our environments; the weather is the total climate; and that climate is antiblack."[9] The chapter makes visible the material and discursive environments that compromise Black (well)-being, giving texture to the atmosphere of antiblackness and addressing the shifting but nonetheless pervasive presence of this violence across the world. Put together, these four chapters convey what it means to experience the weather, a state in which Black people find it difficult to "aspire."[10] In this context, aspiration does not refer to social and economic mobility but rather to a deep concern with the question of Black vitality within a climate that is pervasively anti-Black.

"To care" is the central project of wake work. It is to (at)tend to Black life, Black beings, and Black lives, however and wherever they appear. It is to be concerned for Black folks' health. It is to be committed to *aspiration*, this "violent and life-saving" act of keeping breath in the Black body.[11] Sharpe performs this care throughout her text by sitting and breathing life into unnamed, potentially unclaimed, lives of Black beings deemed property. Sharpe does more than tell us what "wake work" can do—she performs it. Indeed, she approaches those who live in the wake with what we may describe as a Black feminist ethic, one where she can "stand and say . . . the child was black and female and therefore mine."[12] Of course, this child is not always a child. Nor do we have to *know* her in the typical sense of the term. She is not necessarily female either. But we do have to see her, not to rescue her but to behold her in a way that cannot be articulated nor performed by the state nor by capital.

Sharpe holds several Black women throughout *In the Wake*. Some of these women are relatives. Most are not. In *The Forgotten Space*, she asks not to forget Aereile Jackson, but sitting with us too is the "girl child" with the word "ship" taped across her forehead following the 2010 earthquake in Haiti. Wake work demands that we pause and sit with this image and the child within.

To behold her. The label threatens to overwhelm, but Sharpe holds the girl's gaze at length. In reading this image, Sharpe notes that there is a leaf stuck in this young child's hair, styled in braids. "Somebody braided her hair before that earthquake hit," Sharpe writes.[13] To some this may seem a small and rather insignificant observation. It is not. That someone took time to braid her hair is an indication of care. That someone took care means she is cared for, she has someone keeping watch. To note that she has someone at all is to reckon with this young girl as a living Black being. She is not a body-made-into-property to illustrate tragedy, a reductive depiction of what Black life is like in the aftermath of an earthquake, in the ongoing afterlife of slavery. The same level of care is afforded to Mikia Hutchings, Glenda Moore, and others in the text.[14]

Sharpe imbues in her writing a poetic style that draws us in, makes us feel. Individual affective responses will vary. For some it will be illuminating, others cathartic and even rejuvenating. Even so, this book demands a certain kind of responsibility. Readers will likely comment on the book's beauty. The beauty of which they speak may have everything to do with the intimate display of Black pain. If this is all one walks away with, it evidences a kind of misreading that Sharpe warns against in her text. Such a reader submits to the often pornographic treatment of violence against Black people and their responses to these circumstances. A responsible reading practice then is *vital*. By vital, I am gesturing to multiple meanings by signaling its importance as well as the author's demand that we take note of the actual life force of Black people.

In the opening pages of the book, Sharpe tells us that one of her aims is to "find the language for this [wake] work . . . find the words that will articulate care."[15] More important than the new frames and analytics, the potent grammar of wake work, and the vocabulary it offers for writing and thinking blackness—all of which will shift the field of Black studies for years to come—*In the Wake*'s biggest achievement may not be the theoretical and conceptual tools Sharpe offers but the space she opens up for working through the layered geographies of Black life. In this respect, the project of wake work is a collective effort. Sharpe's analytic is an intervention that invites us to revisit, interrogate, and reconceptualize what it means to perform intellectual labor with an element of care, attending to the complexities and contradictions of Black being in the world.

CORNEL GREY is a PhD student at the Women & Gender Studies Institute, University of Toronto. Cornel's research is located within the field of Black studies and queer studies, with a focus on Black geographies. He is concerned with shades and textures of Black diaspora in the Americas and is especially interested in political movements that insist upon Black life amid laws and policies that seek to erase Black presence.

NOTES

1. Christina Sharpe, *In the Wake: On Blackness and Being* (Durham, N.C.: Duke University Press, 2016).

2. Ibid, 73.

3. Sylvia Wynter, "1492: A New World View," in *Race, Discourse, and the Origin of the Americas: A New World View*, ed. Vera Lawrence Hyatt and Rex Nettleford (Washington, D.C.: Smithsonian Institution, 1995), 5–57.

4. Sharpe, *In the Wake*, 13; 132.

5. Saidiya Hartman, "Venus in Two Acts," *Small Axe: A Caribbean Journal of Criticism* 12, no. 2 (26) (June 2008): 1–14; Hartman, *Scenes of Subjection: Terror, Slavery, and Self-Making in Nineteenth-Century America* (Oxford: Oxford University Press, 1997).; Hartman, *Lose Your Mother: A Journey along the Atlantic Slave Route* (New York: Farrar, 2007).

6. Sharpe, *In the Wake*, 5.

7. Ibid., 25.

8. Ibid, 27.

9. Ibid, 104.

10. Ibid, 108.

11. Ibid, 113.

12. Claire Harris, *Fables from the Women's Quarters* (Fredericton, N.B.: Goose Lane Editions, 1984), 38.

13. Ibid, 120.

14. See pages 79–80, 120–22 of Sharpe, *In the Wake*.

15. Ibid, 19.